THE BRONTË STORY

'This is one of those rare books which completely satisfy . . . Mrs Gaskell's is a recognised masterpiece in biography; Miss Lane's reconstruction enriches it . . . There is so much which is so good in her reassessment that in a brief review one is embarrassed by the available riches . . . listing the virtues of this book could go on and on; in the meantime, readers will find them for themselves.' *Guardian*

'This endlessly fascinating story demands an emotional response; sympathy and imagination must be touched, as they are in Margaret Lane's moving account of the most remarkable family of the nineteenth century.'

G. M. Thomson, Evening Standard

'It is quite certain that Charlotte Brontë would not stand on so splendid a pedestal today but for the single-minded devotion of her accomplished biographer.'
Preface to *The Brontës: Life and Letters*
C. SHORTER

The Brontë Story

A RECONSIDERATION
OF MRS GASKELL'S
LIFE OF CHARLOTTE BRONTË
BY
MARGARET LANE
ILLUSTRATED BY
JOAN HASSAL

COLLINS/FONTANA

First published by William Heinemann Ltd 1953
First issued in Fontana 1969
Sixth Impression October 1973

TO MY FATHER

The cover portrait of Charlotte Brontë by
George Richmond R.A. is reproduced by kind
permission of the National Portrait Gallery.

*Printed in Great Britain
Collins Clear-Type Press
London and Glasgow*

CONTENTS

FOREWORD

This book is intended rather for the general reader than for the Brontë specialist, who will be already familiar, perhaps, with nearly everything in it. So much has been written since 1857, when Mrs Gaskell's *Life of Charlotte Brontë* appeared, that the ordinary reader, stretching up a hand to the appropriate shelf in any well-stocked library, may well hesitate. For if so much has been written since, it is reasonable to suppose that there is new material of which Mrs Gaskell knew nothing : and if that is so, which of these newer volumes contains the whole? Besides, Mrs Gaskell has been accused of timid suppressions on the one hand and libellous falsification of character on the other; so what is one to believe? And our conception of character has changed considerably since her day; we ask questions and detect motives to which Mrs Gaskell and her contemporaries would have been deaf and blind.

My aim, therefore, has been to place the reader in a discreet position behind Mrs Gaskell's shoulder, where he can comfortably see what she is writing, and watch her tackle her difficulties as she encounters them; and while he is thus strategically placed, to put into his hand all the material to which Mrs Gaskell had no access, or which, for one good reason or another, she did not use; so that he will, by the time he sees her come to her last page, be able to fill in all the gaps and make his own deductions and interpretations.

This book, in fact, is offered as a sort of footnote to Mrs Gaskell, bringing the reader back at every point to her incomparable text, and at the same time putting him in possession of everything of importance that has come to light in the century since she wrote. Provided with this footnote as well as with her *Life* he will, I hope, have in his hands the whole of the Brontë story.

I have not been able to do this without very extensive quotations from Mrs Gaskell. Where there is nothing to be added to her words, her words are always the best. Since, however, an incessant use of quotation marks in the narrative would be tedious to the eye, I have adopted the device of giving the quotations from Mrs Gaskell simply a wider margin than the main body of the text and enclosing them between distinctive signs. In this way I have hoped to let the story flow without interruption.

MARGARET LANE

I : MR BRONTË'S REQUEST

When Mrs Gaskell arrived in Haworth one afternoon in July in 1855, she was taking the first step in an adventure of twofold importance. She was preparing to display to the world a hidden life, to compose the portrait of a woman of genius. Of this she was seriously aware. She was also (although she could not be sure of this) herself about to produce her literary masterpiece.

Only a few days before, she had received a letter from the Reverend Patrick Brontë, whose daughter Charlotte had died four months ago, at the age of thirty-nine. It had been a surprising letter, for in it Mr Brontë had asked Mrs Gaskell to write a biography, and had expressly said he would wish and expect her to publish it under her own name, 'so that the work might obtain a wide circulation and be handed down to the latest times.' Surprising, because the atmosphere of Haworth Parsonage, and of Charlotte Brontë's own life, had been one of reclusive quiet. She had shrunk, herself, even from the personal recognition which was a fruit of her fame; and the circumstances of her death had been so painful—still young, newly famous, married but nine months, pregnant with her first child—that Mrs Gaskell may well have wondered that Mr Brontë should choose to have Charlotte's life exposed to view.

It was even more extraordinary when one considered that Charlotte's husband, the Reverend Arthur Bell Nicholls, was a man of extreme reticence; one who, she suspected, did not particularly care for his wife's renown. She had never met Mr Nicholls, but she seems to have had a faint distaste for him. What Charlotte had told her about him, before her marriage, had not been attractive. 'He is *not* intellectual,' she had said; '. . . he is a Puseyite and very stiff; I fear it will stand in the way of my intercourse with some of my friends.' And by that, naturally, Mrs Gaskell had understood themselves, the Gaskells, who were Unitarians : for, as Charlotte had written in her undisguised sketch of Mr Nicholls in *Shirley*, 'the circumstance of finding himself invited to tea with a dissenter would unhinge him for a week.' Yet here he was, mentioned in Mr Brontë's letter as approving of the step, and being willing to supply Mrs Gaskell with information. She may well have wondered, as the station fly crawled up the steep road from Keighley, what kind of hindrance as well as help, what veiled hostility or secretiveness, would be waiting for her in the quiet parsonage.

Mrs Gaskell had been in Haworth two years before, when Charlotte was alive, and she knew to the full how quiet the place could be. 'No-one comes to the house,' she had written to a friend after that first visit; 'nothing disturbs the deep repose; hardly a voice is heard; you catch the ticking of the clock in the kitchen, or the buzzing of a fly in the parlour, all over the house.' And Miss Brontë, who had so touched her imagination, had been alive then, so that the life of the house had flowed with a quiet pulse, and had been fed from the strange vitality that was hers, however still and absorbed she sat at the centre of it, making no sound. Whereas now, Charlotte lay under the pavement of Haworth Church; and in the parsonage, as Mrs Gaskell knew, were only the stiff, black, unbending figures of those two clergymen, sitting aloof from one another in their different studies, writing their different sermons; '*ever near* but *ever separate*', as the sexton said; with only their grief to bind them. What real help were they likely to give her, if she undertook this task? What difficult course would she have to steer among these hidden reefs, when she might be told so little and suspect so much?

As the horse plodded the winding road towards Haworth, approaching the precipitous cobbled gully which ended at the church, Mrs Gaskell must have reflected on the five years of her friendship with Charlotte Brontë, and have realised—in spite of regrets for intimacies missed, in spite of the rocks ahead—that she had been offered a perfect subject. From the first moment of meeting Miss Brontë her imagination had wakened to a quivering interest, so that everything Miss Brontë had said or done, her home life, her childhood, her sisters, her father and brother, had been invested with that potent fascination which is the biographer's essential. Contact with Charlotte had fertilised an area of her mind. It had long, unconsciously, been ready for Mr Brontë's request. The seeds were in it already.

When they had first met at Windermere in 1850, Currer Bell, author of *Jane Eyre* and *Shirley*, was already famous; and it had sufficiently got about that this masculine pseudonym concealed a Yorkshire parson's daughter for her identity to be the subject of much inquisitive guessing. They had both been staying with Sir James Kay-Shuttleworth, and Mrs Gaskell had eagerly drunk in a great deal of personal information about her fellow guest, both from Lady Kay-Shuttleworth and from Miss Brontë herself. Fascinated though she was by the little creature whom she found in the drawing-room when she arrived, it is unlikely that Mrs Gaskell, who was a pure novelist and had never written a biography, thought it might ever fall to her to write Charlotte Brontë's life. Besides, Miss Brontë was six years younger than herself, and though she looked delicate there was nothing to suggest that in less than five years she would be dead. So it is all the more interesting to know what were Mrs Gaskell's first impressions, since they were the dropped seeds of the unthought-of book; and by one of those miracles of good fortune which have preserved so many treasures from that letter-writing age her long letter to Catherine Winkworth is still before us.

'I have been spending the week in the same house with Miss Brontë. Now is not this material enough for one letter, let alone my home events? . . . Such a life as Miss B.'s I never heard of before. Lady K.-S. described her home to me as in a village of a few grey stone houses perched up on the north side of a bleak moor . . . There is a court of turf and a stone wall. (No flowers or shrubs will grow there) a straight walk, and you come to the parsonage door with a window on each side of it. The parsonage has never had a touch of paint or an article of new furniture for 30 years; never since Miss B.'s mother died. She was a "pretty young creature" brought from Penzance in Cornwall by the Irish Curate, who got his moorland living. Her friends disowned her at her marriage. She had 6 children as fast as could be; and what with that and the climate, and the strange half-mad husband she had chosen, she died at the end of 9 years. An old woman at Burnley who nursed her at last, says she used to lie crying in bed, and saying "Oh God, my poor children—oh God my poor children!" continually. Mr Brontë vented his anger against *things* not persons; for instance, once in one of his wife's confinements something went wrong, so he got a saw and went and sawed up all the chairs in her bedroom, never answering her remonstrances or minding her tears. Another time he was vexed and took the hearth rug and tied it in a tight bundle and set it on fire in the grate, and sat before it with a leg on each hob, heaping on more coals till it was burnt, no-one else being able to endure in the room because of the stifling smoke. All this Lady K.-S. told me. The sitting-room at the parsonage looks into the Church-yard, filled with graves. Mr B. has never taken a meal with his children since his wife's death unless he invited them to tea—never to dinner. And he has only once left home since to come to Manchester to be operated upon for cataract. . . . Well! these five daughters and one son grew older—their father never taught the girls anything—only the servant taught them to read and write. But I suppose they laid their heads together, for at 12 Charlotte (this one) presented a request to the father that they might go to school; so they were sent to Cowan Bridge (the place where the Daughters of the Clergy were before they were removed to Casterton). There the two elder died in that fever. Miss B. says the pain she suffered from hunger was not to be told, and her two younger sisters laid the foundation of the consumption of which they are now dead. They all came home ill. But the poverty of home was very great ("at 19 I should have been thankful for an allowance of 1d. a week. I asked my father, but he said what did women want with money?"). So at 19 she advertised and got a teacher's place in a school—(where she did not say, only said it was preferable to the governess's place she got afterwards) but she saved up enough to pay for her journey to a school in Brussels. She had never been out of Yorkshire before; and was so frightened when she got to London—she took a cab, it was night, and drove down to the Tower Stairs and went to the Ostend Packet and they refused to take her in; but at last they did. She was in this school at Brussels two years without a holiday except one week with one of her Belgian schoolfellows. Then she came home and her sisters were ill, and her father going blind—so she thought she ought to stay at home. She tried to teach herself drawing and to be an artist, but she could not . . . she had always wished to write and believed that she could; at 16 she had sent some of her poems to Southey, and had "kind, stringent" answers from him. So she and her sisters tried. They kept their initials and took names that would do either for a man or a woman. They used to read to each other when they had written so much—their father never knew a word about it. He had never heard of *Jane Eyre* when, 3 months after its publication, she promised her sisters one day at dinner she would tell him before tea. So she marched into his study with a copy wrapped up and the reviews. She said (I think I can remember the exact words): "Papa, I've been writing a book." "Have you, my dear?" and he went on reading. "But, Papa, I want you to look at it." "I can't be troubled to read MS." "But it is printed." "I hope you have not been involving yourself in any such silly expense." "I think I shall gain money by it. May I read you some reviews?" So she read them; and then she asked him if he would read the book. He said she might leave it, and he would see. But he sent them an invitation to tea that night, and towards the end of tea he said, "Children, Charlotte has been writing a book—and I think it is a better one than I expected." He never spoke about it again till about a month ago and they never dared to tell him of the books her sisters wrote. Just in the success of *Jane Eyre* her sisters died of rapid consumption *unattended by any* doctor, why I don't know. But she says she will have none and her death will be quite lonely; having no friend or relation in the world to nurse her, and her father dreading a sick room above all places. There seems little doubt she herself is already tainted with consumption.'

So there it all was, dashed down in a letter, as one might scrawl the shape of a design on the back of an envelope. Not altogether accurate, perhaps, but the outline was there; and it reflected faithfully the image which had been impressed on her imagination. She was able to fill in some detail the following year, when Charlotte had spent three days with her in Manchester, and, later, two more short visits; and in 1853 Mrs Gaskell had gone to Haworth for a few days, and had seen for herself what life at the parsonage was like. 'The wind,' she wrote afterwards in a letter, 'goes piping and wailing and sobbing round the square unsheltered house in a very strange unearthly way'—though it was only September; and she recorded her sly observation of Mr Brontë. 'What he does with himself through the day I cannot imagine! He is a tall fine looking old man, with silver bristles all over his head; nearly blind. . . . He was very polite and agreeable to me; paying rather elaborate old-fashioned compliments, but I was sadly afraid of him in my inmost soul; for I caught a glare of his stern eyes over his spectacles at Miss Brontë once or twice which made me know my man.'

She now had to deal with Mr Brontë himself, and listen to his proposition, as well as to make acquaintance with Mr Nicholls; and there may well have been some apprehension in her mind as she arrived at the parsonage. But the interview, though necessarily in that house of mourning delicate enough, seems to have been harmonious, and Mrs Gaskell found it possible to discuss her most obvious difficulty. Would there be enough material for a life? Mr Nicholls thought it doubtful. His wife's existence had, in his view, been uneventful; yet

Jane Eyre having had the success it had and being the kind of book it was, he was aware that public curiosity about her would be intensely personal; and as he was a man of strong feelings, who had been deeply in love, he shrank with distaste from the thought of this literary prying. The whole vexed question of biography had, in fact, to be examined and decided at this first interview, with Mr Nicholls representing the private interest—the husband, the widower, who had an aversion from private letters being made public and who preferred that nothing further should be said. Mrs Gaskell, naturally, would take the opposite view; and justly; having a splendid piece of work to her hand and a perfect confidence in her own delicacy and honour. Charlotte Brontë would be safe with her, and they all knew it. The unexpected point of view, perhaps, was Mr Brontë's; for Mrs Gaskell had never thought him appreciative of Charlotte's genius or sympathetic as a father; yet it was his 'impetuous wish' that the biography should be written. Certainly, as the talk deepened through the summer afternoon, his characteristic blend of intellectual pride and personal vanity must gradually have emerged, touched by the pathos which was softening the harsh outlines of his old age. He had been full of drive and ambition as a young man, and nothing had come of it but a handful of still-born verse and pamphlets and his Sunday sermons. His only son, formed, as he believed, for the achievements of genius, had died in disgrace. All his five daughters were dead, and now, near the end of his life, he found himself alone with the Irish curate whom he had hated and despised, and whom at one time he had forbidden Charlotte to marry.

Into this drained life, however, had come a compensation. He had been slow to recognise it, but he now drew comfort and pleasure from Charlotte's fame. After her death, of course, he had adopted the conventional pose of preferring silence; but within a few months the inevitable had happened—articles were appearing in magazines which he liked even less than the thought of a biography. Once the idea had taken root (and the seed had been dropped by Ellen Nussey, Charlotte's lifelong friend, who had been affronted by an article in *Sharpe's Magazine* and had written to Mr Nicholls to point out that if it went uncontradicted the public would be 'left to imbibe a tissue of malignant falsehoods') it developed at once into a dominating interest. So that he became unexpectedly Mrs Gaskell's ally, and overrode his son-in-law's objections; 'not perceiving,' as she told Miss Nussey, 'the full extent of the great interest in her personal history felt by strangers, but desirous above all things that her life should be written, and written by me.'

There were not many of Charlotte's letters in the house; only about a dozen, mostly written to her sister Emily, with one or two to her father and brother and one to her aunt. If Mr Nicholls had kept the letters which Charlotte had written to him before their marriage, he did not disclose them. It was a poor beginning. There was, however, a source of material known to Mr Brontë and Mr Nicholls to which Mrs Gaskell was directed; and which proved so rich that it is doubtful whether, without it, her book could have been written. This was that same Ellen Nussey who had been Charlotte's friend since she was fifteen years old, and to whom she had written scores upon scores of letters. Indeed, for as long as Mr Brontë and Mr Nicholls could remember, whenever Charlotte had been found writing a letter, it was generally to Ellen; and the friendship had been so intimate and the letters so long that Mr Nicholls had never felt quite easy about them. 'Arthur has just been glancing over this note,' Charlotte had added at the end of a letter to Ellen Nussey when she had been four months married; 'He thinks I have written too freely. . . . Arthur says such letters as mine never ought to be kept, they are dangerous as lucifer matches, so be sure to follow a recommendation he has just given, "fire them" or "there will be no more", such is his resolve. I can't help laughing, this seems to me so funny.'

It did not, however, seem funny to Mr Nicholls, who pursued the matter with humourless persistence, and laid it down that unless Ellen promised to burn Charlotte's letters as soon as she had read them, he himself would censor the correspondence. 'Arthur complains that you do not distinctly promise to burn my letters as you receive them. He says you must give him a plain pledge to that effect, or he will read

16

every line I write and elect himself censor. . . . Write him out his promise on a separate slip of paper, in a legible hand, and send it in your next.'

Ellen had kept nearly all of Charlotte's letters for the past twenty years, and if anything were needed to make her value the collection more than she already did, it was Mr Nicholls's prohibition. However, finding herself cornered, she wrote him the required promise, assuring him that 'As you seem to hold in great horror the ardentia verba of feminine epistles, I pledge myself to the destruction of Charlotte's epistles, henceforth, if you pledge yourself to *no* authorship in the matter communicated.' We wonder, as we consider this brief note, whether there is not something rather sly about 'henceforth', as though Miss Nussey meant to rely on it as her excuse for preserving the letters of the past, and burning only those that she might get in the future. Whichever way she meant her promise, we are thankful to know that it was immediately broken, and that Charlotte's letters continued to accumulate as before; so that when Mr Nicholls advised Mrs Gaskell to apply to Miss Nussey for specimens of his wife's correspondence ('especially those of an early date,' he wrote warningly to Miss Nussey, '—I think I understood you to say that you had some . . . not for publication, but merely to give the writer an insight into her mode of thought') she was able to put into Mrs Gaskell's hands an intimate and fairly complete collection.

How we wish that Charlotte's other lifelong friend, Mary Taylor, had been able to do the same! For this other Yorkshire girl who, like Ellen Nussey, had made friends with Charlotte at school, was a person of an altogether different stamp—harsh, independent and mentally alert where Ellen was pious and conventional. She had been able to meet Charlotte on her own intellectual ground, and to discuss matters which would have been shocking or mystifying to Ellen. But alas! Mary had never kept Charlotte's letters, or at least only a few. 'I wish I had kept Charlotte's letters now,' she wrote to Ellen, hearing that Mrs Gaskell was at work; 'though I never felt safe to do so until latterly that I have had a home of my own. They would have been much better evidence than my imperfect recollection, and infinitely more interesting.'

In Ellen Nussey, however, Mrs Gaskell had a source of material and an eager helper such as falls to the lot of very few biographers. She was not in herself an interesting character, being neither remarkable nor particularly intelligent; but, perhaps because of her negative pliability, she had been an excellent confidante for Charlotte. She was affectionate; she was loyal; and she possessed those scrupulous Victorian virtues of truthfulness and delicacy which have so greatly lost prestige in our own times, but which remain the most serviceable foundations of enduring friendship. Charlotte had loved her, though she had known her limitations, as those vital areas which are never approached in the letters bear silent witness; and round Charlotte, Ellen had gradually built up the greatest remaining interest of her life.

This life, like Mr Brontë's, had become more than usually empty since Charlotte's death, and like him she focused a personal and enthralled attention on the biography. She rushed at the subject with the unaffected, unintelligent piety which is the keynote of her nature. She hoped Mrs Gaskell would undertake a 'just and honourable defence'; it was a 'righteous work' to vindicate 'dear C.', and she would do everything in her power to forward it. 'I possess a great many letters,' she wrote, 'for I have destroyed but a small portion of the correspondence, but I fear the early letters are not such as to unfold the character of the writer except in a few points. You perhaps may discover more than is apparent to me. You will read them with a purpose—I perused them only with interests of affection.'

Mrs Gaskell's eye was more penetrating than Miss Nussey's, her understanding deeper, her purpose more mature; and as, during that autumn and winter, she read her way steadily through the parcels of Charlotte's letters, she began to see with marvellous clarity the sombre but fertile landscape through which her search would take her. By the turn of the year she was deeply engaged in her task.

II: HAWORTH PARSONAGE

In the spring and summer of 1856 Mrs Gaskell made a
number of journeys to places connected with Charlotte
Brontë's life. She spent a fortnight in Haworth, staying at the
'Black Bull' with her husband and conducting researches
independently of the parsonage. She went to London, where
she spent many hours with George Smith, Charlotte's publisher and friend, who furnished her with much information
and who had been chosen, not unnaturally, to publish the
biography. She also, conscious of the importance of this
particular mission, went to Brussels. 'In fact,' as she wrote
in the summer to Ellen Nussey, 'I now think I have been
everywhere where she ever lived, except of course her two
little pieces of private governess-ship.' It was a summer spent
in minutely feeling her subject, and discovering its variously
smooth and prickly surfaces.

Her impression of Mr Brontë, which was one of reclusive selfishness combined with a certain moral fearlessness and integrity, had been deepened by what she heard of him in the village; and she felt bound to describe him as truthfully as she dared because of his bearing on Charlotte's life and character. Uncomfortably conscious of his still alert presence in the parsonage, and of herself therefore, as Mary Taylor put it, 'not being at liberty to give a true description of those around', she was often puzzled how to steer a successful course between truth and policy; and when she sent some tentative pages to Mr Smith and Ellen Nussey in private, they both advised her to soften what she had written. 'I thought,' she wrote to Miss Nussey, 'that I carefully preserved the reader's respect of Mr Brontë, while truth and the desire of doing justice to her compelled me to state the domestic peculiarities of her childhood.' But Mr Smith had pencilled cautionary words in the margin which made her 'rather uncomfortable', and Ellen Nussey had replied—having a long personal knowledge of Mr Brontë and none of the publisher's experienced dread of what the reviewers might make of it—'I do not wish anything you have said suppressed, only I think your readers will have to be taught to think kindly of Mr B. . . .'

Then there was Mr Nicholls, who, while not being positively unhelpful, was, somehow, dry and unyielding. She guessed he had material which he did not wish to show, and his reserve and her good breeding being what they were, her delicacy quailed before him.

'Mr N. ought to have no reserve with you,' Ellen Nussey wrote, 'his very affection should make him see it is wisest, best and kindest to tell the whole truth to you in everything that regards her literary life or her domestic virtues. . . . I hope you may be able to open his heart, he spoke in one of his notes to me last year of having implicit confidence in you. I think you may win him by your own heartiness in the work—at any rate you will Mr B., and for a quiet life Mr N. will have to yield where Mr B. is urgent and impatient.' But would he? 'It seems,' wrote Mrs Gaskell, 'as if Mr Brontë's own consent or opinion on these matters had very little weight with Mr Nicholls.'

The parsonage, in fact, was so rich a field for research that it could not be neglected; but it was also the thorniest area that she had to work in. 'I still,' she told Ellen, 'want one or two things to complete my materials, and I am very doubtful if I can get them—at any rate I think they will necessitate my going to Haworth again, and I am literally *afraid* of that.' However, when she finally went she was unexpectedly fortunate, for she was accompanied by Sir James Kay-Shuttleworth, who, like Mr Clement Shorter nearly forty years later, was inhibited by not the smallest feeling of delicacy. Blunt methods, as it surprisingly turned out, were what were most successful with Mr Nicholls. Sir James was a somewhat overwhelming figure, a noted philanthropist and the founder of our modern system of education; if he had a foible, it was to wish to be thought intimate with literary celebrities. It was to indulge this vanity that he had assiduously entertained Mrs Gaskell, and had pressed his benevolent but undesired friendship on Charlotte Brontë. Now that Miss Brontë was dead he by no means relaxed his attention, for, as Mrs Gaskell was quick to perceive, 'Sir J. evidently wants to appear to the world in intimate connexion with her.' He was not the most comfortable companion for such a visit, but his sledge-hammer methods succeeded where Mrs Gaskell's persuasive tact had failed. 'He had not the slightest delicacy or scruple : and asked for an immense number of things, literally taking no refusal. Hence we carried away with us a whole heap of those minute writings . . . the beginning (only about 20 pages) of a new novel which she had written at the end of 1854, before marriage, and I dare say when she was anxious enough. This fragment was excessively interesting.'

The 'minute writings' were, of course, some of those bundles of microscopic works with which Charlotte, Emily, Anne and Branwell Brontë had occupied themselves as children, and of which Mrs Gaskell, conscientiously glancing but doing no more than glance, was to miss the extraordinary significance. Among them she found scraps which were much more obviously valuable and which she seized upon at once—'quantities of fragments very short but very graphic written when she was about 12, giving glimpses of her life at that time, all of which I had to decipher, and interweave with what I had already written—in fact I had to rewrite about 40 pages. They give a much pleasanter though hardly less *queer* notion of the old father.'

Mrs Gaskell was now in the full turmoil of her task, carried away on a tide of creative energy and excitement. She went up to her room 'directly after 9 o'clock breakfast; and came down to lunch at ½ p. 1, up again and write without allowing any temptation to carry me off till 5—or past: having just a run of a walk before 7 o'clock dinner. . . . I could not sleep for thinking of it.'

She had begun: and now that she was away from Haworth she could see how completely the pattern of that grey stone village, with its harsh outlines of parsonage, graveyard and surrounding moors, dominated her theme. There can hardly ever have been a story more powerfully riveted to a place than that of the Brontës to Haworth; and the intensity of their identification with it had been stamped again and again on Mrs Gaskell's perceptions until it seemed to her that the very stones might speak. Here they had been brought up as children; here, with only one or two brief disastrous excursions into the world, they had spent their lives; here they had all, save Anne, died and been buried. The books which had made Charlotte famous had been conceived and written in that little square sitting-room which had not known the touch of paint or the luxury of curtains for more than thirty years. The bitter experience of life which had made her what she was had been endured, day in, day out, in that grey stone house; so that, when one stood at the stair-foot and remembered, the very flagstones seemed possessed of mysterious significance. It was even, and lately, in the very room that Mrs Gaskell had slept in that Charlotte had died.

It is impossible for anyone who goes to the parsonage today to see it with Mrs Gaskell's eyes: it is so subtly changed. The structure of the house is not much altered, except for the large ground-floor room at the side which Mr Brontë's successor added, and the transformation of the back part to suit the functions of a museum, which does not need a kitchen; but the aspect is very different. Trees have been induced to grow as a shelter to the strip of garden, a showy wrought-iron sign hangs out from the side of the house, and the lawn is tended to a suburban perfection. However, there is no need to drive our imaginations to the other extreme, as so many writers on the Brontës have done, and picture the parsonage as almost the last accessible outpost of civilisation, perpetually swept by northern gales and separated by miles of savage moorland from any other habitation. In the Brontës' day it stood, as now, at the head of an unbeautiful but workmanlike and decent Yorkshire village, steeply set on its hill in the grey, green and black of a semi-industrial landscape. It is cobbled, noisy, unpretentious and, to southern eyes at least, a little grim. The graveyard surrounds the house and garden on two sides, and is as full of graves as any place can be. The gravestones do, indeed, seem to press and close in about the place; they crowd and bristle and conceal the turf; and when it rains, the slab surfaces appal the eye with their unbroken gleam. Behind and above the house lie two or three short-cropped, stone-walled fields with stiles. This is the way to the moors. The moors are not sensational, for they appear as a rolling plateau almost devoid of features and drained of colour; one can stand below them and be unaware that they are there. But they are far bigger than one at first imagines, and, to the eye which perceives the beauty of vast, monotonous and unemphatic places, curiously rewarding. The apparent plain is full of folds and hills, where the valley world is lost sight of and drops away; it is seamed with little streams and hidden waterfalls, where clear brown water pours over dappled stones; and the whole expanse is covered with heather and bilberry, in which innumerable larks conceal their nests. It is a landscape which has nothing to do with man, and has little to invite him : but at the end of summer, after ten months of the year offering a blackened and colourless beauty only to the discerning, the moors above Haworth blaze into sudden splendour, and crown the black and green industrial valleys with wave after wave of heather-coloured hills.

Mrs Gaskell, a northerner herself (since she came of Lancashire stock and lived in Manchester), was not appalled by Haworth, as some later writers have allowed themselves to

be. She saw it for what it was—a Yorkshire village in a manu-
facturing district : and she so described it. The inhabitants, of
strong and independent temper, as Yorkshire people always
appear to be, impressed her as somewhat surly and unattractive.
They had their virtues, which are still the same; but she could
not fail to remark the gritty surface. Indeed, that Yorkshire
love of bluntness and contempt for the shifts of tact, that
veneration for money and opinionated self-reliance which one
can still see, today, sometimes developed beyond the bounds of
dignity or virtue, were undoubtedly more strongly marked
a hundred years ago, when the West Riding had less communication with the world and was open to fewer softening
impressions. This character was important, for Charlotte
Brontë had been born and reared in its influence, herself
sharing its virtues and some of its acerbities; and as Mrs Gaskell
analysed and described the Yorkshire temperament it was with
a conscious if sidelong glance at its vestiges in Charlotte.

§ Each man relies upon himself, and seeks no help at the
hands of his neighbour. From rarely requiring the assistance
of others, he comes to doubt the power of bestowing it :
from the general success of his efforts, he grows to depend
upon them, and to over-esteem his own energy and power.
He belongs to that keen, yet short-sighted class, who consider suspicion of all whose honesty is not proved as a sign
of wisdom. The practical qualities of a man are held in
great respect; but the want of faith in strangers and untried
modes of action, extends itself even to the manner in which
the virtues are regarded; and if they produce no immediate
and tangible result, they are rather put aside as unfit for this
busy, striving world; especially if they are more of a passive than an active character. The affections are strong, and
their foundations lie deep : but they are not—such affections
seldom are—widespreading; nor do they show themselves
on the surface. Indeed, there is little display of any of the
amenities of life among this wild, rough population. Their
accost is curt; their accent and tone of speech blunt and
harsh. . . . They have a quick perception of character, and a
keen sense of humour; the dwellers among them must be

24

prepared for certain uncomplimentary, though most likely true, observations, pithily expressed. Their feelings are not easily roused, but their duration is lasting. . . .

Even now, a stranger can hardly ask a question without receiving some crusty reply, if, indeed, he receive any at all. Sometimes the sour rudeness amounts to positive insult. Yet, if the 'foreigner' takes all this churlishness good-humouredly, or as a matter of course, and makes good any claim upon their latent kindliness and hospitality, they are faithful and generous, and thoroughly to be relied upon. §
In this part of the country, as Mrs. Gaskell could not fail to be aware, Protestantism in its many aspects and its least attractive forms had taken hold. The Methodist revival of the eighteenth century had here achieved some of its most sensational salvations and repentances; and though the exaltation of the movement had long since died away, there remained here and there that curious blend of extreme puritanism with unregenerate moral violence which is so strangely found in the temperament of some natural dissenters.

§ The people of this district are 'strong religionists'; only, fifty years ago, their religion did not work down into their lives. Half that length of time back, the code of morals seemed to be formed upon that of their Norse ancestors. Revenge was handed down from father to son as an hereditary duty; and a great capability for drinking, without the head being affected, was considered as one of the manly virtues. . . . The old custom of 'arvills' was as prevalent as ever. The sexton, standing at the foot of the open grave, announced that the 'arvill' would be held at the 'Black Bull', or whatever public house might be fixed upon by the friends of the dead; and thither the mourners and their acquaintances repaired. . . . Among the poor, the mourners were only expected to provide a kind of spiced roll for each person; and the expense of the liquors—rum, or ale, or a mixture of both called 'dog's nose'—was generally defrayed by each guest placing some money on a plate, set in the middle of the table. Richer people would order a dinner for their friends. . . . As few 'shirked their liquor', there were very frequently 'up-and-down fights' before the close of the day; sometimes with the horrid additions of 'pawsing' and 'gouging', and biting. . . .

Into the midst of this lawless, yet not unkindly population, Mr Brontë brought his wife and six little children, in February, 1820. There are those yet alive who remember seven heavily-laden carts lumbering slowly up the long stone street, bearing the 'new parson's' household goods to his future abode.

One wonders how the bleak aspect of her new home— the low, oblong stone parsonage, high up, yet with a still higher background of sweeping moors—struck on the gentle delicate wife, whose health even then was failing. §

In describing the parsonage itself Mrs. Gaskell found no difficulty. It was modest; it was Spartan; but it was not un-homely.

§ The parsonage stands at right-angles to the road, facing down upon the church; so that, in fact, parsonage, church, and belfried school-house form three sides of an irregular oblong, of which the fourth is open to the fields and moors that lie beyond. The area of this oblong is filled up by a crowded churchyard, and a small garden or court in front of the clergyman's house. As the entrance to this from the road is at the side, the path goes round the corner into the little plot of ground. Underneath the windows is a narrow flower border, carefully tended in days of yore, although only the most hardy plants could be made to grow there. Within the stone wall, which keeps out the surrounding churchyard, are bushes of elder and lilac; the rest of the ground is occupied by a square grass plot and a gravel walk. The house is of grey stone, two stories high, heavily roofed with flags, in order to resist the winds which might strip off a lighter covering. It appears to have been built about a hundred years ago, and to consist of four rooms on each story; the two windows on the right (as the visitor stands with his back to the church, ready to enter in at the front door) belonging to Mr Brontë's study, the two on the left to the family sitting-room. Everything about the place tells of the most dainty order, the most exquisite cleanliness. The doorsteps are spotless; the small old-fashioned window-panes glitter like looking-glass. Inside and outside of that house cleanliness goes up into its essence, purity. §

But describing Mr Brontë was another matter. Mrs Gaskell had known him, slightly, for several years; she had stayed in his house, where she had attentively observed the relations between Charlotte and her father; and the con-clusion she had formed was that he was an eccentric, domin-eering, selfish and irascible old man. She was not alone in this view, for Mary Taylor, Charlotte's lifelong friend who had known him since she was a girl, had written to Miss Nussey, 'I can never think without gloomy anger of Charlotte's sacri-fices to the selfish old man'; and it is probable that Mrs Gaskell had seen this letter. Besides, Charlotte had confided in Mrs Gaskell during the painful time before her father had consented to her marriage; and though Charlotte had never blamed him, and had been torn through the whole affair between guilt and duty, Mrs Gaskell had seen easily enough through her harassed loyalty to the discreditable background of his selfishness. The solitary habits, too, which had grown on him with age, and the authoritarian atmosphere of his presence, had deepened her first impression; and she had found that, while not actually disliked (since he kept so much to himself and never interfered with his parishioners), he was very far from popular in the village.

During her first visit to Haworth, when Charlotte was alive, she had naturally talked to the daughter about the father, and from her, sitting over the parlour fire in the eve-ning, had learned much. 'Mr Brontë,' she had written to a friend, as soon as she was home again, 'lives almost entirely in the room opposite. . . . We dined—she and I together—Mr Brontë having his dinner sent to him in his sitting-room according to his invariable custom (fancy it! and only they two left). . . . He is a tall fine-looking old man . . . nearly blind; speaking with a strong Scotch accent (he comes from the North of Ireland), raised himself from the ranks of a poor farmer's son—and was rather intimate with Lord Palmerston at Cambridge, a pleasant soothing reflection now, in his shut-out life. There was not a sign of engraving, map, writing materials, beyond a desk, etc., no books but those contained on two hanging shelves between the windows—his two pipes, etc., a spittoon, if you know what that is.' He was, she said, 'much respected and to be respected. But he ought never to have married. He did not like children; and they had six in six years, and the consequent pinching and family disorder—(which can't be helped), and noise, etc., made him shut himself up and want no companionship—nay be positively annoyed by it. He won't let Miss Brontë accompany him in his walks, although he is so nearly blind; goes out in defiance of her gentle attempts to restrain him, speaking as if she thought him in his second childhood; and comes home moaning and tired :—having lost his way. "Where is my strength gone?" is his cry then, "I used to walk 40 miles a day" . . . Moreover to account for my fear—rather an admiring fear after all—of Mr Brontë, please take into account that though I like beautiful glittering of bright flashing steel I don't fancy firearms at all, at all—and Miss Brontë never remembers her father dressing himself in the morning without putting a loaded pistol in his pocket, just as regularly as he puts on his watch. There was this little deadly pistol sitting down to breakfast with us, kneeling down to prayers at night to say nothing of a loaded gun hanging up on high, ready to pop off on the slightest emergency.'

In her search for material Mrs Gaskell seems not to have paid much attention to Martha Brown, the servant at the parsonage; nor, in particular, to have questioned her at all about Mr Brontë. It is possible that she never thought of it, but more likely that she avoided this obvious course out of a feeling of delicacy. It would not have been easy, after listening to Mr Brontë in the parlour, to have gone for corroboration to the kitchen. But it is a pity, after all, that she did not; for it seems quite certain that Mr Brontë was a more sympathetic character than she knew; that there was a genial and touching as well as a harsh side to his nature, and that Martha was aware of this. Mrs Gaskell, however, prompted perhaps by her desire to know more of those early years before ever Martha Brown had come to the parsonage, took as her informant a 'good old woman' who had been day-nurse to Mrs

Brontë in her last illness, and whom she must have been delighted to find still alive and in Haworth, and apparently in excellent memory. This old woman related anecdotes of Mr Brontë's early married life which, in their very violence and oddity, seemed to fit in so perfectly with what Mrs Gaskell conceived to be his character that she never questioned them. One sees that it would have been difficult to interrogate Mr Brontë, since the anecdotes were so little to his credit; but one is startled by the recklessness with which Mrs Gaskell adopted them. There seems little doubt that by her unconscious selection of evidence she created a legend about Charlotte Brontë's father which, after the manner of legends, contains more of poetic than of actual truth. She seems to have done him less than justice; to have made him more picturesque and less understandable than he really was; and yet to have drawn a portrait which, for all its over-dramatic chiaroscuro, conveys an impression of mass and outline which one feels is true.

§ The Rev Patrick Brontë is a native of the County Down, in Ireland. His father, Hugh Brontë, was left an orphan at an early age. He came from the south to the north of the island, and settled in the parish of Ahaderg, near Loughbrickland. There was some family tradition that, humble as Hugh Brontë's circumstances were, he was the descendant of an ancient family. But about this neither he nor his descendants have cared to enquire. He made an early marriage and reared and educated ten children on the proceeds of the few acres of land which he farmed. This large family were remarkable for great physical strength and much natural beauty. Even in his old age, Mr Brontë is a striking-looking man, above the common height, with a nobly shaped head and erect carriage. In his youth he must have been unusually handsome. §

Mrs Gaskell did not say (and very likely Mr Brontë did not tell her) that the name of this crofter family was Brunty or Bruntee, and that he himself had been entered at St John's College, Cambridge, as Patrick Branty. The improvement of the name to Brontë, which seems to have taken place while he was an undergraduate, had nothing to do with the myth of an 'ancient family' (which was simply a normal manifestation

29

of the grandiose Irish feeling for descent from kings) and was most probably suggested by Lord Nelson's being created Duke of Brontë. The changed name, and the appearance at Cambridge of this almost penniless Irish boy, were tokens of what Mrs Gaskell recognised as his 'extraordinary quickness and intelligence'. It is a familiar phenomenon, the sudden rise to comparative eminence in priesthood, medicine or law of a child reared in primitive poverty in an Irish cabin. Quick intellect and a yearning for education are Celtic traits, and Mr Brontë in his youth was goaded by a powerful mixture of vanity and ambition. How precisely he got to Cambridge, and maintained himself there for nearly four years, until he had taken a degree and holy orders, has never been made clear : he can have done it only on a Spartan level. As a boy in Ireland he had been put into the local weaving trade, and had struggled out of that to become a teacher in the little Protestant parish school of Drumballyroney, where he taught both himself and others until he was twenty-five years old. By this time he seems to have saved a few pounds out of his small earnings, and with this little capital, and a few pounds more subscribed by one or two benevolent Methodist clergymen, who were impressed by his capabilities and evidently thought him a likely recruit to the connection, he made his own way to Cambridge. That his life there must have been of a beggarly simplicity is suggested by a letter from one of these kindly clergymen to another, written at a time when Mr Brontë had been a commoner at St John's College for nearly two years. 'I availed myself as soon as possible of your generous offer to Mr Brontë, and left it without hesitation to himself to fix the limits of his request. He says that £20 per annm. will enable him to go on with comfort, but that he could do with less. He has twice given me some account of his outset to college. . . . He left his native Ireland . . . with seven pounds, having been able to lay by no more after superintending a school for some years. He reached Cambridge before that was expended, and then received an unexpected supply of £5 from a distant friend. On this he subsisted some weeks before entering at St John's, and has since had no other assistance than what the college afforded.' The sums which he drew from college were the emoluments of a scholarship and two exhibitions which he won at Cambridge, and the fees he was able to earn by coaching less promising students. He made enough, and was sufficiently strict with himself on the point of expense, to be able, like a good Irish son, to send his mother £20 a year during this period.

He evidently, and justifiably, convinced a sufficient number of people of his talents; and so, by one means and another, and a little modest help from various quarters, contrived to stay on until he had taken his B.A. degree at the age of twenty-nine, and had been ordained to a curacy in Essex. Here, at Wethersfield in that county, he remained for three years, and came very near to being married. Nobody knows for certain why he did not marry Miss Mary Burder. It has been said that her guardian forbade it and removed her from the neighbourhood; but fifteen years later, when Mary Burder briefly appears once more in Mr Brontë's story, it emerges fairly clearly that he had jilted her; and the suggestion is there that, being ambitious and self-confident, he had felt that by waiting he might possibly do better. At all events, the feelings he left in Mary Burder's breast were of extreme bitterness, as we shall see; and in leaving Essex he went as far away as possible; for in 1812, at the age of thirty-five, and after a brief curacy in Shropshire, we find him at Hartshead, near Dewsbury in Yorkshire; and, what is more interesting, newly married. His bride was Miss Maria Branwell, a native of Penzance and a member of a pious Methodist family.

§ In the early summer of 1812, when she would be twenty-nine, she came to visit her uncle, the Reverend John Fennel, who was at that time a clergyman of the Church of England, living near Leeds, but who had previously been a Methodist minister. Mr Brontë was the incumbent of Hartshead; and had the reputation in the neighbourhood of being a very handsome fellow, full of Irish enthusiasm, and with something of an Irishman's capability of falling easily in love. Miss Branwell was extremely small in person; not pretty, but very elegant, and always dressed with a quiet simplicity of taste, which accorded well with her general character, and of which some of the details call to mind the

31

style of dress preferred by her daughter for her favourite heroines. Mr Brontë was soon captivated by the little, gentle creature and this time declared that it was for life. §

Little and gentle though she was, Miss Branwell was by no means characterless and seems to have been all the happier in accepting the authority of a husband from the consideration that she had, in the past, enjoyed almost too much of her own way. 'For some years I have been perfectly my own mistress,' she wrote to Mr Brontë, 'subject to no control whatever; so far from it that my sisters, who are many years older than myself, and even my dear mother, used to consult me on every occasion of importance, and scarcely ever doubted the propriety of my opinions and actions; perhaps you will be ready to accuse me of vanity in mentioning this, but you must consider that I do not boast of it. I have many times felt it a disadvantage, and although, I thank God, it has never led me into error, yet, in circumstances of uncertainty and doubt, I have deeply felt the want of a guide and instructor.'

The simple wedding arrangements were soon made, and Mrs Gaskell seems to have obtained what details she needed from the descendants of the Branwell family in Cornwall, rather than from Mr Brontë: indeed, we get the impression that he did not tell her much about his wife, and that she perhaps shrank from questioning him. After all, there was not much to tell.

§ The journey from Penzance to Leeds in those days was both very long and very expensive; the lovers had not much money to spend in unnecessary travelling, and, as Miss Branwell had neither father nor mother living, it appeared both a discreet and seemly arrangement that the marriage should take place from her uncle's house. There was no reason either why the engagement should be prolonged. They were past their first youth; they had means sufficient for their unambitious wants; the living of Hartshead is rated in the Clergy List at £202 per annum, and she was in receipt of a small annuity (£50 I have been told) by the will of her father. So, at the end of September, the lovers began to talk about taking a house, for I suppose that Mr Brontë up to that time had been in lodgings; and all went smoothly and successfully with a view to their marriage in the ensuing winter, until November, when a misfortune happened, which she thus patiently and prettily describes:—

'I suppose you never expected to be much the richer for me, but I am sorry to inform you that I am still poorer than I thought myself. I mentioned having sent for my books, clothes, etc. On Saturday evening, about the time when you were writing the description of your imaginary ship-wreck, I was reading and feeling the effects of a real one, having then received a letter from my sister giving me an account of the vessel in which she had sent my box being stranded on the coast of Devonshire, in consequence of which the box was dashed to pieces with the violence of the sea, and all my little property, with the exception of a very few articles, being swallowed up in the mighty deep. If this should not prove the prelude to something worse I shall think little of it, as it is the first disastrous circumstance which has occurred since I left my home.'

The last of these letters is dated December 5th. Miss Branwell and her cousin intended to set about making the wedding-cake in the following week, so the marriage could not be far off. She had been learning by heart a 'pretty little hymn' of Mr Brontë's composing; and reading Lord Lyttelton's 'Advice to a Lady', on which she makes some pertinent and just remarks, showing that she thought as well as read. And so Maria Branwell fades out of sight; we have no more direct intercourse with her; we hear of her as Mrs Brontë, but it is as an invalid, not far from death; still patient, cheerful and pious. The writing of these letters is elegant and neat; while there are allusions to household occupations—such as making the wedding-cake—there are also allusions to the books she has read, or is reading, show-ing a well-cultivated mind. Without having anything of her daughter's rare talents, Mrs Brontë must have been, I imagine, that unusual character, a well-balanced and con-sistent woman. The style of the letters is easy and good; as is also that of a paper from the same hand, entitled 'The

Advantages of Poverty in Religious Concerns', which was written rather later, with a view to publication in some periodical.

She was married, from her uncle's house, in Yorkshire, on the 29th of December, 1812; the same day was also the wedding day of her younger sister, Charlotte Branwell, in distant Penzance. I do not think that Mrs Brontë ever re-visited Cornwall, but she has left a very pleasant impression on the minds of those relations who yet survive; they speak of her as 'their favourite aunt, and one to whom they, as well as all the family, looked up, as a person of talent and great amiability of disposition'; and, again, as 'meek and retiring, while possessing more than ordinary talents, which she inherited from her father, and her piety was genuine and unobtrusive'. §

Mr and Mrs Brontë seem to have been sufficiently in love for their married life to have started full of gaiety and hope; and although the mean little square brick parsonage where they set up house at Hartshead, and the almost sordid street-faced dwelling which went with Mr Brontë's next curacy at Thornton, are discouraging to look at, there is no suggestion that they were disappointed with this beginning. Indeed, at Thornton near Bradford, where Mr Brontë became curate in the spring of 1815, they shared in a good deal of the parish social life, frequenting the usual amount of tea parties and modest visitings; and must certainly (since Mr Brontë could by this time claim a mild celebrity as the author of two books of verse and a small prose work of an improving nature) have been considered an asset to the neighbourhood. But it was not long before Mr Brontë was going out to tea with his parishioners alone, while his wife set about serving her quietly-accepted sentence of continuous pregnancies. Their first child, Maria, was born a year after the marriage, and was followed by a second, Elizabeth, about eighteen months later. The next three came so fast that she can hardly have risen from her lying-in before she had conceived afresh; and then there was a pause of only seventeen months before the birth of the last daughter. 'Pray much for me,' she had written to Mr Brontë before their marriage, 'that I may be made a blessing and not

34

a hindrance to you. Let me not interrupt your studies nor intrude on that time which ought to be dedicated to better purposes.' Poor Mrs Brontë! We wish she could have known that her own time, so heroically employed and quickly over, would produce marvellous fruit. But all she could see, as she lay dying at thirty-eight of cancer (and, one suspects, also of tuberculosis) was that she was leaving six small children alone with their harassed father, and had brought him so much responsibility and sorrow that she had perhaps not been quite the blessing she had meant to be.

§ At Thornton, Charlotte Brontë was born, on the 21st of April, 1816. Fast on her heels followed Patrick Branwell, Emily Jane, and Anne. After the birth of this last daughter, Mrs Brontë's health began to decline. It is hard work to provide for the little tender wants of many young children where the means are but limited. The necessaries of food and clothing are much more easily supplied than the almost equal necessaries of attendance, care, soothing, amusement and sympathy. Maria Brontë, the eldest of six, could only have been a few months more than six years old when Mr Brontë removed to Haworth, on February 25th, 1820. Those who knew her then, describe her as grave, thoughtful and quiet, to a degree far beyond her years. Her childhood was no childhood; the cases are rare in which the possessors of great gifts have known the blessings of that careless happy time; their unusual powers stir within them, and, instead of the natural life of perception—the objective, as the Germans call it—they begin the deeper life of reflection —the subjective.

Little Maria Brontë was delicate and small in appearance, which seemed to give greater effect to her wonderful precocity of intellect. She must have been her mother's companion and help-mate in many a household and nursery experience, for Mr Brontë was, of course, much engaged in his study; and besides, he was not naturally fond of children, and felt their frequent appearance on the scene as a drag both on his wife's strength and as an interruption to the comfort of the household.

Haworth Parsonage is—as I mentioned in the first chapter

—an oblong stone house, facing down the hill on which the village stands, and with the front door right opposite to the western door of the church, distant about a hundred yards. Of this space twenty yards or so in depth are occupied by the grassy garden, which is scarcely wider than the house. The grave-yard goes round house and garden, on all sides but one. The house consists of four rooms on each floor, and is two stories high. When the Brontës took possession, they made the larger parlour, to the left of the entrance, the family sitting-room, while that on the right was appropriated to Mr Brontë as a study. Behind this was the kitchen; behind the former, a sort of flagged store-room. Upstairs were four bed-chambers of similar size, with the addition of a small apartment over the passage, or 'lobby' as we call it in the north. . . . This little upstairs room was appropriated to the children. Small as it was, it was not called a nursery; indeed, it had not the comfort of a fireplace in it; the servants—two rough, affectionate, warm-hearted, wasteful sisters, who cannot now speak of the family without tears—called the room the 'children's study'. The age of the eldest student was perhaps by this time seven. §

Mr Brontë, as Mrs Gaskell learned from the villagers, was not the type of parson to establish a personal intimacy with his flock. He performed his duties conscientiously and, that done, left the parish alone. 'From individuals in the village the family stood aloof, unless some direct service was required, from the first. "They kept themselves very close," is the account given by those who remember Mr and Mrs Brontë's coming among them.' Small wonder, so far as Mrs Brontë was concerned, for with her six children (the youngest, Anne, only a month old when they came to Haworth) she was sufficiently occupied; and was besides, poor woman, already ill. Mr Brontë found the pleasures of life in his own study, where he composed his sermons, read the newspapers, and—intoxicating occupation—wrote poetry. He had published (probably at his own expense) his little volume of *Cottage Poems* the year before his marriage, and another, *The Rural Minstrel*, a year later; and had himself described the exquisite escape from ordinary life which he enjoyed behind the closed door of the parlour.

'When relieved from clerical avocations he was occupied in writing the *Cottage Poems*; from morning till noon, and from noon till night, his employment was full of indescribable pleasure, such as he could wish to taste as long as life lasts. His hours glided pleasantly and almost imperceptibly by, and when night drew on, and he retired to rest, ere his eyes closed in sleep with sweet calmness and serenity of mind, he often reflected that, though the delicate palate of criticism might be disgusted, the business of the day in the prosecution of his humble task was well pleasing in the sight of God, and by His blessing might be rendered useful to some poor soul who cared little for critical niceties.'

It is rare to find genius in a family which has given no hint or promise of its coming, and in Mr Brontë's poetic musings and little prose works, worthless though they are, and in his passion for literary composition, we perceive that craving for self-expression which was to inflame and exalt his children like a fever; and in the Spartan ambition which had lifted him from a poor Irish cabin and brought him through Cambridge to his present clerical dignity and scholarly retirement, that resolution and self-discipline which was a part of his daughters' greatness. For Mr Brontë was a remarkable man, vigorous of intellect, passionate, of complete integrity; a man guilty very often of unconscious selfishness but capable nevertheless of stringent self-denials, imposed as a matter of course and without drama. Mrs Gaskell saw him chiefly as harsh and eccentric, and conceived it her duty not to disguise her impression, since the peculiarities of the father went some way to explain the frustrations, the desperate courage, and also the slight acerbities of the daughter. His qualities of obstinacy and aloofness, his single-minded care for the things of the intellect (however mediocre his own performance) explain still more; and point a finger, inscrutable but steady, in the direction of Emily. That strange mingling of influence, that incalculable blend of experience and heredity which was to produce Charlotte and Emily, had single elements to be found in Mr Brontë, and in great strength and profusion. Mrs Gaskell was fascinated by him, though there was a strain in his personality that she found repellent; and she was a woman

37

who judged men with liking and sympathy. ('I wish I could help taking to men so much more than to women . . . and I wish I could help men taking to me; but I believe we've a mutual attraction of which Satan is the originator.') What is wonderful is that she had the courage—the foolhardiness almost—to be as outspoken as she was, in a book which was bound, sooner or later, to be read with minute attention by Mr Brontë.

§ Mr Brontë was faithful in visiting the sick and all those who sent for him, and diligent in attendance at the schools; so was his daughter Charlotte too; but, cherishing and valuing privacy themselves, they were perhaps over-delicate in not intruding upon the privacy of others.

From their first going to Haworth, their walks were directed rather out towards the heathery moors, sloping upwards behind the parsonage, than towards the long descending village street. A good old woman, who came to nurse Mrs Brontë in the illness—an internal cancer—which grew and gathered upon her, not many months after her arrival in Haworth, tells me that at that time the six little creatures used to walk out, hand in hand, towards the glorious wild moors, which in after days they loved so passionately; the elder ones taking thoughtful care for the toddling wee things.

They were grave and silent beyond their years; subdued, probably, by the presence of serious illness in the house; for, at the time which my informant speaks of, Mrs Brontë was confined to the bedroom from which she never came forth alive. 'You would not have known there was a child in the house, they were such still, noiseless, good little creatures. Maria would shut herself up' (Maria, but seven!) 'in the children's study with a newspaper, and be able to tell one everything when she came out; debates in Parliament, and I don't know what all. She was as good as a mother to her sisters and brother. But there never were such good children. I used to think them spiritless, they were so different to any children I had ever seen. They were good little creatures. Emily was the prettiest.'

Mrs Brontë was the same patient, cheerful person as we

have seen her formerly; very ill, suffering great pain, but seldom if ever complaining; at her better times begging her nurse to raise her in bed to let her see her clean the grate, 'because she did it as it was done in Cornwall'; devotedly fond of her husband, who warmly repaid her affection, and suffered no one else to take the night-nursing; but, according to my informant, the mother was not very anxious to see much of her children, probably because the sight of them, knowing how soon they were to be left motherless, would have agitated her too much. So the little things clung quietly together, for their father was busy in his study and in his parish, or with their mother, and they took their meals alone; sat reading, or whispering low, in the 'children's study', or wandered out on the hill-side, hand in hand. . . .

Mr Brontë wished to make his children hardy, and indifferent to the pleasures of eating and dress. In the latter he succeeded, as far as regarded his daughters; but he went at his object with unsparing earnestness of purpose. Mrs Brontë's nurse told me that one day when the children had been out on the moors, and rain had come on, she thought their feet would be wet, and accordingly she rummaged out some coloured boots which had been given to them by a friend. These little pairs she ranged round the kitchen fire to warm; but when the children came back the boots were nowhere to be found; only a very strong odour of burnt leather was perceived. Mr Brontë had come in and seen them; they were too gay and luxurious for his children, and would foster a love of dress; so he had put them into the fire. He spared nothing that offended his antique simplicity. Long before this, some one had given Mrs Brontë a silk gown; either the make, the colour, or the material was not according to his notions of consistent propriety, and Mrs Brontë in consequence never wore it. But, for all that, she kept it treasured up in her drawers, which were generally locked. One day, however, while in the kitchen, she remembered that she had left the key in her drawer, and hearing Mr Brontë up-stairs, she augured some ill to her dress, and, running up in haste, she found it cut into shreds.

His strong, passionate, Irish nature was, in general, compressed down with resolute stoicism; but it was there notwithstanding all his philosophic calm and dignity of demeanour. He did not speak when he was annoyed or displeased, but worked off his volcanic wrath by firing pistols out of the back-door in rapid succession. Mrs Brontë, lying in bed up-stairs, would hear the quick explosions, and know that something had gone wrong; but her sweet nature thought invariably of the bright side, and she would say, 'Ought I not to be thankful that he never gave me an angry word?' Now and then his anger took a different form, but still was speechless. Once he got the hearth-rug, and stuffing it up the grate, deliberately set it on fire, and remained in the room in spite of the stench, until it had smouldered and shrivelled away into uselessness. Another time he took some chairs, and sawed away at the backs till they were reduced to the condition of stools.

He was an active walker, stretching away over the moors for many miles, noting in his mind all natural signs of wind and weather, and keenly observing all the wild creatures that came and went in the loneliest sweeps of the hills. He has seen eagles stooping low in search of food for their young : no eagle is ever seen on those mountain slopes now. He fearlessly took whatever side in local or national politics appeared to him right. In the days of the Luddites, he had been for the peremptory interference of the law, at a time when no magistrate could be found to act, and all the property of the West Riding was in terrible danger. He became unpopular then among the mill-workers, and he esteemed his life unsafe if he took his long and lonely walks unarmed; so he began the habit, which has continued to this day, of invariably carrying a loaded pistol about with him. It lay on his dressing-table with his watch; with his watch it was put on in the morning; with his watch it was taken off at night. His opinions might be often both wild and erroneous, his principles of action eccentric and strange, his views of life partial, and almost misanthropical; but not one opinion that he held could be stirred or modified by any worldly motive; he acted up to his principles of action; and, if any touch of misanthropy mingled with his view of mankind in general, his conduct to the individuals who came in personal contact with him did not agree with such a view. It is true that he had strong and vehement prejudices, and was obstinate in maintaining them, and that he was not dramatic enough in his perceptions to see how miserable others might be in a life that to him was all-sufficient. But I do not pretend to be able to harmonise points of character, and account for them, and bring them all into one consistent and intelligible whole. The family with whom I have now to do shot their roots down deeper than I can penetrate. I cannot measure them, much less is it for me to judge them. I have named these instances of eccentricity in the father because I hold the knowledge of them to be necessary for a right understanding of the life of his daughter.' §

Mrs Gaskell has been much criticised, and even discredited, for this account of the character and behaviour of Mr Brontë. Was she misled, was she malicious, or did she tell the truth? It is quite certain, at least, that she *believed* she was telling the truth; she had drawn much of her information from Charlotte herself; and if she was at all uneasy at the thought of Mr Brontë's possible annoyance at what she had written, her apprehensions were soothed at first by his reception of it. 'I thank you,' he wrote to Mrs Gaskell in 1857, when she had sent him the published biography, 'for the books you have sent me containing the Memoir of my daughter. I have perused them with a degree of pleasure and pain which can be known only to myself. . . . You have not only given a picture of my dear daughter Charlotte, but of my dear wife, and all my dear children and such a picture, too, as is full of truth and life. The picture of my brilliant and unhappy son, and his diabolical seducer, is a masterpiece. Indeed, all the pictures in the work have vigorous, truthful, and delicate touches in them, which could have been executed only by a skilful female hand.' Mrs Gaskell must have read this letter with sensations of relief, and even with a gratified surprise, for there were many fathers who, however well they might confront the truth about themselves, would have cavilled at her candour about Branwell. But no; Mr Brontë apparently was pleased, and sounded only the mildest note of criticism when he added, 'There are a few trifling mistakes, which, should it be deemed necessary, may be corrected in the second edition.' A few days later he explained, 'The principal mistake in the memoir which I wish to mention is that which states that I laid my daughters under restriction with regard to their diet, obliging them to live chiefly on vegetable food. This I never did.' He had always, he said, knowing his children to be delicate, advised them to wear flannel and to eat as much meat as they could. He particularly wished this to be mentioned in the second edition; and he added in a postscript (as being perhaps of less importance) 'The Eccentrick Movements ascribed to me, at pages 51 and 52, Vol. I—have no foundation in fact.'

This was in April, and the letter is placid enough; but by July the tone has become more anxious, Mr Brontë meanwhile having been considerably annoyed by the officiousness of a Mr William Dearden, who had been an acquaintance of Branwell's, and who had written a defence of Mr Brontë in the *Halifax Examiner* which contradicted very nearly everything that Mrs Gaskell had said. 'I did not know,' he represented Mr Brontë as having said to him, 'that I had an enemy in the world; much less one who would traduce me before my death. Everything in that book which relates to my conduct to my family is either false or distorted. I never committed such acts as are there ascribed to me.' This article had been written and published without Mr Brontë's knowledge, though he admitted to Mrs Gaskell that Mr Dearden had 'call'd on me to make enquiries', and that he, Mr Brontë 'had spoken in the highest terms of the Memoir, mentioning, however, that there were a few statements respecting myself that were erroneous, and which I wish to have omitted in the Third Edition'. (The second had already appeared.) He had never said anything 'intimating in the remotest degree that I considered you an enemy'.

Mr Brontë was clearly upset by this superfluous defence, and all his letters to Mrs Gaskell at this time prove that, whoever may have been making angry protests against her treatment of him, it was not himself. He wanted some far-fetched anecdotes corrected, but for the rest he was quite willing to admit that he had faults. 'I do not deny that I am somewhat eccentric. Had I been numbered amongst the calm, sedate, concentric men of the world, I should not have been as I now am, and I should in all probability never have had such children as mine have been. . . . Only don't set me on in my fury to burning hearthrugs, sawing the backs of chairs, and tearing my wife's silk gowns.' His tone, throughout the whole of this interesting correspondence, is one of tolerance and reasonableness; he is concerned for truth, but beyond that never questions Mrs Gaskell's right to her interpretations. 'I am not in the least offended at your telling me that I have faults; I have many—and, being a Daughter of Eve, I doubt not that you also have some. Let us both try to be wiser and better as Time recedes and Eternity advances.'

The truth about Mr Brontë seems to lie, as truth usually does, in that interesting middle ground between two points of view. He is not an altogether sympathetic character, being too aloof, spartan and, in a sense, unimaginative (in spite of the poems) to evoke much response; too far gone in the unconscious selfishness of the recluse to have any attraction for an affectionate and sociable temper like Mrs Gaskell's. But he is not entirely harsh; he would have gone through life without criticism if he had not inadvertently begotten children of genius; and it is almost impossible, as one follows the fortunes of the family, not to feel a slightly irritable fondness for Mr Brontë.

Did he bring up his children on potatoes, as Mrs Gaskell (and later biographers) believed? Why, no, it seems that they had roasts like other people; though perhaps not very many, since their means were small. And Charlotte, at least in her younger days, seems to have been by preference a vegetarian. 'Her appetite,' said Ellen Nussey, writing her recollections of Charlotte as a schoolgirl, 'was of the smallest; for years she had not tasted animal food; she had the greatest dislike to it; she always had something specially provided for her at our midday repast. Towards the close of the first half-year she was induced to take, by little and little, meat gravy with vegetable, and in the second half-year she commenced taking a very small portion of animal food daily.' And in a fragment of a diary which Emily and Anne kept together when they were young girls we find, 'It is past twelve o'clock. . . . We are going to have for dinner Boiled Beef, Turnips, Potatoes and apple pudding.' So it was evidently Charlotte's vegetarian tendencies which had led Mrs Gaskell astray; and in her account of Mr Brontë's pistol-shooting we find about the same degree of inexactness.

According to Mrs Gaskell, he had been in the habit of working off his 'volcanic wrath' by firing pistols out of the back door in rapid succession. This, says Mr Dearden, claiming to speak for Mr Brontë, is together with the burning of the hearthrug and the sawing up of the chairs, nothing but a 'tissue of falsehoods'. About the chairs and the hearthrug we shall never know; the stories have an air of distortion about them which inclines one to think that they are perhaps untrue. But about the pistols there is no doubt : Mr Brontë loved firearms and always carried them; and Ellen Nussey, in a description which she wrote in middle-age of her first visit to Haworth, remembers Mr Brontë's daily firing of pistols, and gives an explanation. 'Every morning was heard the firing of a pistol from Mr Brontë's room window,—it was the discharging of the loading which was made every night. Mr Brontë's tastes led him to delight in the perusal of battle scenes, and in following the artifice of war; had he entered on military service instead of ecclesiastical, he would probably have had a very distinguished career. The self-denials and privations of camp life would have agreed entirely with his nature, for he was remarkably independant of the luxuries and comforts of life. . . .' So no doubt Mr Brontë discharged his pistols sometimes in an irritable mood, for he seems to have been a man of quick temper, though generally well controlled, and, in his later years, protected by solitary habits from provocation. Not, we are bound to conclude, a comfortable man to live with; for even Mr Dearden's account of the silk gown episode, supplied by Nancy Garrs, the Brontës' servant, has a disconcerting flavour. It was not a silk gown, he insists, but a print one; and the only thing that Mr Brontë objected to was the shape of the sleeves; and it was only the sleeves that

Mr Brontë had cut off, when he found the dress in his wife's bedroom; and Mrs Brontë had shown the mutilated dress to Nancy in the kitchen, 'laughing heartily'. It may have been a joke; but it does not stand high as a domestic pleasantry; and Mr Dearden's defence has the unintentional effect of convincing us of the sweet temper of Mrs Brontë.

If Mrs Brontë had lived, life at Haworth Parsonage might have been very different: but she had only eighteen ailing months at Haworth.

§ Mrs Brontë died in September, 1821, and the lives of those quiet children must have become quieter and lonelier still. Charlotte tried hard, in after years, to recall the remembrance of her mother, and could bring back two or three pictures of her. One was when, some time in the evening light, she had been playing with her little boy, Patrick Branwell, in the parlour of Haworth Parsonage. But the recollections of four or five years old are of a very fragmentary character. §

Those first eighteen months at Haworth had been a dreadful time for Mr Brontë, and he needed all his stoicism to support him. Only a year after he had arrived there with his family of six small children, his wife had taken to her bed, and he had had the anguish for seven months of seeing her slowly dying, while the children themselves ran the course of childish illness. 'All the prudence and skill I could exercise,' he wrote to his former vicar, 'would have availed me nothing had it not been for help *from above*. . . . One day, I remember it well; it was a gloomy day, a day of clouds and darkness, three of my little children were taken ill of a scarlet fever; and, the day after, the remaining three were in the same condition. Just at that time death seemed to have laid his hand on my dear wife. . . . She was cold and silent and seemed hardly to notice what was passing around her.' The children recovered, and Miss Branwell, Mrs Brontë's elder sister, came from Penzance to comfort the stricken family with practical help; but neither her help nor the doctor's could reach Mrs Brontë. 'Death pursued her unrelentingly. Her constitution was enfeebled, and her frame wasted daily; and after above seven months of more agonising pain than I ever saw anyone

45

endure she fell asleep in Jesus.' Mr Brontë now needed more than ever all the comfort he could draw from his religious faith, 'when my dear wife was dead and buried and gone, and when I missed her at every corner, and when her memory was hourly revived by the innocent yet distressing prattle of my children.' His grief for his wife was deep, and none the less painful for his common-sense efforts not to be engulfed by it, but to carry on with the everyday business of life. 'The tide of grief, which once threatened to overwhelm me, has I trust been at its height, and the slowly receding waves often give me a breathing time though there are periods when they swell high and rush momentarily over me. . . .'

The sensible thing, clearly, was to marry again, since the eldest child was still only seven years old; and after a decent interval Mr Brontë addressed himself to this solution of his difficulties. His thoughts turned first to Mary Burder, whom he had courted years ago during his first curacy in Essex, and with whom he appears to have had an understanding which somehow fell short of marriage. He is a little self-conscious in his approach; opens the campaign with a circumspect letter to the lady's mother, in which he mentions, among other topics, that he has an excellent vicarage and is now a widower; and follows this up some three months later, with a letter to Miss Burder herself.

It is a naïve and transparent letter, in which one winces to see Mr Brontë fall into almost every tactical error possible to a man in his somewhat disadvantageous situation. He is delighted, he tells her, to learn that she is '*still* single', and reminded her, '*You* were the *first* whose hand I solicited, and no doubt I was the *first* to whom *you promised to give that hand*. However much you may dislike me now,' he goes on, glancing in passing at whatever it was that had been uncomfortable between them, 'I am sure you once loved me with an unaffected innocent love, and I feel confident that . . . you cannot doubt my love for you. It is now almost fifteen years since I last saw you. This is a long interval of time and may have effected many changes. It has made me look something older. But, I trust I have gained more than I have lost, I hope

46

I may venture to say I am *wiser* and better.' After some references to divine wisdom he mentions the loss of his wife, and the fact that he has 'a *small* but *sweet* little family', and goes on to explain that he wants 'to see a dearly Beloved Friend, kind as I *once* saw her, and as *much* disposed to promote my happiness. If I have ever given her any pain I only wish for an opportunity to make her ample amends, by every attention and kindness.' In short, his 'ancient love is rekindled', and he begs her to say candidly whether Mrs and Miss Burder will receive him 'as an Old Friend' at Finchingfield Park.

It is rarely that a jilted woman has revenge so unexpectedly put into her hand, and we are not astonished to see that Miss Burder made use of it. Her enjoyment rises like warmth from her close, full page, though even her very pleasure is at moments swamped by a recrudescence of bitterness. She has, she says, been looking through his early letters and remembering the past, and 'This review, Sir, excites in my bosom increased gratitude and thankfulness to that wise, that indulgent Providence which then watched over me for good and withheld me from forming in very early life an indissoluble engagement with one whom I cannot think was altogether clear of duplicity.' (Oh, what had Mr Brontë said and done?) 'Happily for me I have not been the ascribed cause of hindering your promotion, of preventing any brilliant alliance, nor have those great and affluent friends that you used to write and speak of witheld their patronage on my account'—a thrust which we may be sure went home where it was intended, to the perpetual curate with six children and £200 a year. No detail of Mr Brontë's letter escapes her waspish attention; each paragraph receives its well-placed sting. 'My present condition upon which you are pleased to remark has hitherto been the state of my choice and to me a state of much happiness,' since she has, as she cannot resist telling him, 'a handsome competency'. As to his own bereaved state and motherless children, 'The Lord,' she suggests, with pious nastiness, 'can supply all your and their need.' Her answer, in fact, is 'a *decided* negative to the desired visit.'

Mr Brontë seems to have been stunned by the vehemence

of this reply, as well he may have been, for it is a letter which only years of resentment and hours of malevolent thought could have produced. It was five months before he could bring himself to answer—a wise delay, since it enabled him to have the last word with decorum. 'When I look at your letter and see it in many parts breathe such a spirit of disdain, hatred and revenge—after the lapse of so long an interval of time—I appear to myself to be in an unpleasant dream; I can scarcely think it a reality.' He asks her pardon for any injury he may have done her in the past, and takes a sorrowful farewell, in which, however, there is a trace of retaliation. 'You may think and write as you please, but I *have not* the *least doubt* that if you had *been mine* you would have been happier than you *now* are or *can* be as one in *single* life.' To this there was only one possibly reply, which Miss Burder was happy enough, after a time, to be able to make. She married a Nonconformist minister of the name of Sibree, and we may be sure she took care that Mr Brontë should hear of the marriage.

There is a tradition that he next proposed to Miss Elizabeth Firth, of Thornton, who had been kind and friendly to the Brontës in the early days of their marriage, and was godmother to Elizabeth and Anne; and that she, too, refused, and a few months later married the vicar of Huddersfield. It seemed that fate, like his own inclination, preferred that Mr Brontë should be solitary, and spend his life more and more steadily closeted in that study where he wrote and read and took his meals alone. We hear no more of any second marriage, and, indeed, the solution which all along had been offering itself was not a bad one. Miss Branwell, his sister-in-law from Penzance, had suggested remaining at Haworth to look after the children. She was unmarried, active, domesticated and—what was equally attractive—had an income of her own. So Miss Branwell took possession of the best bedroom, and shouldered all the female responsibilities of the house, enabling it to settle down once more into its quiet rhythm.

Life at the parsonage was quiet, and in a sense solitary; but it was not unhappy. In our own days of facile communications it is easy to forget how complete, more than a hundred years ago, how absorbing was often the life lived on its own resources by a large family. Brothers and sisters, where there is intelligence and affection and nearness of age, create their own world; they do not need outsiders. In the case of the little Brontës there was also what Mrs Gaskell justly called a 'wonderful precocity of intellect', in itself the most complete protection against boredom. It generated its own heat, and since nothing was lost in sociable trivialities, the solitary parsonage, cut off from the world but abnormally fertile within, became by chance the forcing-house of genius.

Mrs Gaskell did not make the mistake of painting the Brontës' childhood in too sombre colours.

§ The children did not want society. To small infantine gaieties they were unaccustomed. They were all in all to each other. I do not suppose that there ever was a family more tenderly bound to each other. Maria read the newspapers, and reported intelligence to her younger sisters which it is wonderful they could take an interest in. But I suspect that they had no 'children's books', and that their eager minds 'browzed undisturbed among the wholesome pasturage of English literature', as Charles Lamb expresses it. §

Mr Brontë remembered these early years with pleasure, when, thanks to Miss Branwell, he was able to return to the closeted life he preferred, and was gratified by the first suspicions that he had fathered a remarkable family. 'When mere children,' he told Mrs Gaskell, in a letter which she quoted almost in full, 'as soon as they could read and write, Charlotte and her brother and sisters used to invent and act little plays of their own, in which the Duke of Wellington, my daughter Charlotte's hero, was sure to come off conqueror; when a dispute would not unfrequently arise amongst them regarding the comparative merits of him, Buonaparte, Hannibal, and Cæsar. When the argument got warm, and rose to its height, as their mother was then dead, I had sometimes to come in as arbitrator, and settle the dispute according to the best of my judgment. Generally, in the management of these concerns, I frequently thought that I discovered signs of rising talent, which I had seldom or never before seen in any of their age. . . . A circumstance now occurs to my mind which I

49

may as well mention. When my children were very young, when, as far as I can remember, the oldest was about ten years of age, and the youngest about four, thinking that they knew more than I had yet discovered, in order to make them speak with less timidity, I deemed that if they were put under a sort of cover I might gain my end; and happening to have a mask in the house, I told them all to stand and speak boldly from under cover of the mask.

'I began with the youngest (Anne, afterwards Acton Bell), and asked what a child like her most wanted, she answered, "Age and experience." I asked the next (Emily, afterwards Ellis Bell), what I had best do with her brother Branwell, who was sometimes a naughty boy; she answered, "Reason with him, and when he won't listen to reason, whip him." I asked Branwell what was the best way of knowing the difference between the intellects of man and woman; he answered, "By considering the difference between them as to their bodies." I then asked Charlotte what was the best book in the world; she answered, "The Bible." And what was the next best; she answered, "The Book of Nature." I then asked the next what was the best mode of education for a woman; she answered, "That which would make her rule her house well." Lastly, I asked the eldest what was the best mode of spending time; she answered, "By laying it out in preparation for a happy eternity." I may not have given precisely their words, but I have nearly done so, as they made a deep and lasting impression on my memory. The substance, however, was exactly what I have stated.'

§ The strange and quaint simplicity of the mode taken by the father to ascertain the hidden characters of his children, and the tone and character of these questions and answers, show the curious education which was made by the circumstances surrounding the Brontës. They knew no other children. They knew no other modes of thought than what were suggested to them by the fragments of clerical conversation which they overheard in the parlour, or the subjects of village and local interest which they heard discussed in the kitchen. Each had their own strong characteristic flavour.

They took a vivid interest in the public characters, and

the local and the foreign as well as home politics discussed in the newspapers. Long before Maria Brontë died, at the age of eleven, her father used to say he could converse with her on any of the leading topics of the day with as much freedom and pleasure as with any grown-up person. §

So that, however slight their contacts with the outside world, the parsonage children had a life of their own, eccentric, perhaps, but fertile. 'It was not,' as Ellen Nussey remembered, 'the seclusion of a *solitary* person, such as Charlotte endured in after days, and which in time becomes awfully oppressive and injurious. It was solitude and seclusion shared and enjoyed with intelligent companionship, and intense family affection.'

III : COWAN BRIDGE

How was such a family to be educated? Mr Brontë, with his £200 a year, had no choice but to bring them up as cheaply as possible; and he must have rejoiced that, with his early teaching experience and his Cambridge degree, he was himself equipped to teach his only son. No doubt he set about instructing the six of them without misgiving. They could all be taught to read and write and cipher, and Patrick, of course, would be given Latin and Greek. For the female side of the girls' education there was naturally Miss Branwell.

§ Miss Branwell was, I believe, a kindly and conscientious woman, with a good deal of character, but with the somewhat narrow ideas natural to one who had spent nearly all her life in the same place. She had strong prejudices, and soon took a distaste to Yorkshire. From Penzance, where plants which we in the north call greenhouse flowers grow in great profusion, and without any shelter even in the winter, and where the soft warm climate allows the inhabitants, if so disposed, to live pretty constantly in the open air, it was a great change for a lady considerably past forty to come and take up her abode in a place where neither flowers nor vegetables would flourish, and where a tree of even moderate dimensions might be hunted for far and wide; where the snow lay long and late on the moors, stretching bleakly and barely far up from the dwelling which was henceforward to be her home; and where often, on autumnal or winter nights, the four winds of heaven seemed to meet and rage together, tearing round the house as if they were wild beasts striving to find an entrance. She missed the small round of cheerful, social visiting perpetually going on in a country town; she missed the friends she had known from her childhood, some of whom had been her parents' friends before they were hers; she disliked many of the customs of the place, and particularly dreaded the cold damp arising from the flag floors in the passages and parlours of Haworth Parsonage. The stairs, too, I believe, are made of stone; and no wonder, when stone quarries are near, and trees are far to seek. I have heard that Miss Branwell always went about the house in pattens, clicking up and down the stairs, from her dread of catching cold. For the same reason, in the later years of her life, she passed nearly all her time, and took most of her meals, in her bed-room. The children respected her, and had that sort of affection for her which is generated by esteem; but I do not think they ever freely loved her. It was a severe trial for any one at her time of life to change neighbourhood and habitation so entirely as she did; and the greater her merit. §

This state of affairs, of teaching all the little girls together and haphazard, as Mr Brontë and Miss Branwell could manage, might have gone on indefinitely if Mr Brontë had not heard of the Clergy Daughters' School, recently established by the Rev Carus Wilson at Cowan Bridge.[1] The school was accessible from Haworth and extremely cheap, having been founded expressly for the daughters of poor clergymen; and Mr Brontë no doubt considered himself fortunate in finding a well-conducted school for his girls which, being partly a

[1] Maria and Elizabeth had previously been sent, for a time, to a school at Wakefield, perhaps to Miss Richmal Mangnall's, of the Questions.

charity foundation, was within his means. He took his four eldest daughters there in 1824, keeping only Branwell at home, and five-year-old Anne. At this time Maria Brontë was ten years old, Elizabeth nine, Charlotte eight, and Emily not yet seven.

Arriving at this point in her narrative Mrs Gaskell, most justifiably, paused: for here she was entering on controversial and dangerous ground, and knew she must be careful. The Clergy Daughters' School, to which Mr Brontë had sent his four little girls, had provided Charlotte with some of the deepest emotional experiences of her childhood; and in writing *Jane Eyre* she had drawn on her memory of the miseries of eight years old. Lowood, the orphan asylum in *Jane Eyre*, administered by a 'black marble clergyman' who admonishes the children with stories of death-beds and hell, and who is so attentive to frugal detail that he chooses the darning needles himself and inspects the holes in stockings hanging on the line, is a cold, hungry, comfortless place, where the girls suffer much from severity and privation, and where numbers of them die.

'My first quarter at Lowood,' Charlotte had written in *Jane Eyre*, 'seemed an age. . . . Our clothing was insufficient to protect us from the severe cold: we had no boots, the snow got into our shoes and melted there: our ungloved hands became numbed and covered with chilblains, as were our feet: I remember well the distracting irritation I endured from this cause every evening, when my feet inflamed; and the torture of thrusting the swelled, raw, and stiff toes into my shoes in the morning. Then the scanty supply of food was distressing: with the keen appetites of growing children, we had scarcely sufficient to keep alive a delicate invalid. From this deficiency of nourishment resulted an abuse, which pressed hardly on the younger pupils: whenever the famished great girls had an opportunity, they would coax or menace the little ones out of their portion. Many a time I have shared between two claimants the precious morsel of brown bread distributed at tea-time; and after relinquishing to a third half the contents of my mug of coffee, I have swallowed the remainder with an accompaniment of secret tears, forced from me by the exigency of hunger. . . .' Into this place, which looked so pretty and was so unhealthy, came, we remember, an epidemic of typhus. 'Semi-starvation and neglected colds had predisposed most of the pupils to receive infection : forty-five out of the eighty girls lay ill at one time. Classes were broken up, rules relaxed. The few who continued well were allowed almost unlimited license. . . . Many, already smitten, went home only to die : some died at the school, and were buried quietly and quickly, the nature of the malady forbidding delay.'

These descriptions, and the bitter portrait of Mr Brocklehurst, the orphanage's patron and founder, had produced an outcry; for Lowood and the Clergy Daughters' School had been quickly identified, and Mr Carus Wilson and his friends had been indignant. It had never occurred to Charlotte Brontë that the real school would be recognised from her description, or that its details would produce so much angry argument. It was a topic which she and Mrs Gaskell had several times discussed, and Charlotte more than once had said 'that she should not have written what she did of Lowood in *Jane Eyre* if she had thought the place would have been so immediately identified . . . although there was not a word in her account of the institution but what was true at the time when she knew it'. Mrs Gaskell believed that she 'would have been glad of an opportunity to correct the over-strong impression which was made upon the public mind by her vivid picture' : but she knew very well that Charlotte in private maintained that she had not exaggerated. Only a few years before her death she had described it as 'a situation as unhealthy as it was picturesque—low, damp, beautiful with wood and water'; and in a letter to Miss Wooler, her old school-mistress, had reiterated that typhus fever[2] had 'decimated the school periodically, and consumption and scrofula in every variety of form, which bad air and water, and bad, insufficient diet can generate, preyed on the ill-fated pupils'.

Aware that her account of Cowan Bridge School, however careful, would be open to criticism, Mrs Gaskell had made

[2] It is worth remembering that the carrier of typhus is the bodylouse.

55

a special journey to inspect the building which Mr Carus Wilson had enlarged and converted from a row of humble dwellings into a school, and which was now—or what was left of it—partly an untenanted public-house and partly a cottage.

'I can hardly understand how the school there came to be so unhealthy, the air all round about was so sweet and thyme-scented, when I visited it last summer. But at this day, every-one knows that the site of a building intended for numbers should be chosen with far greater care than that of a private dwelling. . . .' Mrs Gaskell had gone into the building, one end of which was almost derelict, 'having all the squalid appearance of a deserted place, which rendered it difficult to judge what it would look like when neatly kept up'. The other end, now a cottage, had still 'the low ceilings and stone floors of a hundred years ago; the windows do not open freely and widely; and the passage up-stairs, leading to the bedrooms, is narrow and tortuous: altogether, smells would linger about the house, and damp cling to it. But sanitary matters were little understood thirty years ago; and it was a great thing to get a roomy building close to the high road, and not too far from the habitation of Mr Wilson, the origina-tor of the educational scheme. There was much need of such an institution; numbers of ill-paid clergymen hailed the pros-pect with joy, and eagerly put down the names of their children as pupils. . . .'

§ Mr Wilson felt, most probably, that the responsibility of the whole plan rested upon him. The payment made by the parents was barely enough for food and lodging; the subscriptions did not flow very freely into an untried scheme; and great economy was necessary in all the domestic arrangements. He determined to enforce this by frequent personal inspection; and his love of authority seems to have led to a great deal of unnecessary and irritating meddling with little matters. Yet, although there was economy in providing for the household, there does not appear to have been any parsimony. The meat, flour, milk, etc., were contracted for, but were of very fair quality; and the dietary, which has been shown to me in manuscript, was

56

neither bad nor unwholesome; nor, on the whole, was it wanting in variety. Oatmeal porridge for breakfast; a piece of oat-cake for those who required luncheon; baked and boiled beef, and mutton, potato-pie, and plain homely puddings of different kinds for dinner. At five o'clock, bread and milk for the younger ones; and one piece of bread (this was the only time at which the food was limited) for the elder pupils, who sat up till a later meal of the same description. Mr Wilson himself ordered in the food, and was anxious that it should be of good quality. But the cook, who had much of his confidence, and against whom for a long time no one durst utter a complaint, was careless, dirty and wasteful. To some children oatmeal porridge is distasteful, and consequently unwholesome, even when properly made; at Cowan Bridge School it was too often sent up, not merely burnt, but with offensive fragments of other substances discoverable in it. The beef, that should have been carefully salted before it was dressed, had often become tainted from neglect; and girls, who were schoolfellows with the Brontës, during the reign of the cook of whom I am speaking, tell me that the house seemed to be pervaded, morning, noon, and night, by the odour of rancid fat that steamed out of the oven in which much of their food was prepared. There was the same carelessness in making the puddings; one of those ordered was rice boiled in water, and eaten with a sauce of treacle and sugar; but it was often uneatable, because the water had been taken out of the rain tub, and was strongly impregnated with the dust lodging on the roof, whence it had trickled down into the old wooden cask, which also added its own flavour to that of the original rain water. The milk, too, was often 'bingy', to use a country expression for a kind of taint that is far worse than sourness, and suggests the idea that it is caused by want of cleanliness about the milk pans, rather than by the heat of the weather. On Saturdays, a kind of pie, or mixture of potatoes and meat, was served up, which was made of all the fragments accumulated during the week. Scraps of meat from a dirty and disorderly larder, could never be very appetising; and, I believe, that this dinner was more loathed than any in the early days of Cowan Bridge School. One may fancy how repulsive such fare would be to children whose appetites were small, and who had been accustomed to food, far simpler perhaps, but prepared with a delicate cleanliness that made it both tempting and wholesome. At many a meal the little Brontës went without food, although craving with hunger. They were not strong when they came, having only just recovered from a complication of measles and whooping-cough : indeed, I suspect they had scarcely recovered; for there was some consultation on the part of the school authorities whether Maria and Elizabeth should be received or not, in July, 1824. Mr Brontë came again, in the September of that year, bringing with him Charlotte and Emily to be admitted as pupils.

It appears strange that Mr Wilson should not have been informed by the teachers of the way in which the food was served up; but we must remember that the cook had been known for some time to the Wilson family, while the teachers were brought together for an entirely different work—that of education. They were expressly given to understand that such was their department; the buying in and management of the provisions rested with Mr Wilson and the cook. The teachers would, of course, be unwilling to lay any complaints on the subject before him; and when he heard of them, his reply was to the effect that the children were to be trained up to regard higher matters than dainty pampering of the appetite, and (apparently unconscious of the fact that daily loathing and rejection of food is sure to undermine the health) he lectured them on the sin of caring over-much for carnal things.

There was another trial of health common to all the girls. The path from Cowan Bridge to Tunstall Church, where Mr Wilson preached, and where they all attended on the Sunday, is more than two miles in length, and goes sweeping along the rise and fall of the unsheltered country, in a way to make it a fresh and exhilarating walk in summer, but a bitter cold one in winter, especially to children whose thin blood flowed languidly in consequence of their half-starved condition. The church was not warmed, there being no means for this purpose. It stands in the midst of fields, and the damp mist must have gathered round the walls, and crept in at the windows. The girls took their cold dinner with them, and ate it between the services, in a chamber over the entrance, opening out of the former galleries. The arrangements for this day were peculiarly trying to delicate children, particularly to those who were spiritless, and longing for home, as poor Maria Brontë must have been. For her ill-health was increasing; the old cough, the remains of the whooping-cough, lingered about her; she was far superior in mind to any of her playfellows and companions, and was lonely amongst them from that very cause; and yet she had faults so annoying that she was in constant disgrace with her teachers, and an object of merciless dislike to one of them, who is depicted as 'Miss Scatcherd' in *Jane Eyre,* and whose real name I will be merciful enough not to disclose. I need hardly say that Helen Burns is as exact a transcript of Maria Brontë as Charlotte's wonderful power of reproducing character could give. Her heart, to the latest day on which we met, still beat with unavailing indignation at the worrying and the cruelty to which her gentle, patient, dying sister had been subjected by this woman. Not a word of that part of *Jane Eyre* but is a literal repetition of scenes between the pupil and the teacher. Those who had been pupils at the same time knew who must have written the book, from the force with which Helen Burns' sufferings are described. They had, before that, recognised the description of the sweet dignity and benevolence of Miss Temple as only a just tribute to the merits of one whom all that knew her appear to hold in honour; but when Miss Scatcherd was held up to opprobrium they also recognised in the writer of *Jane Eyre* an unconsciously avenging sister of the sufferer.

One of these fellow-pupils of Charlotte and Maria Brontë's, among other statements even worse, gives me the following :—The dormitory in which Maria slept was a long room, holding a row of narrow little beds on each side, occupied by the pupils; and at the end of this dormitory there was a small bed-chamber opening out of it, appropriated to the use of Miss Scatcherd. Maria's bed stood nearest to the door of this room. One morning, after she had become so seriously unwell as to have had a blister applied to her side (the sore from which was not perfectly healed), when the getting-up bell was heard, poor Maria moaned out that she was so ill, so very ill, she wished she might stop in bed; and some of the girls urged her to do so, and said they would explain it all to Miss Temple, the superintendent. But Miss Scatcherd was close at hand, and her anger would have to be faced before Miss Temple's kind thoughtfulness could interfere; so the sick child began to dress, shivering with cold, as, without leaving her bed, she slowly put on her black worsted stockings over her thin white legs (my informant spoke as if she saw it yet, and her whole face flushed out undying indignation). Just then Miss Scatcherd issued from her room, and, without asking for a word of explanation from the sick and frightened girl, she took her by the arm, on the side to which the blister had been applied, and by one vigorous movement whirled her out into the middle of the floor, abusing her all the time for dirty and untidy habits. There she left her. My informant says, Maria hardly spoke, except to beg some of the more indignant girls to be calm; but, in slow, trembling movements, with many a pause, she went down-stairs at last—and was punished for being late.

Any one may fancy how such an event as this would rankle in Charlotte's mind. I only wonder that she did not remonstrate against her father's decision to send her and Emily back to Cowan Bridge, after Maria's and Elizabeth's deaths. But frequently children are unconscious of the effect which some of their simple revelations would have in altering the opinions entertained by their friends of the persons placed around them. Besides, Charlotte's earnest, vigorous mind saw, at an unusually early age, the immense importance of education, as furnishing her with tools which she had the strength and the will to wield, and she would be aware that the Cowan Bridge education was, in many points, the best that her father could provide for her.

Before Maria Brontë's death, that low fever broke out, in the spring of 1825, which is spoken of in *Jane Eyre*. Mr Wilson was extremely alarmed at the first symptoms of this; his self-confidence was shaken; he did not understand what kind of illness it could be that made the girls too dull and heavy to understand remonstrances, or be roused by texts and spiritual exhortation; but caused them to sink away into dull stupor, and half-unconscious listlessness. He went to a kind motherly woman, who had had some connection with the school—as laundress, I believe—and asked her to come and tell him what was the matter with them. She made herself ready, and drove with him in his gig. When she entered the school-room, she saw from twelve to fifteen girls lying about; some resting their aching heads on the table, others on the ground; all heavy-eyed, flushed, indifferent, and weary, with pains in every limb. Some peculiar odour, she says, made her recognise that they were sickening for 'the fever'; and she told Mr Wilson so, and that she could not stay there for fear of conveying the infection to her own children; but he half commanded, and half entreated her to remain and nurse them; and finally mounted his gig and drove away, while she was still urging that she must return to her own house, and to her domestic duties, for which she had provided no substitute. However, when she was left in this unceremonious manner, she determined to make the best of it; and a most efficient nurse she proved : although, as she says, it was a dreary time.

Mr Wilson supplied everything ordered by the doctors of the best quality, and in the most liberal manner; he even sent for additional advice, in the person of his own brother-in-law, a very clever medical man in Kirby, with whom he had not been on good terms for some time previously; and it was this doctor who tasted and condemned the daily food of the girls by the expressive action of spitting out a portion which he had taken in order to taste it. About forty of the girls suffered from this fever, but none of them died at Cowan Bridge, though one died at her own home, sinking under the state of health which followed it. None of the Brontës had the fever. But the same causes, which affected the health of the other pupils through typhus, told more slowly, but not less surely, upon their constitutions. The principal of these causes was the food.

The bad management of the cook was chiefly to be blamed for this; she was dismissed, and the woman who had been forced against her will to serve as head nurse, took the place of housekeeper; and henceforward the food was so well prepared that no one could ever reasonably complain of it. Of course it cannot be expected that a new institution, comprising domestic and educational arrangements for nearly a hundred persons, should work quite smoothly at the beginning, and all this occurred during the first two years of the establishment. But Mr Wilson seems to have had the unlucky gift of irritating even those to whom he meant kindly, and for whom he was making perpetual sacrifices of time and money, by never showing any respect for their independence of opinion and action. He had, too, so little knowledge of human nature as to imagine that, by constantly reminding the girls of their dependent position, and the fact that they were receiving their education from the charity of others, he could make them lowly and humble. Some of the more sensitive felt this treatment bitterly, and instead of being as grateful as they should have been for the real benefits they were obtaining, their mortified pride rose up from its fall a hundredfold more strong. Painful impressions sink deep into the hearts of delicate and sickly children. What the healthy suffer from but momentarily, and then forget, those who are ailing brood over involuntarily, and remember long— perhaps with no resentment, but simply as a piece of suffering that has been stamped into their very life. The pictures, ideas, and conceptions of character received into the mind of the child of eight years old, were destined to be reproduced in fiery words a quarter of a century afterwards. She saw only one side, and that the unfavourable side of Mr Wilson; but many of those who knew him, assure me of the wonderful fidelity with which his disagreeable qualities, his spiritual pride, his love of power, his ignorance of human nature and consequent want of tenderness are represented; while, at the same time, they regret that the delineation of these should have obliterated, as it were, nearly all that was noble and conscientious.

The recollections left of the four Brontë sisters at this period of their lives, on the minds of those who associated with them, are not very distinct. Wild, strong hearts, and powerful minds, were hidden under an enforced propriety and regularity of demeanour and expression, just as their faces had been concealed by their father, under his stiff, unchanging mask. Maria was delicate, unusually clever and thoughtful for her age, gentle, and untidy. Of her frequent disgrace from this last fault—of her sufferings, so patiently borne—I have already spoken. The only glimpse we get of Elizabeth, through the few years of her short life, is contained in a letter which I have received from 'Miss Temple'. 'The second, Elizabeth, is the only one of the family of whom I have a vivid recollection, from her meeting with a somewhat alarming accident, in consequence of which I had her for some days and nights in my bedroom, not only for the sake of greater quiet, but that I might watch over her myself. Her head was severely cut, but she bore all the consequent suffering with exemplary patience, and by it won much upon my esteem. Of the two younger ones (if two there were) I have very slight recollections, save that one, a darling child, under five years of age, was quite the pet nursling of the school.' This last would be Emily. Charlotte was considered the most talkative of the sisters—a 'bright, clever, little child'. Her great friend was a certain 'Mellany Hane' (so Mr Brontë spells the name), a West Indian, whose brother paid for her schooling, and who had no remarkable talent except for music, which her brother's circumstances forbade her to cultivate. She was 'a hungry, good-natured, ordinary girl', older than Charlotte, and ever ready to protect her from any petty tyranny

63

or encroachments on the part of the elder girls. Charlotte always remembered her with affection and gratitude.

I have quoted the word 'bright' in the account of Charlotte. I suspect that this year of 1825 was the last time it could ever be applied to her. In the spring of it, Maria became so rapidly worse that Mr Brontë was sent for. He had not previously been aware of her illness, and the condition in which he found her was a terrible shock to him. He took her home by the Leeds coach, the girls crowding out into the road to follow her with their eyes over the bridge, past the cottages, and then out of sight for ever. She died a very few days after her arrival at home. Perhaps the news of her death, falling suddenly into the life of which her patient existence had formed a part, only a little week or so before, made those who remained at Cowan Bridge look with more anxiety on Elizabeth's symptoms, which also turned out to be consumptive. She was sent home in charge of a confidential servant of the establishment; and she, too, died in the early summer of that year. Charlotte was thus suddenly called into the responsibilities of eldest sister in a motherless family. She remembered how anxiously her dear sister Maria had striven, in her grave, earnest way, to be a tender helper and a counsellor to them all; and the duties that now fell upon her seemed almost like a legacy from the gentle little sufferer so lately dead.

Both Charlotte and Emily returned to school after the Midsummer holidays in this fatal year. But before the next winter it was thought desirable to advise their removal, as it was evident that the damp situation of the house at Cowan Bridge did not suit their health. §

This moving account of Charlotte's ten months at Cowan Bridge, based as it was on what Mrs Gaskell had learned from Charlotte herself, scrupulously weighed and checked against what she heard from old pupils who had been at the Clergy Daughters' School at the same time, and who from their own memories augmented what she already knew of Maria Brontë, nevertheless started an ominous crackle of controversy, which spread and grew louder in the first weeks after publication until it threatened to develop into a dangerous blaze. Mr Carus Wilson's son wrote indignant and complaining letters, both to Charlotte Brontë's husband and to the newspapers, quoting from the sympathetic letters which, he claimed, had been received by his family in great numbers, protesting that Mrs Gaskell's account of the school was unjustified, and that her portrait of Mr Wilson was a slander on a noble, conscientious, charitable and well-loved clergyman. Mr Nicholls, surprisingly, came out of his customary silence, and in defence of Mrs Gaskell and his wife engaged in a long and spirited exchange of letters in *The Halifax Guardian*. Old pupils of Cowan Bridge offered their testimony on both sides, and the vehemence of Mr Carus Wilson's supporters (who were preparing a 'vindication') was so great, and their threat of a libel action so alarming, that Mrs Gaskell's publishers thought it prudent to soften the harshness of her account in the next edition. Accordingly, but reluctantly (for she was convinced of the truth of all that she had said), Mrs Gaskell bent to the storm, and the third edition appeared with a number of passages cut out and a paragraph or two added in cautious justification of Mr Wilson.

That version of *The Life of Charlotte Brontë* which is published today, is fortunately, the first. Time has gradually obliterated the indignation of the Carus Wilsons; it is Mrs Gaskell's description that remains. But did she, so far as we can ever be certain, speak the truth? We cannot be certain : yet it seems, it really seems, as though she did; or at least that she faithfully drew one profile of a face which may have had other aspects; had she seen these, they might have softened the cruelty of her single impression. Mrs Gaskell's book, unlike *Jane Eyre*, is a record and an interpretation of fact; and although the evidence on both sides is positive and copious, the opposing parties flatly contradicting one another, it does not seem that she has been seriously unjust.

It is true that discipline and privations would make a deeper and bitterer impression on a sickly and imaginative child than on one naturally cheerful and robust; it is also true that the motives which Mr Wilson thought he pursued, and the principles which he believed he upheld, are in themselves good. But Carus Wilson seems to have been a man deeply self-deceived, and to have deceived some of his contemporaries as well. He cannot, however, altogether convince a posterity which has been taught to look below the conscious surface, and to accept without flinching the possibility that there may be some very unprepossessing reasons for being righteous. Carus Wilson gave money, time and energy to projects which he fully believed were for the help and betterment of mankind; there is some evidence that he had his lighter moments and his amiable side; but no-one who has ever glanced into his own works, his little tracts and books written for children, can really believe that he was a much wronged man, or fail to see the neurotic obsessed with power, going about his chastening work with all the innocent zeal of the unconscious sadist. His books are full of whippings and death-beds, and the wrath of God suddenly and justly visited on children. Mr Wilson's God is a swift admonisher and punisher, a God whose hell is always busy and full. In following Him, he served a deity very much to his liking, in the happy certainty that he had a moral excuse for every stringency and discipline. It was only unlucky for him that at the beginning he had among the Clergy Daughters a still, quiet, abnormally sensitive child of eight who would never forgive him, and who took most woundingly to heart a meanness in management and a rigour of discipline which left no mark on some of the other children.

The truthfulness of that child's evidence against Mr Wilson and his institution seems to be supported by the first prospectus of the Clergy Daughters' School, several copies of which are still in existence.[8] It was circulated by Mr Carus Wilson when the school opened in the spring of 1824, the year in which the little Brontës were sent there, and we may conclude that Mrs Gaskell never saw a copy, since she took her particulars of the school from the entrance rules given in the Governors' Report of eighteen years later. This prospectus on two points is unexpectedly illuminating—the extent to which Cowan Bridge was a family concern, providing niches and salaries for male and female Wilsons; and the possible

---

[8] There is a copy in the Brontë Parsonage Museum at Haworth.

identity of 'Miss Scatcherd', whose real name Mrs Gaskell was 'merciful enough not to disclose', and whose shadow falls across the printed sheet in the person of 'Miss Finch, Singing and Scourgemistress' This part of the prospectus is curious, and worth examining.

PATRON	W. W. C. Wilson, M.P.
RECTOR AND THEOLOGICAL LECTURER	
	Rev W. Wilson, M.A.
ASSISTANT LECTURERS	
In Housekeeping, Domestic Economy	
	Rev R. Wilson, M.A.
Elocution, Ventriloquy	Rev Edward Wilson
Latin, Greek and Philosophy	Rev Ian Blythe
Female managing Assistants, Teachers, Head Manager	
and Teacher in Arithmetic & Dressmaking	
	Mrs W. Wilson
English, Reading and Poetry	Miss Jane Thompson
Singing and Scourgemistress	Miss Finch

Miss Finch, Miss Thompson, Mr Blythe and the Wilsons are described as 'professional teachers of more than ordinary talent'. Their abilities, says Mr Carus Wilson, 'need no comment from me; they have already distinguished themselves by their accomplishments. I could afford instances of such, but seeing they are members for the most part of my own family, I refrain from motives of delicacy. . . .' (One wonders what paucity of suitable accomplishments among his relations had driven Mr Wilson to list Ventriloquy among the subjects to be taught to the daughters of clergymen.)

'The female teachers I have engaged to be constantly resident at College (excepting my sister whom domestic afflictions must necessarily detain at her father's house during the winter session), at a salary of fifty guineas per an. each.

'All the teachers named in the prospectus receive the above mentioned sum as being teachers, etc., excepting Miss Finch (a lady well known for the pious fortitude and resignation with which she has borne various trying afflictions) who has engaged for a very trifling remuneration to assist me in regulating the *Discipline* of the College.'

We do not know whether Miss Finch was the original of Miss Scatcherd, but the presence of a Scourgemistress is significant in our estimate of the character of the place, even though we refuse to be prejudiced by her pious fortitude and resignation and the fact that she was willing to perform her duties for a wage which even the frugal Mr Wilson describes as 'very trifling'.

Another document which unintentionally hints at the conditions prevailing at Cowan Bridge during that first year is the school register; and this, again, we may suppose that Mrs Gaskell never saw, since she made no use of the interesting material it contained, and nowhere refers to it. Later biographers have drawn on those extracts which were printed in the *Journal of Education* in 1900, and which give particulars of the Brontë sisters themselves—('Charlotte Brontë. Entered August 10, 1824. Writes indifferently. Ciphers a little and works neatly. Knows nothing of grammar, geography, history, or accomplishments. Altogether clever of her age, but knows nothing systematically. Left school June 1, 1825. Governess')—but none seems to have examined any other part of the book, or to have noticed that the number of deaths and withdrawals during the first eighteen months is so high as to suggest that something was seriously amiss.

From the register, then, we find that seventy-seven children were entered at Cowan Bridge in the first two years, and that by the end of the second year twenty-eight of the number had been removed. One, as we see from a brief entry, died at Cowan Bridge. Three, including Maria and Elizabeth Brontë, 'left school in ill health and died in a decline'. One 'left school in ill health, 13th February, died April 28th, 1825'. Another 'left school in ill health 3rd September 1825', and another 'left on account of ill health which incapacitated her from further study'. Another 'went home in good health April 2nd, 1825, died of typhus fever April 23rd'. Of the remaining twenty who were removed it is recorded simply that they 'left'. Charlotte and Emily Brontë were among these, and since children do not leave school in such numbers without good reason it seems fair to conclude that there was something approaching panic among the parents.

The Clergy Daughters' School undoubtedly improved as time went on, and even at the beginning it is possible that the school and its founder were less bad than Mrs Gaskell believed or Charlotte Brontë remembered: but even so, they seem to have been horrible enough.

IV : THE SECRET WORLD

It was now the autumn of 1825. Maria and Elizabeth were dead, and the four remaining children, of whom Charlotte, now nine years old, was the eldest, were all at home together at the parsonage, at the beginning of that long period of seclusion and quiet which was to have so profound an effect on all their lives.

It is impossible to exaggerate the importance, to the receptive and fertile minds of these extraordinary children, of the next five years; though they are years in which, to the uninitiated eye, nothing seems to happen. Mrs Gaskell, conscientiously looking into those bundles of microscopic writings which (thanks to Sir James Kay-Shuttleworth's insistence) had been put into her hands by Mr Nicholls, saw that the children were busy and occupied, though none of them went to school; that they played highly elaborate creative games, in which their father's political interests were precociously reflected; and that they had a new friend and source of domestic comfort in the kitchen. But she did not look any further than seemed necessary into the juvenilia, which were in any case very difficult to decipher; and she thus allowed to slip through her fingers a wonderful key to the nature and source of Charlotte's mature work, and to much that is mysterious in the work of Emily. Mrs Gaskell was not much interested in Emily Brontë. Hers was a nature—gentle, affectionate and sociable—which would have found Emily farouche and unattractive; she was concerned only with Charlotte's relation to her sister, for as yet no-one but Charlotte had perceived that Emily was the greater of the two. As for the strange and vivid light which those writings shed on Charlotte's imaginative life, it is certain that Mrs Gaskell would have shrunk from it. The light, brilliant and interesting, is also lurid. It throws into relief outlines which Mrs Gaskell, for the sake of her womanly admiration of Miss Brontë, perhaps preferred not to see. They are shapes which in a sense justify the puritanical uneasiness over her work which was betrayed by some of Charlotte Brontë's contemporaries, showing us, as they do, among many other interesting scenes, the erotic Byronic landscape which is the unseen but palpable background of all her work. It has remained for our own day, and the minute patience of American scholarship, to unravel and employ the clue which was dropped as a tangled skein into Mrs Gaskell's hand.

For the moment, however, we will look at the scene as Mrs Gaskell saw it, for Haworth Parsonage at this time is not by any means the gloomy and solitary place that it became. It is a place where four marvellously gifted and affectionate children are inhabiting their private world, absorbed in interests and activities which are unusual but happy, and drawing from their father's strangely equalitarian company the intellectual vigour and independence which it was in him to bestow. They are thrown entirely upon their own resources for amusement, and their happiest hours are spent, not with their father or Miss Branwell, but with the servant Tabitha Aykroyd in the kitchen.

§ About this time, an elderly woman of the village came to live as servant at the parsonage. She remained there, as a member of the household, for thirty years; and from the length of her faithful service, and the attachment and respect which she inspired, is deserving of mention. Tabby was a thorough specimen of a Yorkshire woman of her class,

71

in dialect, in appearance, and in character. She abounded in strong practical sense and shrewdness. Her words were far from flattery; but she would spare no deeds in the cause of those whom she kindly regarded. She ruled the children pretty sharply; and yet never grudged a little extra trouble to provide them with such small treats as came within her power. In return, she claimed to be looked upon as a humble friend; and, many years later, Miss Brontë told me that she found it somewhat difficult to manage, as Tabby expected to be informed of all the family concerns, and yet had grown so deaf that what was repeated to her became known to whoever might be in or about the house. To obviate this publication of what it might be desirable to keep secret, Miss Brontë used to take her out for a walk on the solitary moors; where, when both were seated on a tuft of heather, in some high lonely place, she could acquaint the old woman, at leisure, with all that she wanted to hear.

Tabby had lived in Haworth . . . when there were no mills in the valleys, and when all the wool-spinning was done by hand in the farm-houses round. . . . No doubt she had many a tale to tell of by-gone days of the countryside; old ways of living, former inhabitants, decayed gentry, who had melted away, and whose places knew them no more; family tragedies, and dark superstitious dooms; and in telling these things without the least consciousness that there might ever be anything requiring to be softened down, would give at full length the bare and simple details.

Miss Branwell instructed the children at regular hours in all she could teach, making her bed-chamber into their school-room. Their father was in the habit of relating to them any public news in which he felt an interest; and from the opinions of his strong and independent mind they would gather much food for thought. . . . Charlotte's deep, thoughtful spirit appears to have felt almost painfully the tender responsibility which rested upon her with reference to her remaining sisters. She was only eighteen months older than Emily; but Emily and Anne were simply companions and playmates, while Charlotte was motherly friend and guardian to both; and this loving assumption of duties beyond her years, made her feel considerably older than she really was.

Patrick Branwell, their only brother, was a boy of remarkable promise, and, in some ways of extraordinary precocity of talent. Mr Brontë's friends advised him to send his son to school; but, remembering both the strength of will of his own youth and his mode of employing it, he believed that Patrick was better at home, and that he himself could teach him well, as he had taught others before. So Patrick, or as his family called him—Branwell, remained at Haworth, working hard for some hours a day with his father; but, when the time of the latter was taken up with his parochial duties, the boy was thrown into chance companionship with the lads of the village—for youth will to youth, and boys will to boys.

Still, he was associated in many of his sisters' plays and amusements. These were mostly of a sedentary and intellectual nature. I have had a curious packet confided to me, containing an immense amount of manuscript, in an inconceivably small space; tales, dramas, poems, romances, written principally by Charlotte, in a hand which it is almost impossible to decipher without the aid of a magnifying glass. . . . §

This was the parcel of tiny manuscripts which Sir James Kay-Shuttleworth had extracted from Mr Nicholls, and which Mrs Gaskell had turned over in the hope of finding something to her purpose. Some of them, less than two inches square, had the appearance of printed books, and had been written by hand in microscopic script, sewn together and bound in wrapping paper. Some were a little larger, with elaborate decorations and title-pages, and a few were small notebooks of the kind that could be bought for a penny or twopence; in one of these Mr Brontë (apparently no friend to the secrecies of microscopic script) had written 'All that is written in this book must be in a good, plain and legible hand'. To decipher the whole of these tiny fragments was unthinkable; Mrs Gaskell contented herself with transcribing two or three. One was a list of Charlotte's works written during the year 1829 to

1830, when she was thirteen, with the dates, titles and contents of twenty-two volumes, which Mrs Gaskell included in her biography 'as a curious proof how early the rage for literary composition had seized upon her'. This list, for sheer bulk, was formidable, and the tininess of the books themselves was no clue to their contents; some of them contained twenty thousand words.

§ As each volume contains from sixty to a hundred pages . . . the amount of the whole seems very great. . . . So much for the quantity; the quality strikes me as of singular merit for a girl of thirteen or fourteen. Both as a specimen of her prose style at this time, and also as revealing something of the quiet domestic life led by these children, I take an extract from the introduction to *Tales of the Islanders* the title of one of their *Little Magazines* :—

'June the 31st, 1829

'The play of the *Islanders* was formed in December, 1827, in the following manner. One night about the time when the cold sleet and stormy fogs of November are succeeded by the snow-storms, and high piercing night-winds of confirmed winter, we were all sitting round the warm blazing kitchen fire, having just concluded a quarrel with Tabby concerning the propriety of lighting a candle, from which she came off victorious, no candle having been produced. A long pause succeeded, which was at last broken by Branwell saying, in a lazy manner, "I don't know what to do." This was echoed by Emily and Anne.

'*Tabby.* "Wha ya may go t' bed."

'*Branwell.* "I'd rather do anything than that."

'*Charlotte.* "Why are you so glum to-night, Tabby? Oh! suppose we had each an island of our own."

'*Branwell.* "If we had I would choose the Island of Man."

'*Charlotte.* "And I would choose the Isle of Wight."

'*Emily.* "The Isle of Arran for me."

'*Anne.* "And mine should be Guernsey."

'We then chose who should be chief men in our islands. Branwell chose John Bull, Astley Cooper, and Leigh Hunt; Emily, Walter Scott, Mr Lockhart, Johnny Lockhart; Anne,

Michael Sadler, Lord Bentinck, Sir Henry Halford. I chose the Duke of Wellington and two sons, Christopher North and Co., and Mr Abernethy. Here our conversation was interrupted by the, to us, dismal sound of the clock striking seven, and we were summoned off to bed.'

What was 'the play of the *Islanders*', this game which apparently produced a copious literature? To pursue it seemed neither interesting nor fruitful, and Mrs Gaskell chose the next fragment not for its information on the children's 'plays' (which it named without describing) but because it sketched a lively domestic scene, and 'gives some idea of the sources of their opinions'.

THE HISTORY OF THE YEAR 1829

'Once Papa lent my sister Maria a book. It was an old geography book; she wrote on its blank leaf, "Papa lent me this book." This book is a hundred and twenty years old, it is at this moment lying before me. While I write this I am in the kitchen of the Parsonage, Haworth; Tabby, the servant, is washing up the breakfast-things, and Anne, my youngest sister (Maria was my eldest), is kneeling on a chair, looking at some cakes which Tabby had been baking for us. Emily is in the parlour, brushing the carpet. Papa and Branwell are gone to Keighley. Aunt is up-stairs in her room, and I am sitting by the table writing this in the kitchen. Keighley is a small town four miles from here. Papa and Branwell are gone for the newspaper, the *Leeds Intelligencer*, a most excellent Tory newspaper, edited by Mr Wood, and the proprietor, Mr Henneman. We take two and see three newspapers a week. We take the *Leeds Intelligencer*, Tory, and the *Leeds Mercury*, Whig, edited by Mr Baines, and his brother, son-in-law, and his two sons, Edward and Talbot. We see the *John Bull*; it is a high Tory, very violent. Mr Driver lends us it, as likewise *Blackwood's Magazine*, the most able periodical there is. The Editor is Mr Christopher North, an old man seventy-four years of age; the 1st of April is his birth-day; his company are

Timothy Tickler, Morgan O'Doherty, Macrabin Mordecai, Mullion, Warnell, and James Hogg, a man of most extraordinary genius, a Scottish shepherd. Our plays were established; *Young Men*, June, 1826; *Our Fellows*, July, 1827; *Islanders*, December, 1827. These are our three great plays, that are not kept secret. Emily's and my best plays were established the 1st of December, 1827; the others March, 1828. Best plays mean secret plays; they are very nice ones. All our plays are very strange ones. Their nature I need not write on paper, for I think I shall always remember them. The *Young Men's* play took its rise from some wooden soldiers Branwell had; *Our Fellows* from *Æsop's Fables*; and the *Islanders* from several events which happened. I will sketch out the origin of our plays more explicitly if I can. First, *Young Men*. Papa bought Branwell some wooden soldiers at Leeds; when Papa came home it was night, and we were in bed, so next morning Branwell came to our door with a box of soldiers. Emily and I jumped out of bed, and I snatched up one and exclaimed, "This is the Duke of Wellington! This shall be the Duke!" When I had said this, Emily likewise took up one and said it should be hers; when Anne came down, she said one should be hers. Mine was the prettiest of the whole, and the tallest, and the most perfect in every part. Emily's was a grave-looking fellow, and we called him "Gravey". Anne's was a queer little thing, much like herself, and we called him "Waiting-Boy". Branwell chose his, and called him "Buonaparte".' §

Looking further with her magnifying glass, Mrs Gaskell decided that she had quoted enough. The volume of childish work was impressive, and some of it interesting; but most of it seemed incomprehensible rubbish. She added only one of the pieces of bombastic nonsense-writing which she found so puzzling—'It is well known that the Genii have declared that unless they perform certain arduous duties every year, of a mysterious nature, all the worlds in the firmament will be burnt up, and gathered together in one mighty globe, which will roll in solitary grandeur through the vast wilderness of space, inhabited only by the four high princes of the Genii, till time shall be succeeded by Eternity. . . .'—to illustrate a peculiarity which struck her very forcibly as she deciphered passages of Charlotte's early writing: 'While her description of any real occurrence is, as we have seen, homely, graphic and forcible, when she gives way to her powers of creation, her fancy and her language alike run riot, sometimes to the very borders of apparent delirium. . . . It is not unlikely,' she concludes, referring to the meaningless grandiose passage she has just quoted, 'that the foregoing letter may have had some allegorical or political reference, invisible to our eyes, but very clear to the bright little minds for whom it was intended. Politics were evidently their grand interest; the Duke of Wellington their demi-god.'

Now these little manuscripts, which Charlotte had kept all her life, are more interesting than Mrs Gaskell knew. It is not certain how many of them she saw; there are perhaps a hundred still in existence, and there were certainly more in Mr Nicholls's bundle[1] To decipher them all would have

---

[1] The little manuscripts remained at Haworth in Mr. Nicholls's possession until after the death of Mr. Brontë. Mr. Nicholls was not given the living, and he then retired to his home in Ireland, taking his wife's letters and personal relics with him; and there they lay undisturbed until 1894, when Mr. Clement Shorter, already well known as a literary journalist, went to Ireland at the instigation of Mr. T. J. Wise (book collector and, as it has since appeared, literary forger) to buy up any available Brontëana. Mr. Nicholls sold him the letters and juvenile manuscripts, which had lain wrapped in newspaper at the bottom of a cupboard for more than thirty years, 'and where,' as he afterwards wrote to Mr. Shorter, 'had it not been for your visit, they must have remained during my lifetime, and most likely afterwards have been destroyed'. The letters were published by Mr. Shorter and formed the basis of his *Charlotte Brontë and her Circle*, and other compilations. The little manuscripts were broken up by Mr. Wise, who selected a few specimens for his own library and, following his usual practice as a literary speculator, gradually introduced the rest into the saleroom. They were eagerly bought by collectors and soon became widely scattered through Europe and America. Fortunately a good number came finally into the hands of Mr. Henry H. Bonnell of Philadelphia, who bequeathed them to the Brontë Museum at Haworth, where they may be seen by the curious.

taken her outside the scope of her biography; besides, the fruits of such tedious labours are of the kind that ripens only with time. It remained for Miss F. E. Ratchford, librarian of Texas University, who for many years had been transcribing specimens whenever she had access to them and pondering the results, to realise that they are 'a closely connected series of stories, poems, novels, histories and dramas, having a common setting and common characters, written through the sixteen years between 1829 and 1845, a period comprehending approximately one-third of Charlotte's life'.

This highly complex creation, which took so strong a hold on their imagination that all four children passed their entire youth under its influence, and even in maturity remained addicted to it like a drug, began in 1826 when, as Charlotte recorded, Mr Brontë brought Branwell the wooden soldiers from Leeds. The children invented names and characters for the soldiers and supplied them with a continuous history of adventure, in which everything that caught their fancy—a book, or something that Tabby had told them or that Papa had read aloud from the newspaper, was incorporated and made use of. In this there was nothing unusual; most children thrown upon their own resources will produce play sagas which can be both complicated and extended. What was extraordinary about the Brontës' games was that they produced an extensive and precocious literature, and, as the children grew up, provided a fantasy world which for all of them, at various times, became a substitute for life. The mature work of Charlotte and Emily cannot be fully understood without some knowledge of the play-sagas of their childhood, and the violent, long-drawn, uninhibited daydream life to which these gave rise; and even Branwell's obscure tragedy emerges more coherently when our enquiry into his character and talents has been taken back to this significant point. To sensitive natures dismayed by life—and it seems that the four of them were all, for different reasons, so dismayed—there is great comfort and great danger in the possession of an absorbing daydream in which to hide one's head. 'Life as we find it,' says Freud, 'is too hard for us; it entails too much pain, too many disappointments, impossible tasks. We cannot do without palliative remedies . . . powerful diversions of interest, which lead us to care little about our misery; substitutive gratifications, which lessen it; and intoxicating substances, which make us insensitive to it. Something of this kind is indispensable.' Daydreams, which are nothing if not 'a powerful diversion of interest', have been made suspect in our time by psycho-analysis, and certainly they conceal temptations to inaction and to various paralysing refusals of life; but they also provide a forcing-ground for the imagination. So wise a thinker as Bertrand Russell has pointed out that they are not wholly evil, but an essential part of the life of the creative mind. The danger, he says, is that 'when throughout a long life there is no means of relating them to reality they easily become unwholesome and even dangerous to sanity.' This is, to a marked degree, what happened to Branwell; and Emily Brontë is perhaps the only writer of genius we know of who completely rejected actual life and embraced, with perfect steadiness, a passionate and poetic existence lived entirely at a high level of the imagination. Some poets—Coleridge through opium, Wordsworth in his moments of mystical experience, Blake—have reached levels of intuition and expression with which ordinary life and consciousness have nothing to do; but Emily Brontë seems to have lived her whole creative life as poet and novelist at this level, without the aid of any drug beyond the obsessive daydream which all four children had variously created. As we shall see, Charlotte in maturity recognised the dangers of the dream and consciously broke out of it, though not without anguish, and not before it had conferred its curious bloom on many areas of her mind. Emily stayed resolutely within it, like some self-communing votary in her cell, and by so doing achieved freedom for the development of her genius; an unself-conscious masculine freedom which in real life her difficult temperament might never have allowed. Branwell dwelt in the drug-like dream too long, taking refuge from his fears and secret inadequacies; on all of them its influence was profound.

This secret life, then, began when Charlotte was not yet ten years old, and in following her development as Mrs Gaskell made it out, and the less clearly defined lives of her brother and sisters, it is important to remember that it runs below for many years as a hidden, continuous flow. Mrs Gaskell will not refer to it again; but we shall have several occasions for returning to it; and it is therefore worth while to pause even at the beginning and look more closely at those elaborate games which contain the seeds of an undreamed-of future.

The play based on the original wooden soldiers was known as 'the *Young Men's* play', and lasted for a year, to be succeeded by a similar game, *Our Fellows*, which took its characters from *Æsop's Fables*. The next was the *Islanders*, in which each child peopled an island with a set of favourite heroes; the islands enlarged to continents, the heroes developed characters startlingly unlike the respectable public men so precociously chosen, and as the play gathered momentum the four children began to write their chronicles. It was not only that the doings of the islanders had to be recorded in histories or reported in tiny magazines and newspapers; the characters themselves proved almost without exception to be fertile authors, necessitating the continuous production of plays, poems and romances, which in their turn had to be well or scathingly reviewed in still further microscopic publications. The tiny size of all these volumes, and the phenomenal density of their laborious eye-destroying script, seem to have been originally due to a desire to make them proportionate to the wooden soldiers; or to imitate the miniature paper-bound juvenile books and tracts which could be bought for a penny or twopence and were familiar to all nineteenth-century children; but smallness had great advantages as well; it economised paper, which could probably only be begged in scraps and odd sheets; and it ensured secrecy, since to adult eyes the script is practically unreadable. Secrecy was a point of some importance, for, as Charlotte had observed, 'Best plays mean secret plays; they are very nice ones. All our plays are very strange ones. Their nature I need not write on paper, for I think I shall always remember them.' Their secret has kept successfully for more than a century.

The fever of self-expression which possessed the Brontë

children must sometimes have taken them outside the limits of their plays; indeed, Charlotte's earliest known work, written when she was twelve years old, begins ordinarily enough in nursery-author tradition, 'There was once a little girl and her name was Ane . . .'; but these aberrations were evidently rare, and from the establishment of the secret plays these alone seem to have provided all that the children desired in the way of material. Every scrap of likely information that came their way was thrust into the crucible of the game and transformed by fancy; the most ordinary things produced bizarre results. The eighteenth-century geography book which Mr Brontë had lent Maria (the Rev J. Goldsmith's *Grammar of General Geography*) let fall a fertilising shower of maps and place-names, altering the whole nature of the play and changing its scene to a wildly imagined continent of Africa. *The Arabian Nights,* now read and absorbed, one supposes, in one of the current simplified and shortened versions, inspired the children to a self-dramatisation which permitted an actual share in the adventures of their characters: they became genii, directing the fortunes of war, reviving the dead, performing all the magical and godlike tasks for which genii are so useful. Chief Genius Tallii, Chief Genius Brannii, Chief Genius Emmii and Chief Genius Annii now come and go in the chronicles on wings of lightning, and with peals of thunder reveal themselves to the Young Men as their masters. 'I am the Chief Genius Brannii. With me there are three others. She, Wellesley, who protects you, is named Tallii; she who protects Parry is named Emmii; she who protects Ross is called Annii. Those lesser ones whom ye saw are Genii and Fairies, our slaves and minions. . . . We are the guardians of you all.' (The passage which had puzzled Mrs Gaskell as being 'wild weird writing,' language 'run riot sometimes to the very borders of apparent delirium', is simply a minatory declaration of the omnipotence of the Genii and the playworld's dependence even for existence on their will and pleasure.)

To explore at length this labyrinth of childish writing can be no possible pleasure to the general reader; it induces even a kind of dizziness, being so copious, unformed, extravagant and diffuse; and the value of its rewarding fragments is rarely intrinsic. Yet even at this early stage, when the children are in the shapeless beginnings of their collaboration, there are pebbles of evidence to be picked up which will prove far from trivial; and later, as we shall see, an examination of the adolescent writings will dredge up a curious and significant harvest. At the present moment, considering only the five years in which the children were left together and alone at Haworth, the long, quiet, fertile and surely happy interval between the griefs of Cowan Bridge and the time when Charlotte was sent once more to school, we can discover among the tiny pages, so ceaselessly written, printed, bound and catalogued on the kitchen table, much that will give substance to their characters.

Charlotte and Branwell, as we might expect, since they are older than the other two, are the prime movers in all the plays and the chief instigators of adventures; and here at once it is possible to perceive their differences. Charlotte's imaginings are Gothic, romantic, full of descriptions of persons, scenery and weather, experimentally pursuing first one line and then another, reflecting a precocious range of intellectual interests and as much concerned with character as with narrative. The tone is sometimes sophisticated and adult, often high-flown and overcharged, occasionally simple and telling, as when the cobbled streets and blustery weather of Haworth break through the artificial descriptions of an imaginary Africa. Her output is so prodigious that it suggests not only a most unchildish concentration on this chosen play but a disregard of all other possibilities of amusement. The intensity of her application can be judged from a note she made herself on a tiny hand-printed volume of nearly three thousand words which she wrote when she was thirteen. 'I began this Book on the 22 of February 1830 and finished it on the 23 of February 1830 doing 3 pages on the first day and 11 on the second. On the first day I wrote an hour and a half in the morning, and an hour and a half in the evening. On the second day I wrote a quarter of an hour in the morning 2 hours in the afternoon and a quarter of an hour in the evening making in the whole 5 hours and a half.'

Branwell's production in this early period is equally large, and he evidently threw himself into their creative play as passionately as his sister, writing a long and detailed *History of the Young Men* in a variety of carefully copied styles, and a weighty series of *Letters from an Englishman* which report, in a very close-packed manner, the imaginary country's military campaigns, revolutions and political problems. Both these works, which are extraordinary productions for a boy of twelve, clearly reflect the models which Branwell copied and which were largely the same as Charlotte's—the books they read and the newspapers and periodicals which came to the parsonage. There is, however, this difference to be noticed between the early work of the two children: Charlotte's, for all its Gothic extravagance, is never safe to dismiss as merely tedious; in nearly every page there is a phrase, an idea, a line of description which catches the attention: whereas Branwell's, as correct as hers and as abundant, and written undoubtedly with no less extraordinary zest, achieves a dullness which makes it almost unreadable. His battles, slaughterings and heavy humours weary the eye to the point where it no longer takes in the sense, which is exactly what happens to anyone who has the stamina to follow the deadening tramp, tramp of Branwell's poetry. It is a relief when an ordinary schoolboy relish of horror breaks out, and we find ourselves suddenly at home in the reassuring prose of boys' literature— 'At these words, knowing I was to be dissected alive, I shrieked out and fell into a swoon. When I recovered, I found myself lying bound to a large oak table which, as well as the floor of the room, was covered with dried blood . . .' or its equivalent in verse—

> They flayed him and then roasted him with salt,
> And laid him on a gridiron to roast alive.
> And oh! the horrid yells that burst from him
> Was like the roaring of wind 'mid trees
> And rocks and mountains in a misty vale,
> Until at last they slowly died away
> Into a low hoarse murmur, then were gone,
> And naught was heard but dripping blood and fat
> Into the raging fire which blazed around.

It would be a mistake, however, to dismiss Branwell's childish productions as being without talent. Their bulk alone, the assiduity with which he pursued his campaigns and discoveries and elections through volume after volume, the tireless regularity of his verse, the minuteness of observation reflected in the making up of his books and magazines, the delicate lettering and bibliographical detail of their title pages, all show him to have been a boy of exceptional talent and enthusiasm, with a nicety of perception and a dexterity which suggest the craftsman rather than the writer. It is no wonder, since he was the only boy in a family of girls, and had, besides, the engaging manner and confident readiness in conversation that his sisters so conspicuously lacked, that Branwell was regarded by the whole family as the one marked out for achievement and success. Yet, to anyone who patiently reads through the available volumes of transcripts, it plainly emerges that in Branwell's work something important is missing. It fails to interest. It is clogged with that curious deadness notice-able in so much correct writing which has somehow failed to convey the excitement that inspired it. Charlotte's early writing, on the other hand, though it has its sterile tracts, lights up from time to time with colour and mockery; her Byronic villainesses, in their 'usual attire of crimson velvet robe and black plumes', have a theatrical brilliance that at least beguiles the eye, and the ear is often startled into attention by the oddly compelling rhythm of scattered sentences.

Nothing written by Emily or Anne remains from this first period. Perhaps, being younger than Charlotte and Branwell, they may have taken no part in the making of the little books at first; certainly no contribution from the Chief Geniuses Emmii or Annii is to be found in the volumes that survive, and references to them in the various works of Charlotte and Branwell suggest that they took part in most of the plays in a controlled and subsidiary manner, following the traditional course of younger sisters. Once Emily appears in Branwell's magazine, bringing him a small yellow book of poems. 'She gave it to me saying that it was the Poems of that Ossian of whom so much has been said, but whose works could never be got'—an incident which plunged Charlotte and Branwell at once into the controversy concerning the genuineness of Macpherson's translations from the Gaelic, and inspired Branwell to make one of his characters the author of a 'Commentary on Ossian 29 vols. folio.' (This work was reviewed in the Magazine with enviable candour by one of its editors—'This is one of the most long winded books that have ever been printed we must now conclude for we are dreadfully tired.') And there are references both in prose and verse suggesting that Emily and Anne everywhere supported the senior genii and brought up the rear.

> I see, I see appear
>   Awful Brannii, gloomy giant,
> Shaking o'er earth his blazing air,
>   Brooding on blood with drear and vengeful soul
> He sits enthroned in clouds to hear his thunders roll.
>   Dread Tallii next like a dire eagle flies
> And on our mortal miseries feasts her bloody eyes.
>   Emmii and Annii last with boding cry
> Famine and war foretell and mortal misery.

It was not, apparently, until Charlotte went away to school for the second time that Emily and Anne established their independent games, leaving Branwell to chronicle the wars and rebellions of the Young Men by himself. This happened in January 1831, when Charlotte, now nearly fifteen, was sent to Miss Wooler's school at Roe Head, about twenty miles from Haworth. Why Charlotte alone was given this second chance of systematic education is not clear; it seems probable that Miss Elizabeth Firth, the kind friend of the Brontës' Thornton days, who was godmother to Elizabeth and Anne (and to whom Mr Brontë as a widower is said to have proposed) had offered to bear the expense of sending one of the girls to school. Miss Firth was now married to the vicar of Huddersfield, and having besides a small fortune of her own was in very comfortable circumstances. She had certainly visited the little Brontës at Cowan Bridge, and continued to visit Charlotte at Miss Wooler's and to show her much kindness; so that she may well have taken this means of helping the family in which she remained always benevolently interested.

Charlotte made the journey to Roe Head in a covered cart, miserable at leaving home and oppressed by the coming ordeal of facing strangers, but no doubt fortified to some extent by the satisfaction of at last being put in the way of education. The Brontës' passionate respect for education is one of their most purely Celtic traits; to the children, no less than to their father, it appeared always as the prize which must be won at all costs, resolution supplying the means which poverty denied. So the adventures and chronicles of the secret kingdom were broken off and the children made a mournful and deliberate end of Glass Town, the capital city, taking a ritual farewell in solemn verse:

No mortal may further the vision reveal;
Human eye may not pierce what a spirit would seal.
The secrets of genii my tongue may not tell,
But hoarsely they murmured: 'Bright city farewell!'

V : MISS WOOLER'S

Miss Wooler's school at Roe Head, about twenty miles from Haworth, was of a kind plentiful enough in the nineteenth century, but not to be found today. The number of pupils was small (it varied between seven and ten while Charlotte was there), and the teachers naturally possessed neither degrees nor diplomas, since this was long before the days of higher education for women. Classes were necessarily small, and manners formal; the girls addressed each other as 'Miss Brontë', 'Miss Nussey', 'Miss Taylor' until at least half a year's acquaintance had justified the use of Christian names. There were no organised games or any form of athletics. The girls took their exercise in country walks and in such simple games of ball as could be played in the fields and garden; on wet days they walked for hours and hours round the school-room, arm in arm. It was as different as can well be imagined from the large, noisy, athletic and highly organised girls' school which would be typical today, but it was perhaps none the worse for that. Miss Wooler and her sister were women of some education and of refined manners, the small number of pupils made individual interest and teaching possible, and there was a comfortable family atmosphere about the place which must have done something to diminish homesickness. It was, in fact, a place where Charlotte could very suitably set about the serious business of training herself to be a governess.

Her determination on this point was not the result of any romantic notions about independence, but of the obvious necessity for all of them to be self-supporting. Mr Brontë's two hundred pounds a year was not enough to keep his children in idleness, and after his death, so far as they knew, they would have nothing. The only brilliant and interesting possibilities, of course, would be Branwell's; for the girls, without forfeiting gentility there was only one profession open—to be governesses.

With all her Celtic passion for education and her belief that it was their one means of 'getting on', Charlotte had none of the temperament of the good teacher, and even in these early years must have been uneasily aware that teaching, for her, would be a perpetual struggle. She was shy, and a governess was obliged to earn her living among strangers. She was small and delicate, and a governess's first requirement was robust health. Nevertheless, since it was the only course open to her, she controlled her shrinking nerves as well as she could, and resolutely set her mind towards Roe Head and Miss Wooler's.

She was already, at fifteen, with her serious, intelligent face and unfashionable clothes, not very different in appearance from the grave, self-contained person whom Mrs Gaskell knew; already she had something of the composed manner, the dowdy fastidiousness of dress, of the mature Charlotte Brontë and of her own heroines.

§ In 1831, she was a quiet, thoughtful girl, of nearly fifteen years of age, very small in figure—'stunted' was the word she applied to herself—but as her limbs and head were in just proportion to the slight, fragile body, no word in ever so slight a degree suggestive of deformity could properly be applied to her; with soft, thick, brown hair, and peculiar eyes, of which I find it difficult to give a description, as they appeared to me in her later life. They were large and well shaped; their colour a reddish brown; but if the iris was closely examined, it appeared to be composed of a great variety of tints. The usual expression was of quiet, listening intelligence; but now and then, on some just occasion for vivid interest or wholesome indignation, a light would shine out, as if some spiritual lamp had been kindled, which glowed behind those expressive orbs. I never saw the like in any other human creature. As for the rest of her features, they were plain, large, and ill set; but, unless you began to catalogue them, you were hardly aware of the fact, for the eyes and power of the countenance over-balanced every physical defect; the crooked mouth and the large nose were forgotten, and the whole face arrested the attention, and presently attracted all those whom she herself would have cared to attract. Her hands and feet were the smallest I ever saw; when one of the former was placed in mine, it was like the soft touch of a bird in the middle of my palm. The delicate long fingers had a peculiar fineness of sensation, which was one reason why all her handiwork, of whatever kind—writing, sewing, knitting—was so clear in its minuteness. She was remarkably neat in her whole personal attire; but she was dainty as to the fit of her shoes and gloves.

I can well imagine that the grave serious composure, which, when I knew her, gave her face the dignity of an old Venetian portrait, was no acquisition of later years, but dated from the early age when she found herself in the position of an elder sister to motherless children. But in a girl only just entered on her teens, such an expression would be called (to use a country phrase) 'old-fashioned'; and in 1831, the period of which I now write, we must think of her as a little, set, antiquated girl, very quiet in manners, and very quaint in dress; for besides the influence exerted by her father's ideas concerning the simplicity of attire befitting the wife and daughters of a country clergyman, her aunt, on whom the duty of dressing her nieces principally devolved, had never been in society since she left Penzance eight to nine years before, and the Penzance fashions of that day were still dear to her heart. §

'I first saw her,' wrote Mary Taylor, writing to Mrs Gaskell from New Zealand, with a freshness of recollection after

twenty-five years which made her long letter a treasure to
Charlotte's biographer, 'coming out of a covered cart, in very
old-fashioned clothes, and looking very cold and miserable.
She was coming to school at Miss Wooler's. When she
appeared in the school-room, her dress was changed, but just
as old. She looked a little old woman, so short-sighted that she
always appeared to be seeking something, and moving her
head from side to side to catch a sight of it. She was very shy
and nervous, and spoke with a strong Irish accent. When a
book was given her, she dropped her head over it until her
nose nearly touched it, and when she was told to hold her head
up, up went the book after it, still close to her nose, so that
it was not possible to help laughing.'

Ellen Nussey, who, a new girl herself, found Charlotte
crying behind the schoolroom curtains on her first day at
Roe Head, retained a less grotesque impression. 'Charlotte's
appearance did not strike me at first as it did others. I saw
her grief, not herself particularly, till afterwards. She never
seemed to me the unattractive little person others designated
her, but certainly she was at this time anything but *pretty*;
even her good points were lost. Her naturally beautiful hair
of soft silky brown being then dry and frizzy-looking, screwed
up in tight little curls, showing features that were all the
plainer from her exceeding thinness and want of complexion
. . . A dark, rusty-green stuff dress of old-fashioned make
detracted still more from her appearance; but let her wear
what she might, or do what she would, she had ever the
demeanour of a born gentlewoman.'

These two girls, whose first impressions of Charlotte were
to be so vividly remembered, were to become her lifelong
friends and consequently of great importance to her biographer.
Ellen Nussey in particular, with her incomparable hoard of
Charlotte's letters from schooldays till death, was indeed to
be Mrs Gaskell's chief source of material. Ellen seems always
to have been a gentle, charming person, conventional, pious,
unintellectual, faithful, discreet—the perfect confidante for
stormier, stronger natures. Charlotte was drawn to her at
once, and the two were soon on terms of affectionate intimacy;
an intimacy qualified, however, by Charlotte's instinctive aware-

ness of her friend's limits. Mary Taylor was an altogether different type, and Mrs Gaskell may well have regretted, when she perceived the quality of the long letter which reached her from New Zealand, that it was not she who had remained in England, and preserved Charlotte's half of an immense correspondence; for she had been able to share with Charlotte all those interests and ideas which both of them knew it was useless to discuss with Ellen. Mary came of a radical family, and was a natural rebel. She was outspoken where Ellen was tactful, original where Ellen was conventional, and revolutionary in matters in which Ellen and Charlotte would stand together against change. 'I have two studies,' Charlotte wrote to Ellen Nussey nine years after this first meeting: 'you are my study for the success, the credit, and the respectability of a quiet, tranquil character; Mary is my study for the contempt, the remorse, the misconstruction which follow the development of feelings in themselves noble, warm, generous, devoted and profound, but which, being too fully revealed, too frankly bestowed, are not estimated at their real value. I never hope to see in this world a character more truly noble. She would die willingly for one she loved. Her intellect and attainments are of the very highest standard.'

Unfortunately Mary Taylor had destroyed all Charlotte's letters, but she was able to send Mrs Gaskell a pointed and faithful acount of what Charlotte had been like as a schoolgirl.

'We thought her very ignorant, for she had never learnt grammar at all, and very little geography. She would confound us by knowing things that were out of our range altogether. She was acquainted with most of the short pieces of poetry that we had to learn by heart; would tell us the authors, the poems they were taken from, and sometimes repeat a page or two, and tell us the plot. She had a habit of writing in italics (printing characters), and said she had learnt it by writing in their magazine. They brought out a "magazine" once a month, and wished it to look as like print as possible. She told us a tale out of it. No one wrote in it, and no one read it, but herself, her brother, and two sisters. She promised to show me some of these magazines, but retracted it afterwards, and would never be persuaded to do so. In our play hours she sate, or stood still, with a book, if possible. Some of us once urged her to be on our side in a game at ball. She said she had never played, and could not play. We made her try, but soon found that she could not see the ball, so we put her out. She took all our proceedings with pliable indifference, and always seemed to need a previous resolution to say "No" to anything. She used to go and stand under the trees in the play-ground, and say it was pleasanter. She endeavoured to explain this, pointing out the shadows, the peeps of sky, &c. We understood but little of it. She said that at Cowan Bridge she used to stand in the burn, on a stone, to watch the water flow by. I told her she should have gone fishing; she said she never wanted. She always showed physical feebleness in every-thing. She ate no animal food at school. It was about this time I told her she was very ugly. Some years afterwards, I told her I thought I had been very impertinent. She replied, "You did me a great deal of good, Polly, so don't repent of it." She used to draw much better, and more quickly, than anything we had seen before, and knew much about celebrated pictures and painters. Whenever an opportunity offered of examining a picture or cut of any kind, she went over it piece-meal, with eyes close to the paper, looking so long that we used to ask her "what she saw in it". She could always see plenty, and explained it very well. She made poetry and draw-ing at least exceedingly interesting to me; and then I got the habit, which I have yet, of referring mentally to her opinion on all matters of that kind, along with many more, resolving to describe such and such things to her, until I start at the re-collection that I never shall.

We used to be furious politicians, as one could hardly help being in 1832. She knew the names of the two ministries; the one that resigned, and the one that succeeded and passed the Reform Bill. She worshipped the Duke of Wellington, but said that Sir Robert Peel was not to be trusted; he did not act from principle like the rest, but from expediency. I, being of the furious radical party, told her "how could any of them trust one another; they were all of them rascals!" Then she would launch out into praises of the Duke of Wellington, referring to his actions; which I could not contradict, as I knew nothing about him. She said she had taken interest in politics ever since she was five years old. She did not get her opinions from her father—that is, not directly—but from the papers, &c., he preferred.

'She used to speak of her two elder sisters, Maria and Elizabeth, who died at Cowan Bridge. I used to believe them to have been wonders of talent and kindness. She told me, early one morning, that she had just been dreaming; she had been told that she was wanted in the drawing-room, and it was Maria and Elizabeth. I was eager for her to go on, and when she said there was no more, I said, "but go on! *Make it out*! I know you can." She said she would not; she wished she had not dreamed, for it did not go on nicely; they were changed; they had forgotten what they used to care for. They were very fashionably dressed, and began criticising the room, etc.

'This habit of "making out" interests for themselves, that most children get who have none in actual life, was very strong in her. The whole family used to "make out" histories, and invent characters and events. I told her sometimes they were like growing potatoes in a cellar. She said, sadly, "Yes! I know we are!" . . . This is the epitome of her life. At our house'—where Charlotte visited the Taylors and enjoyed the noisy vitality of the whole talkative intelligent family—'she had just as little chance of a patient hearing, for though not school-girlish, we were more intolerant. We had a rage for practicality, and laughed all poetry to scorn. Neither she nor we had any idea but that our opinions were the opinions of all the *sensible* people in the world, and we used to astonish each other at every sentence. . . . Charlotte, at school, had no plan of life beyond what circumstances made for her. She knew that she must provide for herself, and chose her trade; at least, she chose to begin it at once. Her idea of self-improvement ruled her even at school. It was to cultivate her tastes. She always said there was enough of hard practicality and *useful* knowledge forced on us by necessity, and that the thing most needed was to soften and refine our minds. She picked up every scrap of information concerning painting, sculpture, poetry, music, etc., as if it were gold.'

Miss Nussey did not provide Mrs Gaskell with any written account of Charlotte's schooldays at Roe Head; she produced letters and willingly answered questions, and since she and Mrs Gaskell easily kept in touch, nothing further seemed necessary. Fourteen years after the publication of the biography, however, feeling perhaps that there was more to be said, she wrote down in full her recollection of Charlotte at this time, and this account contains many details which Mrs Gaskell would undoubtedly have used if she had known of them. Charlotte's vegetarianism, for instance, over which there had been so much argument, here appears as a habit which she gradually gave up at school; one gets the impression that it was a matter of preference, rather than obedience to an imposed principle.

Her sense of duty and responsibility, which was at once a burden and a source of strength to her throughout life, was already, apparently, abnormally developed. 'She always seemed to feel that a deep responsibility rested upon her; that she was an object of expense to those at home, and that she must use every moment to attain the purpose for which she was sent to school, i.e., to fit herself for governess life. . . . She did not play or amuse herself when others did. When her companions were merry round the fire, or otherwise enjoying themselves during the twilight, which was always a precious time of relaxation, she would be kneeling close to the window busy with her studies, and this would last so long that she would be accused of seeing in the dark.' Though she did not join in ordinary games she was found useful in a different sort of entertainment, where imagination was called for, and Miss Nussey had even kept a speech which Charlotte had written (in fine Angrian vein) for a mock-coronation which the girls had held one half-holiday. 'Powerful Queen! accept this Crown, the symbol of dominion, from the hands of your faithful and affectionate subjects! And if their earnest and united wishes have any efficacy, you will long be permitted to reign over this peaceful, though circumscribed empire. . . .' And she was greatly in demand as a teller of dormitory thrillers. 'She brought together all the horrors her imagination could create,' from surging seas, raging breakers, towering castle walls, high precipices, invisible chasms and dangers. Having wrought these materials to the highest pitch of effect, she brought out, in almost cloud-height, her somnambulist, walking on shaking turrets. . . .' Small wonder that one of her audience was seized with palpitations, and that all 'late talking' was afterwards forbidden by Miss Wooler.

It was not an unhappy time. Miss Wooler herself was a serious and talented woman, well able to convey enthusiasm and to inspire affection. Ellen Nussey remembered her at this time as 'short and stout, but graceful in her movements, very fluent in conversation and with a very sweet voice. . . . Personally Miss Wooler was like a lady abbess. She wore white, well-fitting dresses, embroidered. Her long hair plaited, formed a coronet, and long large ringlets fell from her head to shoulders. She was not pretty nor handsome, but her quiet dignity made her presence imposing.' Mrs Gaskell had met her and found her not unhelpful, though she had refused to ask Charlotte's biographer to her own home. The meeting had eventually been brought about by Miss Nussey at Brookroyd, and Mrs Gaskell was able to see clearly enough that, however reserved Miss Wooler might be towards herself, she had had a happy and congenial influence on Charlotte.

§ Miss Wooler had a remarkable knack of making them feel interested in whatever they had to learn. They set to their studies, not as to tasks or duties to be got through, but with a healthy desire and thirst for knowledge, of which she had managed to make them perceive the relishing savour. They did not leave off reading and learning as soon as the compulsory pressure of school was taken away. They had been taught to think, to analyse, to reject, to appreciate. Charlotte Brontë was happy in the choice made for her of the second school to which she was sent. There was a robust freedom in the out-of-doors life of her companions. They played at merry games in the fields round the house: on Saturday half-holidays they went long scrambling walks down mysterious shady lanes, then climbing the uplands, and thus gaining extensive views over the country, about which so much had to be told, both of its past and present history. §

Miss Wooler had lived all her life in that part of Yorkshire, and well remembered the troubled times of the Luddite riots, when mills were attacked and owners ambushed by workers who found their living threatened by the introduction of machinery. She could tell exciting stories of the riots, and point to the very field where an armed rising had taken place; the woods and valleys were alive with recent revolutionary history. These stories, which all the girls enjoyed, impressed Charlotte's imagination all the more because her father, during his curacy at Hartshead, had been in the very thick of the disturbances, and his enjoyment of this violent interlude, when he had supported the militant anti-revolutionary clergy of the district, and had first taken to carrying arms, was one of his favourite themes during family breakfast. Miss Wooler's stirring tales, and seeing the very places where the troubles had been, quickened Charlotte's response to her father's stories. A part of her mind received a fertilising seed, as Mrs Gaskell's had when she had first seen Haworth, and eagerly absorbed it.

There were few excitements, apart from those of the imagination, at Roe Head, and when after eighteen months Charlotte was ready to leave, one catches a hint that, in spite of her quiet happiness there, she regretted for a moment the strenuous application which had kept her apart from the normal life of the school. 'The last day Charlotte was at school,' Ellen Nussey remembered, 'she seemed to realise what a sedate, hard-working season it had been to her. She said, "I should for once like to feel *out and out* a schoolgirl; I wish something would happen! Let us run round the fruit garden (running was what she never did); perhaps we shall meet someone, or we may have a fine for trespass." She evidently was longing for some never-to-be-forgotten incident. Nothing, however, arose from her little enterprise. She had to leave school as calmly and quietly as she had there lived.'

VI : GROWING UP

There now followed three more years of quiet at Haworth, years in which the four children were all at home together and nothing had happened, yet, to cloud the future. Mrs Gaskell was able to turn to the earliest of Charlotte's letters to Ellen Nussey, for by this time their friendship was well established and long communicative letters were passing between them.

Since the letters to Ellen were Mrs Gaskell's chief, indeed her only, source of material for this seemingly uneventful period, she not unnaturally formed the impression that the friendship was Charlotte's chief preoccupation, and that the emotional, sometimes despondent tone of the letters was a clue to the whole state of the writer's mind. Nothing, however, could have been more misleading, for though Mrs Gaskell made faithful use of her material, she could not know that it was incomplete, and that beneath the surface of life at Haworth there had been a yeasty turmoil of activity, pleasure, interest, fantasy and experiment of which Ellen knew nothing.

She had known nothing because the Brontës' dream world, to which Charlotte eagerly returned as soon as she came home, and in which Branwell, Emily and Anne had been absorbed all the time she was away, had become more secret as it increased in emotional intensity. Never again shall we find Charlotte telling anyone, as she had once told Mary Taylor, about their 'magazines'; the thing had reached the level of addiction, and from now on was concealed under an immense reserve. When Charlotte gave Ellen an account of her life at the parsonage she did not so much as hint at the enjoyments which were filling the leisure and absorbing the energy of them all.

'An account of one day is an account of all. In the morning, from nine o'clock till half-past twelve, I instruct my sisters, and draw; then we walk till dinner-time. After dinner I sew till tea-time, and after tea I either write, read, or do a little fancy-work, or draw, as I please. Thus, in one delightful, though somewhat monotonous course, my life is passed. I have been only out twice to tea since I came home. We are expecting company this afternoon, and on Tuesday next we shall have all the female teachers of the Sunday-school to tea.' It sounds tame enough; yet behind the demure communication, 'after tea I either write, read, or do a little fancy-work', there lies concealed an extraordinary possiblity—that the year 1833, when Charlotte was seventeen, was the most productive of her life.

Of this, however, Mrs Gaskell naturally knew nothing. The Charlotte that she evoked at this period was Ellen Nussey's Charlotte, her 'dear C.'; and the lurid life of the imagination which Charlotte and Branwell were sharing at this time, and which we shall consider presently, casts none of its light on the delicate, quiet picture.

In looking over the earlier portion of the correspondence, Mrs Gaskell is

§ struck afresh by the absence of hope, which formed such a strong characteristic in Charlotte. At an age when girls, in general, look forward to an eternal duration of such feelings as they or their friends entertain, and can therefore see no hindrance to the fulfilment of any engagements dependent on the future state of the affections, she is surprised that 'E.' keeps her promise to write. In after-life, I was painfully impressed with the fact, that Miss Brontë never dared to allow herself to look forward with hope; that she had no confidence in the future; and I thought, when I heard of the sorrowful years she had passed through, that it had been this pressure of grief which had crushed all buoyancy of expectation out of her. But it appears from the letters, that it must have been, so to speak, constitutional; or, perhaps, the deep pang of losing her two elder sisters combined with a permanent state of bodily weakness in producing her hopelessness. If her trust in God had been less strong, she would have given way to unbounded anxiety, at many a period of her life. §

'I am slow, *very* slow,' Charlotte had written to Ellen, 'to believe the protestations of another; I know my own sentiments, I can read my own mind, but the minds of the rest of man and woman kind are to me sealed volumes, hieroglyphical scrolls, which I cannot easily either unseal or decipher. Yet time, careful study, long acquaintance, overcome most difficulties.' Her extreme diffidence in forming friendships was perhaps, as Mrs Gaskell guessed, in part due to the influence of Mr Brontë, who, with a practical cynicism more Yorkshire than Irish, considered 'distrust of others as a part of that knowledge of human nature on which he piqued himself. His precepts to this effect, combining with Charlotte's lack of hope, made her always fearful of loving too much; of wearying the objects of her affection; and thus she was often trying to restrain her warm feelings, and was ever chary of that presence so invariably welcome to her true friends.'

The friendship with Ellen, however, in spite of Charlotte's caution, ripened fast. At first they corresponded in French, with a touching determination on self-improvement; but Ellen quickly broke down under the effort and Charlotte was not sorry to abandon it: schoolgirl French was a hampering medium for a friendship which had become not only affectionate but emotional. There comes at times, indeed, an almost loverlike note in Charlotte's letters to Ellen during the next two years, a note on which modern readers have sometimes too significantly paused. If there is a trace of homosexual feeling in these letters it marks only that universal stage of adolescence, when the emotional nature is stirring and awake, yet not totally aware. It yearns after love, and bestows it where it can, on either sex, on friends, on animals, on fantasies. A great deal of the passionate vitality now awakening in Charlotte was directed, as we shall see, into the Byronic fantasy-world of her own imagining, where it had free range, released from the censorship of her puritan conscience; some of its ardour and yearning overflowed into little crises of religious emotion and of tenderness for Ellen. The phase was brief. The friendship soon settled down into the normal, affectionate relationship that it remained; and the feverish touch in the early letters would be scarcely worth commenting on if it had not, in recent years, attracted too much sophisticated attention.

In the first September after leaving school, Charlotte was invited to visit Ellen at Birstall, and stayed with her for a fortnight. We still have (which Mrs Gaskell had not) Miss Nussey's own careful account of the visit, written from her excellent memory in middle-age, and her first-hand description is more vital than any paraphrase:

'Charlotte's first visit from Haworth was made about three months after she left school. She travelled in a two-wheeled gig, the only conveyance to be had in Haworth except the covered cart which brought her to school. Mr Brontë sent Branwell as an escort; he was *then* a very dear brother, as dear to Charlotte as her own soul; they were in perfect accord of taste and feeling, and it was mutual delight to be together.

'Branwell probably had never been far from home before; he was in wild ecstasy with everything. He walked about in unrestrained boyish enjoyment, taking views in every direction of the old turret-roofed house, the fine chestnut trees on the lawn . . . and a large rookery, which gave to the house a good background—all these he noted and commented upon with perfect enthusiasm. He told his sister he "was leaving her in paradise, and if she were not intensely happy she never would be!" Happy, indeed, she then was, *in himself*, for she, with her own enthusiasms, looked forward to what her brother's great promise and talent might effect. He would at this time be between fifteen and sixteen years of age.

'The visit passed without much to mark it (at this distance of time) except that we crept away together from household life as much as we could. Charlotte liked to pace the plantations or seek seclusion in the fruit garden; she was safe from visitors in these retreats. She was so painfully shy she could not bear any special notice. One day, on being led into dinner by a stranger, she trembled and nearly burst into tears; but notwithstanding her excessive shyness, which was often painful to others as well as herself, she won the respect and affection of all who had opportunity enough to become acquainted with her.'

The following summer the visit was returned, and Ellen came to Haworth; and here again her own words have the freshness and value, the incomparable poetic quality of recollection. 'Even at this time, Mr Brontë struck me as looking very venerable. . . . His manner and mode of speech always had the tone of high-bred courtesy. He was considered something of an invalid, and always lived in the most abstemious and simple manner.'

(Mr Brontë's health is something of a puzzle. He must have possessed considerable stamina to have endured the Spartan conditions of his youth and to have come unscathed through the lean years at Cambridge; he was a great walker, and died at the age of eighty-four, having outlived all his children. Yet even as early as Charlotte's first term at Roe Head we learn from his letters that he has been suffering from inflammation of the lungs, and is 'very delicate'. 'I fear,' he told Charlotte's godmother, 'I shall never fully recover. I sometimes think that I shall fall into a decline.' The consumptive tendency, if it ever threatened, did not develop, but he seems to have suffered for many years from a digestive disorder. At all events, he adopted the mode of self-treatment which common sense would suggest for such an ailment, eating little and carefully, and enjoying the quiet luxury of dining alone. This régime, begun when the children were small, became a lifelong habit, and probably preserved him into his comparatively healthy old age, though it never, it seems, completely cured him of his trouble.)

'His white cravat was not then so remarkable as it grew

to be afterwards. He was in the habit of covering this cravat himself. We never saw the operation, but we always had to wind for him the white sewing-silk which he used. Charlotte said it was her father's one extravagance—he cut up yards and yards of white lutestring (silk). . . . Mr Brontë's cravat went into new silk and new size without taking any off, till at length nearly half his head was enveloped in cravat. His liability to bronchial attacks, no doubt, attached him to this increasing growth of cravat.

'Miss Branwell was a very small, antiquated lady. She wore caps large enough for half a dozen of the present fashion, and a front of light auburn curls over her forehead. She always dressed in silk. She had a horror of the climate so far north, and of the stone floors in the parsonage. She amused us by clicking about in pattens whenever she had to go into the kitchen or look after household operations.

'She talked a great deal of her younger days; the gayeties of her dear native town Penzance, in Cornwall; the soft, warm climate, etc. The social life of her younger days she used to recall with regret; she gave one the idea that she had been a belle among her own home acquaintances. She took snuff out of a very pretty gold snuff-box, which she sometimes presented to you with a little laugh, as if she enjoyed the slight shock and astonishment visible in your countenance. In summer she spent part of the afternoon in reading aloud to Mr Brontë. In the winter evenings she must have enjoyed this; for she and Mr Brontë had often to finish their discussions on what she had read when we all met for tea. She would be very lively and intelligent, and tilt arguments against Mr Brontë without fear.

' "Tabby", the faithful, trustworthy old servant, was very quaint in appearance—very active, and, in these days, the general servant and factotum. We were all "childer" and "bairns" in her estimation. . . .

'Emily Brontë had by this time acquired a lithesome, graceful figure. She was the tallest person in the house, except her father. Her hair, which was naturally as beautiful as Charlotte's, was in the same unbecoming tight curl and frizz, and there was the same want of complexion. She had very beautiful eyes—kind, kindling, liquid eyes; but she did not often look at you; she was too reserved.' ('I distinguish reserve from shyness,' wrote Mrs Gaskell, who clearly was not attracted by what she learned of Emily, 'because I imagine shyness would please, if it knew how; whereas, reserve is indifferent whether it pleases or not. Anne, like her eldest sister, was shy; Emily was reserved.') 'Their colour might be said to be dark grey, at other times dark blue, they varied so. She talked very little. She and Anne were like twins—inseparable companions, and in the very closest sympathy, which never had any interruption.

'Anne—dear, gentle Anne—was quite different in appearance from the others. She was her aunt's favourite. Her hair was a very pretty, light brown, and fell on her neck in graceful curls. She had lovely violet-blue eyes, fine pencilled eyebrows, and clear, almost transparent complexion. She still pursued her studies, and especially her sewing, under the surveillance of her aunt. Emily had begun to have the disposal of her own time.'

Emily was not idle, however, for she was having piano lessons and doing her share of the housework; nor was life at the parsonage quite so regular and sedate as Ellen's narrative suggests. The following year Emily and Anne wrote a loose page of diary together, sitting in the kitchen, which makes a very homely and easy-going impression : 'It is past twelve o'clock Anne and I have not tidied ourselves, done our bed work, or done our lessons and we want to go out to play. We are going to have for dinner Boiled Beef, Turnips, potatoes and apple pudding. The kitchin is in a very untidy state Anne and I have not done our music exercise which consists of *b major* Taby said on my putting a pen in her face Ya pitter pottering there instead of pilling a potate. I answered O Dear, O Dear, O Dear I will derectly With that I get up, take a knife and begin pilling. . . .' This oddly childish and touching fragment was not seen by Mrs Gaskell; it came to light forty years after the writing of the biography, when Mr Nicholls, now an old man and living in Ireland, found this and three other fragments screwed into a corner of an old box. 'They are sad reading, poor girls!' he wrote to Clement Shorter.

To return to Ellen Nussey's narrative: 'Branwell studied regularly with his father, and used to paint in oils, which was regarded as study for what might be eventually his profession. All the household entertained the idea of his becoming an artist, and hoped he would be a distinguished one.

'In fine and suitable weather delightful rambles were made over the moors, and down into the glens and ravines that here and there bróke the monotony of the moorland. . . . Emily, Anne and Branwell used to ford the streams, and sometimes placed stepping-stones for the other two. . . . Emily especially had a gleesome delight in these nooks of beauty—her reserve for the time vanished. One long ramble made in these early days was far away over the moors to a spot familiar to Emily and Anne, which they called "The Meeting of the Waters". It was a small oasis of emerald green turf, broken here and there by small clear springs; a few large stones served as resting-places. . . . Emily, half reclining on a slab of stone, played like a young child with the tadpoles in the water, making them swim about, and then fell to moralising on the strong and the weak, the brave and the cowardly, as she chased them with her hand. No serious care or sorrow had so far cast its gloom on nature's youth and buoyancy, and nature's simplest offerings were fountains of pleasure and enjoyment. . . .'

The parsonage then had been even plainer and barer than when Mrs Gaskell saw it, but even in those early years had shown a certain fastidiousness and taste. The interior 'lacked drapery of all kinds. Mr Brontë's horror of fire forbade curtains to the windows, they never had these accessories to comfort and appearance' (they would have shutters, however) 'till long after Charlotte was the only inmate of the family sitting-room. She then ventured on the innovation . . . it did not please her father, but it was not forbidden.

'There was not much carpet anywhere except in the sitting-room, and on the study floor. The hall floor and stairs were done with sand-stone, always beautifully clean, as everything was about the house; the walls were not papered, but stained in a pretty dove-coloured tint; hair-seated chairs and mahogany tables, book-shelves in the study, but not many of these elsewhere. Scant and bare indeed, many will say, yet it was not a scantness that made itself felt. Mind and thought, I had almost said elegance, but certainly refinement, diffused themselves over all, and made nothing really wanting.

'A little later on, there was the addition of a piano. Emily, after some application, played with precision and brilliancy. Anne played also, but she preferred soft harmonies and vocal music. She sang a little; her voice was weak, but very sweet in tone.

'Mr Brontë's health caused him to retire early. He assembled his household for family worship at eight o'clock; at nine he locked and barred the front door, always giving as he passed the sitting-room door a kindly admonition to the "children" not to be late; half-way up the stairs he stayed his steps to wind up the clock. . . . The only dread he had was of *fire*, and this dread was so intense it caused him to prohibit all but silk or woollen dresses for his daughters; indeed, for anyone to wear any other kind of fabric was almost to forfeit his respect.' (His obsession had, apparently, a reasonable foundation, for in 1844, while writing to the *Leeds Mercury* on this favourite topic, he produced horrifying data : 'I have been at Haworth for more than twenty years, and during that long interval of time, as far as I can remember, I have performed the funeral service over ninety or a hundred children, who were burnt to death in consequence of their clothes having taken fire, and on enquiry in every case I have found that the poor sufferers had been clothed in either cotton or linen.')

Pet animals were an important part of life at the parsonage. At the time of Ellen's first visit there appears to have been only one; but the diary fragment quoted above opens with the words, 'I fed Rainbow, Diamond, Snowflake, Jasper pheasant,' which suggests that their numbers rapidly increased in spite of Miss Branwell's objections. 'During Miss Branwell's reign at the parsonage,' Ellen remembered, 'the love of animals had to be kept in due subjection. There was then but one dog, which was admitted to the parlour at stated times. Emily and Anne always gave him a portion of their breakfast, which was, by their own choice, the old north-country diet of oatmeal porridge. Later on, there were three household pets—the tawny, strong-limbed Keeper, Emily's favourite : he was so completely under her control, she could quite easily make him spring and roar like a lion. She taught him this kind of occasional play without any coercion. Flossy—long, silky-haired, black and white Flossy—was Anne's favourite; and black Tom, the tabby, was everybody's favourite. It received such gentle treatment it seemed to have lost cat's nature, and subsided into luxurious amiability and contentment. The Brontës' love of dumb creatures made them very sensitive of the treatment bestowed upon them. For anyone to offend in this respect was an infallible bad sign, and a blot on the disposition.'

The household which Ellen visited in the summer of 1833 was, indeed, an extremely happy one; a good deal cut off, it is true, from the rest of the world, both by the remoteness of the place and also by temperament; but so busy with its own concerns, with such unusual resources in its own company, that it was impossible to be either bored or lonely. Ellen herself made an extremely favourable impression. 'Were I to tell you,' Charlotte wrote, 'of the impression you have made on everyone here, you would accuse me of flattery. Papa and aunt are continually adducing you as an example for me to shape my actions and behaviour by. Emily and Anne say "they never saw anyone they liked so well as you". And Tabby, whom you have absolutely fascinated, talks a great deal more nonsense about your ladyship than I care to repeat.'

The friendship with Ellen soon fell into its characteristic pattern, with Charlotte the dominant, Ellen the receptive partner. Ellen was flatteringly anxious for Charlotte's advice on every subject except, perhaps, religion; on this point she was conscious of a piety superior to Charlotte's, and with youthful seriousness exhorted and admonished. On points of character, however, or self-improvement, it was Charlotte's word and authority that she relied on, and with justice, for nearly all Charlotte's letters of this period are admirable for their good-humour and good sense.

'In your last, you request me to tell you of your faults. Now, really, how can you be so foolish! I *won't* tell you of your faults, because I don't know them. What a creature would that be, who, after receiving an affectionate and kind letter from a

beloved friend should sit down and write a catalogue of defects
by way of answer! Imagine me doing so, and then consider
what epithets you would bestow on me. Conceited, dogmatical,
hypocritical, little humbug, I should think, would be the mildest. Why, child! I've neither time nor inclination to reflect on
your *faults* when you are so far from me, and when, besides,
kind letters and presents, and so forth, are continually bringing forth your goodness in the most prominent light. Then, too,
there are judicious relations always round you, who can much
better discharge that unpleasant office. I have no doubt their
advice is completely at your service; why then should I intrude
mine? If you will not hear *them*, it will be vain though one
should rise from the dead to instruct you.'

Ellen, however, recognising her friend's far superior abilities,
did not give up her habit of asking advice, and Charlotte's
answer to a request for a list of books for her 'perusal' throws
an interesting light on the Brontës' adolescent reading.

'If you like poetry, let it be first-rate; Milton, Shakespeare,
Thomson, Goldsmith, Pope (if you will, though I don't admire
him), Scott, Byron, Campbell, Wordsworth, and Southey. Now,
don't be startled at the names of Shakespeare and Byron. Both
these were great men, and their works are like themselves. You
will know how to choose the good, and to avoid the evil; the
finest passages are always the purest, the bad are invariably
revolting; you will never wish to read them over twice. Omit
the comedies of Shakespeare and the *Don Juan*, perhaps, the
Cain, of Byron, though the latter is a magnificent poem, and
read the rest fearlessly; that must indeed be a depraved mind
which can gather evil from *Henry VIII*, from *Richard III*, from
Macbeth, and *Hamlet*, and *Julius Cæsar*. Scott's sweet, wild,
romantic poetry can do you no harm. Nor can Wordsworth's,
nor Campbell's nor Southey's—the greatest part at least of his;
some is certainly objectionable. For history, read Hume, Rollin,
and the *Universal History*, if you *can*; I never did. For fiction,
read Scott alone; all novels after his are worthless. For biography, read Johnson's *Lives of the Poets*, Boswell's *Life of
Johnson*, Southey's *Life of Nelson*, Lockhart's *Life of Burns*,
Moore's *Life of Sheridan*, Moore's *Life of Byron*, Wolfe's
Remains. For natural history, read Bewick and Audubon, and

Goldsmith and White's *History of Selborne*. For divinity, your brother will advise you there. I can only say, adhere to standard authors, and avoid novelty.'

From this list we see that the Brontës had a sufficiently wide range of books to choose from. We know that as they grew older they made use of the Keighley Mechanics' Institute library, and probably borrowed books as well from Ponden Hall, two miles from Haworth, where the Heatan family owned a good private library and were personally friendly. The parsonage itself possessed a fair though not impressive number of books. When Mrs Gaskell stayed there during Charlotte's lifetime she had been struck by the fact that the books were principally Charlotte's—'two recesses, on each side of the high, narrow, old-fashioned mantel-piece, filled with books—books given to her, books she had bought, and which tell of her individual pursuits and tastes: *not* standard books' : but in Mr Brontë's study there were 'no books but those contained on two hanging shelves between the windows', and she was moved to wonder how he passed the time. But in the earlier days, with Mr Brontë still active and the children reading and borrowing, to say nothing of Miss Branwell with her narrow but powerful vein of Methodist literature, books seem to have been more plentiful.

§ The well-bound were ranged in the sanctuary of Mr Brontë's study; but the purchase of books was a necessary luxury to him, and as it was often a choice between binding an old one, or buying a new one, the familiar volume, which had been hungrily read by all the members of the family, was sometimes in such a condition that the bed-room shelf was considered its fitting place. Up and down the house, were to be found many standard works of a solid kind. Sir Walter Scott's writings, Wordsworth's and Southey's poems were among the lighter literature; while, as having a character of their own—earnest, wild, and occasionally fanatical —may be named some of the books which came from the Branwell side of the family—from the Cornish followers of the saintly John Wesley—and which are touched on in the account of the works to which Caroline Helstone had access in *Shirley* :—'Some venerable Lady's Magazines, that had once performed a voyage with their owner, and undergone a storm'—(possibly part of the relics of Mrs Brontë's possessions, contained in the ship wrecked on the coast of Cornwall)—'and whose pages were stained with salt water; some mad Methodist Magazines full of miracles and apparitions, and preternatural warnings, ominous dreams, and frenzied fanaticism; and the equally mad letters of Mrs Elizabeth Rowe from the Dead to the Living. §

Mad they may have been, and perhaps laughed at by Charlotte and Branwell in private and weeded out of the bookshelves when Miss Branwell was gone; but it would be a mistake to underestimate the Methodist influence on the whole Brontë family. Mrs Brontë and Miss Branwell were strong Methodists. In his youth Mr Brontë himself seems to have skirted the Methodist fringe; Mr Tighe, whose children he had taught in Ireland, was an ardent friend of Wesley's, and it seems more than likely that Mr Brontë was helped through Cambridge, and to his earliest living, by Methodist influence, in the belief that he would make a useful recruit to the connection. Mr Brontë remained, however, in the Church of England, though not wholly unsympathetic to the evangelical movement. His own early poems echo Charles Wesley's hymns to the point of plagiarism; he had followed a Methodist predecessor in the living of Haworth, and liked to think that Wesley himself had stayed at the parsonage when he was preaching in Yorkshire. It is interesting, too, to remember that the Rev Carus Wilson, under whose rule Mr Brontë placed his daughters at Cowan Bridge, was an evangelical clergyman, firm in the doctrine of salvation by faith, not works.

On the Brontë children the effects of such intimacy with Methodism were various. It left its mark on all their poetry, particularly on Emily's, which often moves in the measures of Methodist hymns. On Anne it laid its most unhappy behest, infecting her with the morbid fear of personal damnation which darkened her youth. Charlotte appears to have been momentarily touched by this, but her robuster nature rose above it, and she seems, like Emily, to have been by temperament impatient of the lurid Methodist ideas of hell and punishment. On Branwell the pressure of so much religious emphasis was to destroy belief.

Branwell at this time was still the brilliant darling of the family. He had none of his sisters' reticence and shyness; on the contrary, he possessed that wonderful facility in conversation which too often carries away the creative energy in talk. 'Nature,' as Charlotte was ready to admit, 'had favoured him with a fairer outside, as well as a finer constitution, than his sisters.' He was by inclination sociable, and so lively and attractive a companion that, again unlike his sisters, even in Haworth he had his convivial circle. He belonged, following the Byronic fashion, to a boxing club, which met and sparred in an upper room in the village; he was a member of the local Freemasons' lodge, The Three Graces, which met at the 'Black Bull'; and managed at the same time to perform the perhaps not very exacting duties of secretary to the Haworth Temperance Society. In spite of his lack of schooling he was well-read, like all the family, and his classical studies under his father seem to have been pursued to uncommonly good effect, since some of his most able poetry is concerned with Greek and Roman themes, and his translation of the first book of the *Odes of Horace* has received respectful recognition even in our own time.[1] His furious literary urge seemed even greater than his sisters', driving him to an almost frenetic production of poems, imaginary histories and prose tales, which in sheer quantity, though not in quality, surpass Charlotte's. In talking and writing his precocious facility was extraordinary, and his talents extended to music and painting as well. While Anne learned to play songs and hymns and Emily grew into a pianist of respectable amateur quality, Branwell achieved, again apparently without much effort, a showy level of execution and a passion for church music; he was accustomed to play emotionally for hours on the church organ. But it was in painting that Branwell showed his greatest promise, or at least the talent which, in the eyes of his father and sisters, seemed most likely to offer him a living. He was not the only

[1] Mr. John Drinkwater edited and privately printed this translation in 1923, with a commendatory preface.

one who had dwelt with longing on this idea; all the girls were addicted to drawing, and Charlotte, as she had told Mrs Gaskell in the early days of their acquaintance, had herself at this time had a romantic hope of being an artist, and to this end had weakened her eyesight by copying 'nimini-pimini copper-plate engravings out of annuals . . . every little point put in, till at the end of six months she had produced an exquisitely faithful copy of the engraving'. She was strongly drawn to the art, but compelled at last to admit she had no talent. 'I sat bent over my desk, drawing—' she was to write later, in *Villette*, 'that is, copying an elaborate line-engraving, tediously working up my copy to the finish of the original, for that was my practical notion of art; and strange to say, I took extreme pleasure in the labour, and could even produce curiously finished facsimiles of steel or mezzotinto plates— things about as valuable as so many achievements in worsted work, but I thought pretty well of them in those days.'

In her brother's case, however, there was a definite gift which seemed to promise well, and by the time he was eighteen his painting had sufficiently impressed his father for Mr Brontë to engage a visiting art master. With this tuition Branwell made good progress, and it was eventually decided that he should study in London.

§ In the middle of the summer of 1835, a great family plan was mooted at the parsonage. The question was, to what trade or profession should Branwell be brought up? He was now nearly eighteen; it was time to decide. He was very clever, no doubt; perhaps, to begin with, the greatest genius in this rare family. The sisters hardly recognised their own, or each others' powers, but they knew *his*. The father, ignorant of many failings in moral conduct, did proud homage to the great gifts of his son; for Branwell's talents were readily and willingly brought out for the entertainment of others. Popular admiration was sweet to him. And this led to his presence being sought at 'arvills' and all the great village gatherings, for the Yorkshire men have a keen relish for intellect; and it likewise procured him the undesirable distinction of having his company recommended by the landlord of the 'Black Bull' to any chance traveller who might happen to feel solitary or dull over his liquor. 'Do you want some one to help you with your bottle, sir? If you do, I'll send up for Patrick' (so the villagers called him till the day of his death, though in his own family he was always 'Branwell'). And while the messenger went, the landlord entertained his guest with accounts of the wonderful talents of the boy, whose precocious cleverness, and great conversational powers, were the pride of the village. The attacks of ill-health to which Mr Brontë had been subject of late years, rendered it not only necessary that he should take his dinner alone (for the sake of avoiding temptations to unwholesome diet), but made it also desirable that he should pass the time directly succeeding his meals in perfect quiet. And this necessity, combined with due attention to his parochial duties, made him partially ignorant how his son employed himself out of lesson-time. His own youth had been spent among people of the same conventional rank as those into whose companionship Branwell was now thrown; but he had had a strong will, and an earnest and persevering ambition, and a resoluteness of purpose which his weaker son wanted.

It is singular how strong a yearning the whole family had towards the art of drawing. Mr Brontë had been very solicitous to get them good instruction; the girls themselves loved everything connected with it—all descriptions or engravings of great pictures; and, in default of good ones, they would take and analyse any print or drawing which came in their way, and find out how much thought had gone to its composition, what ideas it was intended to suggest, and what it *did* suggest. In the same spirit, they laboured to design imaginations of their own; they lacked the power of execution, not of conception. At one time, Charlotte had the notion of making her living as an artist, and wearied her eyes in drawing with pre-Raphaelite minuteness, but not with pre-Raphaelite accuracy, for she drew from fancy rather than from nature.

But they all thought there could be no doubt about Branwell's talent for drawing. I have seen an oil painting of his, done I know not when, but probably about this time. It was a group of his sisters, life-size, three-quarters' length; not much better than sign-painting, as to manipulation; but the likenesses were, I should think, admirable. I could only judge of the fidelity with which the other two were depicted, from the striking resemblance which Charlotte, upholding the great frame of canvas, and consequently standing right behind it, bore to her own representation, though it must have been ten years and more since the portraits were taken. The picture was divided, almost in the middle, by a great pillar. On the side of the column which was lighted by the sun, stood Charlotte, in the womanly dress of that day of gigot sleeves and large collars. On the deeply shadowed side, was Emily, with Anne's gentle face resting on her shoulder. Emily's countenance struck me as full of power; Charlotte's of solicitude; Anne's of tenderness. The two younger seemed hardly to have attained their full growth, though Emily was taller than Charlotte; they had cropped hair, and a more girlish dress. I remember looking on those two sad, earnest, shadowed faces, and wondering whether I could trace the mysterious expression which is said to foretell an early death. I had some fond superstitious hope that the column divided their fates from hers, who stood apart in the canvas, as in life she survived. I liked to see that the bright side of the pillar was towards *her*—that the light in the picture fell on *her* : I might more truly have sought in her presentment—nay, in her living face—for the sign of death in her prime. They were good likenesses, however badly executed. From thence I should guess his family augured truly that, if Branwell had but the opportunity, and, alas! had but the moral qualities, he might turn out a great painter.

The best way of preparing him to become so appeared to be to send him as a pupil to the Royal Academy. I dare say he longed and yearned to follow this path, principally because it would lead him to that mysterious London—that Babylon the great—which seems to have filled the imaginations and haunted the minds of all the younger members of this recluse family. To Branwell it was more than a vivid imagination, it was an impressed reality. By dint of studying maps, he was as well acquainted with it, even down to its by-ways, as if he had lived there. Poor misguided fellow! this craving to see and know London, and that stronger craving after fame, were never to be satisfied. He was to die at the end of a short and blighted life. But in the year of 1835, all his home kindred were thinking how they could best forward his views, and how help him up to the pinnacle where he desired to be. What their plans were, let Charlotte explain. These are not the first sisters who have laid their lives as a sacrifice before their brother's idolised wish. Would to God they might be the last who met with such a miserable return! §

There is no doubt that whatever Mr Brontë could squeeze from his stipend was being spent at this time on Branwell's future. There was nothing over for the girls: from now on they must prepare to stand on their own. Emily was to go to school at Miss Wooler's and Charlotte to return there as a teacher, the expense of the one being met out of the wages of the other. Anne was, for the present, to stay at home. The girls did not question this arrangement; the spending of all available money on the only son was a convention too traditional for argument; and the sum which could be devoted even to Branwell must have been pitifully small. 'We are all about to divide, break up, separate,' Charlotte wrote to Ellen Nussey. 'Emily is going to school, Branwell is going to London, and I am going to be a governess. This last determination I formed myself, knowing that I should have to take the step some time, "and better sune as syne", to use the Scotch proverb; and knowing well that Papa would have enough to do with his limited income, should Branwell be placed at the Royal Academy, and Emily at Roe Head. . . . Emily and I leave home on the 27th of this month; the idea of being together consoles us both somewhat, and, in truth, since I must enter a situation, "My lines have fallen in pleasant places". I both love and respect Miss Wooler.'

Other biographers have followed Mrs Gaskell's lead in pitying the sisters for their sacrifice, but in reality the arrangement was, had they but known it, as inauspicious for Branwell as it was for them, since he possessed to an extreme degree that kind of temperament which collapses under pressure, and his going to London precipitated his first failure. Like many a seeming genius, he found the test of performance impossible to face because nothing he could ever do could reach the expected standard. So long as he was not actually put to the proof he could, like a prodigious child, live brilliantly on promise. His creative urge could drive him in one direction after another, his undoubted talents could expand, and his own hope and vanity, unchilled by outside criticism, could pursue a large untroubled dream of fame. Only when reality, the enemy, obtruded itself did the bubble collapse, and the wretched boy, terrified of failure to a degree unknown to those who have never been under a comparable pressure towards success, would desperately cast about for ways of escape. The means of escape were not many, but there were a few; and among them were the illusions of drink and opium.

It is not known at what age Branwell began his experiments with laudanum, but he was certainly no stranger to alcohol in his teens, and it was an easy step to a drug so readily available. The biographers who have been shocked by the opium-taking of his early twenties forget the extreme ease with which, in his time, anyone could buy laudanum. Drams of this simple solution of opium in alcohol, of which De Quincey had written with poetic fervour and which Coleridge and other literary men had made fashionable, could be purchased from any apothecary for a few pence, and without opprobrium, since it was in universal domestic use as an anodyne. Mrs Gaskell herself had had occasion to use it, and had discussed with Charlotte its effects—'vivid and exaggerated presence of objects, of which the outlines were indistinct or lost in golden mist'; and a few weeks after she had returned to Manchester after staying with Charlotte at Haworth, Elizabeth Barrett Browning was writing to her from Italy, 'Such a summer we have had here! Nothing makes a strong woman of me,—but I ride about the mountains on a donkey in a round peasant's hat for which I should be pelted in Manchester, and see such divine visions as of a new heaven and new earth from the summits as you cannot dream of in England except when you are poetical or take opium. . . .' No sensible person endured a toothache or neuralgia without recourse to it; it was readily prescribed by physicians, even for children; and was, indeed, almost the nineteenth-century equivalent of the aspirin. Branwell may thus very easily have come to it first as to a simple remedy, and have been drawn gradually into a more habitual use when he discovered its characteristic effects, which to his unstable nature were peculiarly attractive.

The effect of laudanum is not erotic. It seems, on the contrary, to produce very often an illusion of intellectual brilliance in which everything is comprehensible and everything possible. It offers particular rewards to the writer and artist because the dreams it induces persist in waking memory; they are accessible to the conscious mind and so are a source of imaginative material. It is able, too, to compose a harassed and despairing mood and induce a delicious temporary tranquillity, full of confidence. 'You, I believe,' wrote Coleridge to his brother, 'know how divine that repose is, what a spot of enchantment, a green spot of fountain and flowers and trees in the very heart of a waste of sands.' Small wonder that Branwell, as the years went by and it became ever more mercilessly clear that he would never fulfil his early promise, should take refuge in the friendly drug which gave him temporary mastery over his unmanageable world.

There is no evidence that the habit ever reached the degree of addiction, or that it seriously affected his health, which was in any case not robust. Certainly at the time of his going to London to be an art student the habit had not yet been formed; but this is nevertheless a convenient place to consider Branwell's drug-taking, since the passionate need of *some* drug, and the ability to generate their own imaginative intoxicants, were to some degree characteristic of all the Brontës.

They all four possessed, in greater or less degrees, that genius which apprehends its own imaginative life as fully and vividly as real experience. The mature work of Charlotte and Emily is trembling with this power; it lays the reader at once under its spell. 'It has become the fashion,' says one perceptive critic,[2] 'to exalt Emily and debase Charlotte, in utter ignorance that their genius—the ability to realise the imaginative with the vivid intensity of the actual—was identical, and that Emily's one point of superiority was her full surrender to the creative spirit which Charlotte fought with all the strength of her tyrannical conscience.' To this type of creative genius there is a vital prerequisite—the ability to withdraw into one's own imagination with a completeness of absorption akin to trance. It is at this point that we begin to see a possible connection between Branwell's opium and the all-absorbing imaginative play-world in which they all lived; lived, too, to an age which makes it clear that it ceased to be a game in the childish sense and became a powerful drug-like substitute for experience. Those incandescent imaginations, abnormally sensitive and abnormally strong, felt with peculiar intensity the universal human desire for protective illusion. They all, in childhood, immersed themselves in the absorbing imaginative shadow-world, the 'drug-like Brontë dream'. Charlotte at twenty-five, realising the strength of the obsession and its dangers, broke out of it with anguish, and not before it had left its permanent, and valuable, mark. Emily never abandoned it, but grew up on the other side of the frontier, a freer and more baffling genius than her sister. Anne, sensitive and talented, a Brontë without genius, shared Emily's dream as long as she could, and then was drawn off into the sadder and lonelier depths of religious melancholy. All three sisters produced, as it were, their drug out of their own being. Branwell alone, sharing the gift and burden of the Brontë temperament, and thrown out of balance under pressure of his own problem, took to the easier intoxications of brandy and opium.

This, however, is to look some distance ahead. When Branwell went to London to be an art student the only drug he knew was one he shared with Charlotte: an addiction to 'the infernal world', 'the world below', the world of Douro, Percy, Northangerland and Angria. Though Charlotte was now nineteen and Branwell eighteen, their long-standing collaboration

[2] Miss F. E. Ratchford in *The Brontës' Web of Childhood.* (Columbia University Press, 1941.)

had lost none of its intensity; on the contrary, their absorption in it was so great that Branwell seems to have found in it his only consolation, both after the mysterious failure of the Academy project and the separation from Charlotte when she returned to Roe Head.

Nobody knows, and nobody is likely to know now, exactly what happened on Branwell's visit to London. He had apparently written to the secretary of the Royal Academy school for permission to enroll his name as a prospective student, but there is no evidence that he ever sat for the necessary examination, and it is possible that, on the strength of such work as he was able to submit, he was discouraged from doing so. We know only that he spent some time in sight-seeing, visiting Westminster Abbey (which he was later able to draw with some accuracy from memory) and a celebrated rendezvous of the boxing fancy, the Castle Tavern in Holborn. After a time, without explanation, we find him again at home, and nothing more is said of his studying art. The only hint is contained in an account he himself wrote the following May of a visit of one of his Angrian heroes to 'Verdopolis'. This hero spends his time in sight-seeing, in lying listlessly on the sofa in his hotel, neglecting to present his letters of introduction and 'feeding his feelings with little squibs of rum'. He is described as having an 'instinctive fear of ending his pleasure by approaching reality'—a fear which we may suppose by this time Branwell understood very well. But we are not justified in accepting this fanciful account as autobiography; it is worth remembering only as a barely possible clue to a mysterious incident.

VII : AMBITIONS AND FRUSTRATIONS

The Academy project, then, had ended in failure, but Branwell, unknown to his father, had another iron in the fire to which he began to give his anxious attention. If he could not be an artist he would be a writer. He was convinced of his own talent in either field, and now, buoyed up by the torrent of verse and prose which had poured from his pen ever since he could remember, he applied himself to the long, chilling and embittering task of convincing the world. He opened his campaign with a shower of letters on the editor of *Blackwood's*:

'Sir,
     Read what I write.
     And would to heaven you could believe it true, for then you would attend to and act upon it. I have addressed you twice before, and now I do it again. . . .
     Now, sir, to you I appear writing with conceited assurance: *but I am not*, for I know myself so far as to believe in my own originality, and on that ground I desire of you admittance into your ranks. And do not wonder that I apply so determinedly, for . . . the idea of striving to aid

another periodical is *horribly repulsive*. My resolution is to devote my ability to you, and for God's sake, till you see whether or not I can serve you, do not so coldly refuse my aid. All, sir, that I require of you is—*that you would in answer to this letter request a specimen or specimens of my writing, and I even wish that you would name the subject on which you would wish me to write.* . . . Now, sir, do not act like a commonplace person, but like a man willing to examine for himself. . . .'

The editor of *Blackwood's*, no doubt professionally sensitive to the faint but authentic lunatic undertone, took no notice; and even a fourth letter, enclosing a long poem in two parts entitled *Misery* and imploring the editor, in printed capitals, to 'CONDEMN NOT UNHEARD', went, like its predecessors, unanswered. Disappointed, but not yet altogether able to believe in this stone wall of indifference, Branwell now began to press for an interview, declaring that 'a journey of three hundred miles shall not deter me', and with his unhappy knack for saying precisely the thing most likely to procure a snub, made certain that the door of *Blackwood's* would be closed against him. 'Will you still so wearisomely refuse me a word when you can neither know what you refuse nor whom you are refusing? Do you think your magazine so perfect that no addition to its power would be either possible or desirable?' But no answer came, and after another and final appeal Branwell sent a specimen of his prose to Wordsworth. 'My aim, sir,' he wrote, 'is to push out into the open world, and for this I trust not poetry alone; that might launch the vessel, but could not bear her on. Sensible and scientific prose . . . would give a further title to the notice of the world; and then again poetry ought to brighten and crown that name with glory. . . . Surely, in this day, when there is not a writing poet worth a sixpence, the field must be open, if a better man can step forward.' Unmoved by such singularly tactless logic, and disgusted by the mixture of 'gross flattery' and 'plenty of abuse' in this egregious letter, Wordsworth, too, let Branwell go unanswered. Charlotte, who at about the same time (and no doubt in consultation with her brother) had sent a letter and a bundle of poems to Southey, fared rather better, for although the Laureate's answer was discouraging—'kind and admirable, a little stringent' was how she described it later to Mrs Gaskell—he did at least reply, and even sent a second and more benevolent letter when she had written to thank him. She possessed, he considered, 'and in no inconsiderable degree', the faculty of verse, but he thought her absorption in day-dreams peculiar and dangerous. 'The daydreams in which you habitually indulge are likely to induce a distempered state of mind; and in proportion as all the ordinary uses of the world seem to you flat and unprofitable, you will be unfitted for them without becoming fitted for anything else. Literature cannot be the business of a woman's life, and it ought not to be. The more she is engaged in her proper duties, the less leisure will she have for it, even as an accomplishment and a recreation. To those duties you have not yet been called, and when you are you will be less eager for celebrity. You will not seek in imagination for excitement. . . .' This was a cooling dose, and on first reading Southey's letter Charlotte felt only shame and regret that she had ever troubled him with her effusions; a 'painful heat' rose to her face when she thought of the quires of paper she had so naïvely covered, and which now were nothing more than a source of confusion. 'But,' she told him, 'after I had thought a little and read it again and again, the prospect seemed to clear. You do not forbid me to write; you do not say that what I write is utterly destitute of merit. You only warn me against the folly of neglecting real duties, for the sake of imaginative pleasures; of writing for the love of fame; for the selfish excitement of emulation. You kindly allow me to write poetry for its own sake, provided I leave undone nothing which I ought to do, in order to pursue that single, absorbing, exquisite gratification. . . .'

This solitary gratification, absorbing and exquisite because of her singular powers of inducing it, in spite of Southey's warning increased its hold when she returned to Miss Wooler's. This time she was accompanied by Emily, but the support was short-lived; Emily suffered so excruciatingly from home-sickness that she had to be sent back, and Charlotte herself fell gradually into an unexplained neurasthenia, which she aggravated by a more and more compulsive resort to her imaginative drug.

Though she was depressed by the loss of Emily, Charlotte understood very well the necessity of letting her go home. 'The change from her own home to a school, and from her own very noiseless, very secluded, but unrestricted and unartificial mode of life, to one of disciplined routine (though under the kindest auspices) was what she failed in enduring. Her nature proved too strong for her fortitude. Every morning, when she woke, the vision of home and the moors rushed on her, and darkened and saddened the day that lay before her. Nobody knew what ailed her but me. I knew only too well. In this struggle her health was quickly broken : her white face, attenuated form, and failing strength, threatened rapid decline. I felt in my heart she would die, if she did not go home, and with this conviction obtained her recall. She had only been three months at school; and it was some years before the experiment of sending her from home was again ventured on.' Here, Charlotte is not quite accurate. Emily went as a teacher to Miss Patchett's Academy at Law Hill the following year, and again suffered so much that she was allowed to return after only six months' drudgery. It really seemed as though Emily, enclosed already within the contemplative cell of her own temperament, were one of those rare creatures who cannot live outside their own narrow territory; she craved the restrictive and sustaining closeness of the parsonage almost as if she had been born into the world against her will, and Haworth were a womb.

§ This physical suffering on Emily's part when absent from Haworth, after recurring several times under similar circumstances, became at length so much an acknowledged fact, that whichever was obliged to leave home, the sisters decided that Emily must remain there, where alone she could enjoy anything like good health. She felt it twice again in her life; once going as teacher to a school in Halifax for six months, and afterwards accompanying Charlotte to Brussels for ten. When at home, she took the principal part of the cooking upon herself, and did all the household ironing; and after Tabby grew old and infirm, it was Emily who made all the bread for the family; and any one passing by the kitchen-door, might have seen her studying German out of an open book, propped up before her, as she kneaded the dough; but no study, however interesting, interfered with the goodness of the bread, which was always light and excellent. Books were, indeed, a common sight in that kitchen; the girls were taught by their father theoretically, and by their aunt practically, that to take an active part in all household work was, in their position, woman's simple duty; but, in their careful employment of time, they found many an odd five minutes for reading while watching the cakes, and managed the union of two kinds of employment better than King Alfred. §

Emily's place at Miss Wooler's was taken by Anne, and Charlotte applied herself with a kind of dreary stoicism to her work as a teacher. The causes of her unhappiness during this second period at Miss Wooler's, which lasted nearly three years, were all subjective. In spite of the long hours and the small pay, there was no apparent reason why she should not have been content, or at least resigned; she was following the accepted course for a poor parson's daughter. 'I went to see her,' Mary Taylor told Mrs Gaskell, 'and asked her how she could give so much for so little money, when she could live without it. She owned that, after clothing herself and Anne, there was nothing left, though she had hoped to be able to save something. She confessed it was not brilliant, but what could she do?' A more potent cause of her increasing neurasthenia was the frustration of a creative spirit tied down to petty tasks and deadening monotony. Charlotte was now twenty; she had been writing prodigiously for years; she was perfectly aware of her unusual powers and of the compelling inner necessity to explore her genius. She found herself at this point cut off from home, from leisure and from Angria, with every drop of her mental and physical vitality wrung out of her by the interminable school-room day, the teaching, correcting, supervising and mending which occupied all ill-paid governesses in private schools from dawn till dark. No conflict is more destructive than frustration; in Charlotte a morbid sensitiveness and irritability began to appear, and by the time that Miss Wooler moved her school from Roe Head to the far less healthy and pleasant surroundings of Dewsbury Moor, she had sunk to a morbid degree of nervous debility. For the first time we find her hog-ridden by that religious melancholy which tormented Anne; her letters to Ellen have a sentimental despair about them quite foreign to her muscular intellect, but which must have given great pleasure to her pious friend. 'If I could always live with you and daily read the Bible with you, if your lips and mine could at the same time drink the same draught from the same pure fountain of mercy, I hope, I trust, I might one day become better, far better, than my evil wandering thoughts, my corrupt heart, cold to the spirit and warm to the flesh, will now permit me to be. I often plan the pleasant life which we might lead together, strengthening each other in that power of self-denial, that hallowed and glowing devotion which the past saints of God often attained to. My eyes fill with tears . . . longing for holiness which I shall *never, never attain*—smitten at times to the heart with the conviction that ——'s ghastly Calvinistic doctrines are true—darkened in short by the very shadows of Spiritual Death! If Christian perfections be necessary to Salvation I shall never be saved, my heart is a real hot-bed for sinful thoughts. . . .' And again, 'If you knew my thoughts, the dreams that absorb me, and the fiery imagination that at times eats me up, and makes me feel society, as it is, wretchedly insipid, you would pity and I dare say despise me.'

Her imagination, indeed, in which she took refuge as in a hiding-place where consolations and adventures never admitted by the conscious mind could be enjoyed, was never more vividly at work than during this time. One gets the impression that the intensity of her realisations brought her to the verge of trance. 'In such moods as these,' she wrote to Ellen, 'it is my nature to seek repose in some calm tranquil idea, and I have now summoned up your image to give me rest. There you sit, upright and still, in your black dress, and white scarf, and pale marble-like face—just like reality. I wish you would speak to me. . . .'

But it was not in the evocation of Ellen's calming presence that she tasted the fierce joys of her imaginative drug. Those fantasies that occupied her in every moment that she dared bestow on them, fantasies throbbing with an erotic pulse which would have startled Mrs Gaskell if she had come upon it, were all of the violent Byronic world she shared with Branwell; a world where heroes were amoral and unscrupulous, 'viciously beautiful', handsome dukes who possessed noble wives and passionate mistresses, who begot bastards, ruined their friends, and were at all times wonderfully eccentric and sardonic and sadistic. These creatures of fantasy, wicked, thrilling and adored, she summoned at will, and as often as she dared. 'I saw them stately and handsome . . . eyes smiling, and lips moving in audible speech that I knew better almost than my brother's and sisters' . . . what glorious associations crowded upon me, what excitement heated my face and made me clasp my hands in ecstasy! . . . how few,' she confided to her journal, 'would believe that from sources purely imaginary such happiness could be derived! Pen cannot portray the deep interest of the scenes, of the continued train of events I have witnessed. . . . What a treasure is thought! What a privilege is reverie! I am thankful I have the power of solacing myself with the dream of creations whose reality I shall never behold. May I never lose that power.'

The power to daydream, the 'system strange as some religious creed', was gathering strength, not losing it, and her pen both could and did portray its visions, in a style in which the compelling rhythms of her later work are already audible. She is carried away in contemplation of an Angrian hero: 'And then in his eye there is a shade of something, words cannot express what . . . a gleam, scarcely human, dark and fiend-like. . . . Once that marvellous light fell on me; and long after I beheld it vanish, its memory haunted me like a spirit. The sensation which it excited was very singular. I felt as if he could read my soul; and, strange to tell, there was no fear lest he should find sinful thoughts and recollections there, but a harassing dread lest anything good might arise which would awake the tremendous power of sarcasm that I saw lurking in every feature of his face.' Her heroines of this period are often absurdly extravagant, in the Gothic mode, but the speech of one, at least, has the note of controlled but authentic passion which was later to disturb the readers of *Jane Eyre*: 'The fact is I have far keener feelings than any other human being I ever knew. I have seen a hundred times beautiful women round me, compared with whom I was in appearance only a puppet; and in mind, in imagination, I knew them dull, apathetic, cold to me . . . and if Lord Douro ever thinks to be loved again with half the burning intensity with which I *have* loved him, with which I *do* love him, with which, if he were torturing me, I *should* love him, he is deluded.'

How could the classroom and the written task detain her, when in every unguarded moment the temptation was there to step across the frontier into scenes like these? 'Never shall I, Charlotte Brontë,' she wrote in her journal, 'forget what a voice of wild and wailing music now came thrilling to my mind's, almost my body's ear, nor how distinctly I, sitting in the schoolroom at Roe Head, saw the Duke of Zamorna leaning against that obelisk . . . I was quite gone. I had really, utterly forgot where I was and all the gloom and cheerlessness of my situation. I felt myself breathing quick and short as I beheld the Duke lifting up his sable crest, which undulated as the plume of a hearse waves to the wind. . . . "Miss Brontë, what are you thinking about?" said a voice, and Miss Lister thrust her little rough, black head into my face.'

Branwell, at home, was as ardently imagining and describing Angrian adventures, and brother and sister kept up a copious correspondence, chronicling for one another 'the on-goings of the infernal world'. Word from Branwell that Zamorna had retreated from burning Adrianopolis and destroyed his palace rather than leave it to the foe, stimulated her as no piece of actual news had power to do: 'Last night I did indeed lean upon the thunder-waking wings of such a stormy blast as I have seldom heard blow, and it whirled me away like heath in the wilderness for five seconds of ecstasy; and as I sat by myself in the dining-room while all the rest were at tea, *the trance seemed to descend on a sudden*, and verily this foot trod the war-shaken shores of the Calabar, and these eyes saw the defiled and violated Adrianopolis shedding its lights on the river from lattices whence the invader looked out.'

Much has been written of the possible influence of the Brontës on one another, particularly of the part played by Branwell in the development of his sisters' genius; the ideas that he may have provided, even (as his most extreme partisans have believed) the part he may actually have written of *Wuthering Heights*. The very full research which has recently been made into the juvenilia, and into Branwell's later writings, leaves no grounds for supposing him equipped for any sustained effort on his sisters' level: he was no more capable of writing *Wuthering Heights* than of becoming a painter of the first rank, or a major poet: but it will be helpful to remember that in their earliest adult years there was a very close degree of collaboration between the four, a common ground where they freely shared emotions, characters, ideas. Branwell's closest literary alliance, it is true, was always with Charlotte; at the time of her first departure for Miss Wooler's the four had divided into two creative pairs, Branwell and Charlotte continuing with Angria, Emily and Anne withdrawing into the fantasy of Gondal. But Branwell and Emily were much at home together during the three years of Charlotte's second absence, and though Branwell was chiefly occupied with Angrian history and Emily with Gondal poetry and legend, one cannot but suppose that they often discussed their work, and that whatever fertilising contact Branwell may have made with Emily's incalculable imagination was made during this period.

Little is known about Emily's Gondal chronicles. Unlike Charlotte's and Branwell's histories and romances they have not survived, or, if they have, they have never come to light. They may still, indeed, be lying in newspaper at the bottom of some unlikely cupboard, or in a forgotten croquet-box in a rectory attic: such things have been known. But the best that can be done in their absence is to reconstruct the saga from the poems it contained which have notably remained to us; and this has been very ably done.[1] One cannot assess the prose or the imaginative quality. The saga was apparently as complicated and long-drawn-out as anything undertaken by Charlotte and Branwell; it was perhaps even longer and

[1] In *The Brontës: Charlotte and Emily*, by Laura L. Hinkley; 1947.

certainly as extravagant and fantastic; but there is nothing to suggest the romantic eroticism pervading Charlotte's later juvenilia. Emily and Anne seem to have pursued their wars, chronicled their passions and deaths and tragic births on a colder, more stylised, almost sexless level. But it is idle to guess at the feeling or quality of the whole work when all we have left are its occasional poems. The creative pattern which we shall, however, do well to keep in mind at the moment is a fourfold one, in which the three sisters and the brother each bear an independent and at the same time collaborative part—Charlotte at Roe Head and Dewsbury Moor, unhappy, neurasthenic, enormously productive both on her own account and in collaboration with Branwell; Branwell at home, writing almost without pause as the pressure of his own first failures and disappointments bears down upon him; Emily, except for two short periods always at home, writing poetry, constructing her enormous chronicles, sending news of Gondal to her collaborator, Anne. And perhaps—since what is more likely?—both giving and absorbing much as she wrote in the dining-room alone with her volatile and far from reticent brother.

Anne's part in the four-fold pattern is necessarily shadowy, since her share in Gondal is as unknown as Emily's, and her sad little hymns and poems would never, by themselves, arrest attention. All we can learn of her during her period of pupillage at Miss Wooler's is that she became very ill there, and that Charlotte was angry because Miss Wooler did not seem to take the illness seriously.

§ Anne had a slight cough, a pain at her side, a difficulty of breathing. Miss Wooler considered it as little more than a common cold; but Charlotte felt every indication of incipient consumption as a stab at her heart, remembering Maria and Elizabeth, whose places once knew them, and should know them no more.

Stung by anxiety for this little sister, she upbraided Miss Wooler for her fancied indifference to Anne's state of health. Miss Wooler felt these reproaches keenly, and wrote to Mr Brontë about them. He immediately sent for his children, who left Dewsbury Moor the next day. Meanwhile,

Charlotte had resolved that Anne should never return as a pupil, nor she herself as a governess. But, just before she left, Miss Wooler sought for the opportunity of an explanation of each other's words, and the issue proved that 'the falling out of faithful friends, renewing is of love'. And so ended the first, last, and only difference Charlotte ever had with good and kind Miss Wooler. §

Miss Wooler seems, indeed, to have been to blame in her impatience with what she regarded as Charlotte's fancies, for Anne had already had one serious illness while she was at Roe Head, and had been considered so much in danger that a clergyman had been sent for. This we know from the recollections of the Rev James la Trobe, minister of the Moravian church at Mirfield at that time, who was summoned to Anne's sick-bed. 'She was suffering from a severe attack of gastric fever which brought her very low, and her voice was only a whisper; her life hung on a slender thread.' He found her distressed by some religious difficulty, 'but her heart opened to the sweet views of salvation, pardon and peace in the blood of Christ . . . and had she died then, I should have counted her His redeemed and ransomed child.' After the second illness and the quarrel with Miss Wooler, Charlotte returned to Dewsbury alone. 'From that time,' Mary Taylor told Mrs Gaskell, 'her imaginations became gloomy or frightful; she could not help it, not help thinking. She could not forget the gloom, could not sleep at night, nor attend in the day.'

§ She went back to her work, and made no complaint, hoping to subdue the weakness that was gaining ground upon her. About this time, she would turn sick and trembling at any sudden noise, and could hardly repress her screams when startled. This showed a fearful degree of physical weakness in one who was generally so self-controlled; and the medical man, whom at length, through Miss Wooler's entreaty, she was led to consult, insisted on her return to the parsonage. She had led too sedentary a life, he said; and the soft summer air, blowing round her home, the sweet company of those she loved, the release, the freedom of life in her own family, were needed, to save either reason or life. §

T.B.S. 129 E

So they were once more all together at Haworth, in a last peaceful and happy lull before they were separated by the necessity of earning a living, and before the shadow that was slowly creeping over Branwell had been noticed by anyone. It is a time given over largely to cooking and housework, for Tabby, now nearly seventy, has fallen in the village street and broken her leg, and they refuse to have her sent away, and yet are unable to replace her. 'Since the event we have been almost without assistance,' Charlotte wrote to Ellen, reluctantly putting off a promised visit, '—a person has dropped in now and then to do the drudgery, but we have as yet been able to procure no regular servant; and, consequently, the whole work of the house, as well as the additional duty of nursing Tabby, falls on ourselves.' It was the kind of inconvenience they could very well bear; they were all together, and Tabby made a fairly rapid recovery. Soon Mary Taylor and her younger sister Martha were staying at the parsonage, and the place echoed with the voices of six young people in a normal state of good spirits. 'They are making such a noise about me I cannot write any more,' Charlotte scribbled to Ellen, 'Mary is playing on the piano, Martha is chattering as fast as her little tongue can run; and Branwell is standing before her, laughing at her vivacity. . . . A calm and even mind like yours,' she added, 'cannot conceive the feelings of the shattered wretch who is now writing to you, when, after weeks of mental and·bodily anguish not to be described, something like peace began to dawn again.'

The next few months were full of changes. Branwell, veering back from literature to art, persuaded his father to set him up in a studio in Bradford, where he would earn his living as a portrait painter. This venture was less ambitious than it would seem today, for at that time the provincial portrait painter still occupied the position from which he was soon to be ousted by the photographer. Well-to-do trades-men and their families had their likenesses taken in oils as a matter of course, and Branwell might well have made a toler-able living if he had really possessed the talent that everyone believed in, or if he had been capable of sustained effort, or if he had not been unstable, precocious, attractive and twenty-one. As it was, he apparently failed to find sitters and got mildly into debt. Mr Brontë quickly tired of this unprofitable enterprise and after only a few months of freedom Branwell was called home.

Mr Brontë himself was low-spirited and far from well, and had written to the Pastoral Aid Society for a grant to enable him to keep a curate. 'My own health is generally but *very* delicate,' he wrote to a friend, ' . . . indeed I have never been very well since I left Thornton.' He missed the offices of a wife, who would normally have shouldered much of the teaching and visiting. Miss Branwell still presided over his household, but she, like himself, was over sixty and spent most of her time in her bedroom; no parish help was to be looked for from that quarter. His daughters taught regularly in the Sunday school whenever they were at home, but Charlotte and Anne were preparing to go out as governesses and Emily had taken over the work of the house. As for Branwell, who had made some false starts but was still the darling genius of the family, it was becoming plain that, whatever he might achieve in other fields, he was not a likely candidate for holy orders. So Mr Brontë wrote to the Bishop and to his clerical acquaintance, begging them to find him a suitable assistant, a man active as well as zealous, free from any evangelical taint which might lead him to 'deem it his duty to preach the appalling doctrines of personal Election and Reprobation'.

In spite of his youthful flirtation with the Methodists Mr Brontë had remained a plain Church of England man, and on the niceties of dogma his mind was clear. Evangelicalism, alive with dissent and heresy, was all around; scarcely a parish in Yorkshire but had the infection. All the more important, then, to make sure that his own curate should be above suspicion, since 'inconvenience might arise from a collision with my future Assistant in our preaching and exhortation'.

It is the moment when the first of the curates is about to arrive in Haworth with his corded box and go into lodgings in the village, in the sexton's compressed little cottage next door to the school; the first of those rather unsatisfactory and (except for William Weightman) unattractive young men who were now to become a part of the parsonage life; one of whom they would grow fond of and eventually mourn; one of whom, in the end, Charlotte would marry.

'Marriage did not enter into the scheme of her life,' wrote Mrs Gaskell, but this, except in a special sense, cannot be true. Matrimony, then as now, entered into the scheme of every young woman's life, with a preponderance of social pressure difficult to realise in our different century. It is easy to forget how strong that pressure was, how much to be dreaded the obloquy of the spinster. Marriage was the desired, the only socially acceptable escape from the life which Charlotte saw stretching wearily in front of her; yet so fundamental to her was the romantic attitude that at twenty-three she rejected without hesitation her first two offers of marriage.

The first of these had much to recommend it. The Rev Henry Nussey, Ellen's brother, was a serious young clergyman who (if Mrs Gaskell was right in supposing him to be the model for St John Rivers in *Jane Eyre*) was of a singularly correct and even handsome appearance. Charlotte dearly loved Ellen, esteemed and 'had a kindly leaning towards' her brother, and was tempted by the consideration that, if she married Henry, her friend would be able to come and live with them. 'Yet I had not,' she told Ellen after she had refused him, 'and could not have that intense attachment which would make me willing to die for him; and, if ever I marry, it must be in that light of adoration that I will regard my husband.'

To Henry Nussey she had written, 'You do not know me; I am not the serious, grave, cool-headed individual you suppose; you would think me romantic and eccentric; you would say I was satirical and severe.' And to Ellen she was even more explicit. 'I was aware that Henry knew so little of me he could hardly be conscious to whom he was writing. Why, it would startle him to see me in my natural home character; he would think I was a wild, romantic enthusiast indeed. I could not sit all day long making a grave face before my husband. I would laugh, and satirise, and say whatever came into my head first. And if he were a clever man, and loved me, the whole world weighed in the balance against his smallest wish should be light as air. Could I, knowing my mind to be such as that, conscientiously take a grave, quiet young man like Henry?'

Charlotte's instinct in this case was sound, since everything we now know of Henry Nussey suggests a frigid and sententious prig. His diary, whose secrets, of course, were never known to Charlotte, betrays the fact that, having made up his mind to marry, he had drawn up a list of prospects, with Charlotte Brontë occupying second place. 'On Tuesday last received a decisive reply from M.A.L.'s papa; a loss, but I trust a providential one. . . . God knows best what is good for us, for His church, and for His own glory. Write to a Yorkshire friend, C.B.' And a little later, 'Received an unfavourable reply from C.B. The will of the Lord be done.' It is perhaps not surprising that when Mr Nussey did eventually find a wife, and one, moreover, with 'a handsome fortune', the marriage proved unhappy.

The second proposal was from another clergyman, whose offer Charlotte dismissed as an amiable but unlikely joke. 'I have an odd circumstance to relate to you,' she wrote to Ellen, 'prepare for a hearty laugh! The other day, Mr Hodgson, a vicar, came to spend the day with us, bringing with him his own curate. The latter gentleman, by name Mr Price, is a young Irish clergyman, fresh from Dublin University. It was the first time we had any of us seen him, but, however, after the manner of his countrymen, he soon made himself at home. His character quickly appeared in his conversation; witty, lively, ardent, clever too; but deficient in the dignity and discretion of an Englishman. At home, you know, I talk with ease, and am never shy—never weighed down and oppressed by that miserable *mauvaise honte* which torments and constrains me elsewhere. So I conversed with this Irishman, and laughed at his jests; and, though I saw faults in his character, excused them because of the amusement his originality afforded. I cooled a little, indeed, and drew in towards the latter part of the evening, because he began to season his conversation with something of Hibernian flattery, which I did not quite relish. However, they went away, and no more was thought about them. A few days after, I got a letter, the direction of which puzzled me, it being in a hand I was not accustomed to see. Evidently, it was neither from you nor Mary, my only correspondents. Having opened and read it, it proved to be a declaration of attachment and proposal of matrimony, expressed in the ardent language of the sapient young Irishman! I hope you are laughing heartily. This is not like one of my adventures, is it? It more nearly resembles Martha's. I am certainly doomed to be an old maid. Never mind, I made up my mind to that fate ever since I was twelve years old.'

She was resolved to arrive at independence by going out as a governess, and this she and Anne, with more apprehension than enthusiasm, set about achieving. They were temperamentally unfitted for the work, as innumerable governesses must have been in an age which offered teaching as the only possible livelihood for a gentlewoman. Mrs Gaskell, said to be skilful in the choice of governesses for her own children, understood Charlotte's unsuitability very well.

§ Neither she nor her sisters were naturally fond of children. The hieroglyphics of childhood were an unknown language to them, for they had never been much with those younger than themselves. I am inclined to think, too, that they had not the happy knack of imparting information, which seems to be a separate gift from the faculty of acquiring it; a kind of sympathetic tact, which instinctively perceives the difficulties that impede comprehension in a child's mind, and that yet are too vague and unformed for it, with its half-developed powers of expression, to explain by words. Consequently, teaching very young children was anything but a 'delightful task' to the three Brontë sisters. With older girls, verging on womanhood, they might have done better, especially if these had any desire for improvement. But the education which the village clergyman's daughters had received, did not as yet qualify them to undertake the charge of advanced pupils. They knew but little French, and were not proficients in music; I doubt whether Charlotte could play at all. But they were all strong again, and, at any rate, Charlotte and Anne must put their shoulders to the wheel. One daughter was needed at home, to stay with Mr Brontë and Miss Branwell; to be the young and active member in a household of four, whereof three—the father, the aunt, and faithful Tabby—were past middle age. And Emily, who suffered and drooped more than her sisters when away from Haworth, was the one appointed to remain. Anne was the first to meet with a situation. §

In April 1839 Anne went as governess to Mrs Ingham of Blake Hall, Mirfield, and the following month Charlotte was placed in a situation near Skipton, with Mrs Sidgwick of Stonegappe.

VIII : THE GOVERNESS

'I now think,' wrote Mrs Gaskell to Ellen Nussey, before she began to write her life of Charlotte, "I have been everywhere where she ever lived, except of course her two little pieces of private governess-ship.' Why of course? Perhaps because Charlotte's experience as a nursery governess, important because of the fruit it eventually bore in *Jane Eyre*, was in fact extremely brief : she was two months with Mrs Sidgwick as a 'temporary', and less than nine months with Mrs White. Also, Mrs Gaskell may well have felt that no good could come of interviewing the Whites or the Sidgwicks : Charlotte and Anne had published their opinion of the employers of governnesses, and Charlotte in her letters had been even more outspoken. Mrs Gaskell clearly felt that here was an occasion for delicate avoidance.

§ I intend carefully to abstain from introducing the names of any living people, respecting whom I may have to tell unpleasant truths, or to quote severe remarks from Miss Brontë's letters; but it is necessary that the difficulties she had to encounter in her various phases of life, should be fairly and frankly made known, before the force 'of what was resisted' can be at all understood. I was once speaking to her about *Agnes Grey*—the novel in which her sister Anne pretty literally describes her own experience as a governess—and alluding more particularly to the account of the stoning of the little nestlings in the presence of the parent birds. She said that none but those who had been in the position of a governess could ever realise the dark side of 'respectable' human nature; under no great temptation to crime, but daily giving way to selfishness and ill-temper, till its conduct towards those dependent on it sometimes amounts to a tyranny of which one would rather be the victim than the inflicter. . . . Among several things of the same kind, which I well remember, she told me what had once occurred to herself. She had been entrusted with the care of a little boy, three or four years old, during the absence of his parents on a day's excursion, and particularly enjoined to keep him out of the stable-yard. His elder brother, a lad of eight or nine, and not a pupil of Miss Brontë's, tempted the little fellow into the forbidden place. She followed, and tried to induce him to come away; but, instigated by his brother, he began throwing stones at her, and one of them hit her so severe a blow on the temple that the lads were alarmed into obedience. The next day, in full family conclave, the mother asked Miss Brontë what occasioned the mark on her forehead. She simply replied, 'An accident, ma'am,' and no further inquiry was made; but the children (both brothers and sisters) had been present, and honoured her for not 'telling tales'. From that time, she began to obtain influence over all, more or less, according to their different characters; and as she insensibly gained their affection, her own interest in them was increasing. But one day, at the children's dinner, the small truant of the stable-yard, in a little demonstrative gush, said, putting his hand in hers, 'I love 'ou, Miss Brontë.' Whereupon, the mother exclaimed, before all the children, 'Love the *governess*, my dear!' §

As with Cowan Bridge, there has been no lack of defenders of Charlotte Brontë's employers, and there are some convincing scraps of evidence that Charlotte was a difficult governess, constrained, melancholy, ill at ease, and perpetually on the defensive. There can be no possible doubt that all three sisters were by temperament and physique totally unsuited to the livelihood they had chosen. But when this is said, and the subjective nature of much of their suffering remembered, there remains a weight of blame which must fairly be laid at the door of the Whites, the Blakes, the Robinsons and the Sidgwicks. Even in our own time it is a ticklish matter to make a governess happy. She is a solitary, in the family but not of it; she has not even a nurse's established intimacy with her children; and only an exceptional woman can discipline herself to be quite free from a perpetually watchful anxiety about her position. The Victorian governess was in a far worse case. Lodged uncomfortably in a little vacuum of her own between the family and the servants, she was too often at the mercy of people to whom it never occurred that she deserved consideration. The servants resented her as a dependant whom it was troublesome to wait upon; she was as ill-paid as they, and yet obliged to maintain her precarious position as a gentlewoman. Added to this, she was employed in a society which, having a vast pool of cheap labour at its disposal, had not yet learned the necessity of considerate treatment; and she too often found herself, as Charlotte and Anne Brontë undoubtedly did, at the beck and call of families who were on their way up in the world, and saw no reason to lessen their own importance by studying their own or their children's behaviour to the governess. Mrs Gaskell, more cautious here than in some other matters, refrained from quoting from the bitterest of Charlotte's letters; even so, the ones she gives are miserable enough, and each sentence bears the stamp of emotional truth.

'I have striven hard to be pleased with my new situation,' she wrote to Emily. 'The country, the house and the grounds are, as I have said, divine; but, alack-a-day! there is such a thing as seeing all beautiful around you—pleasant woods, winding white paths, green lawns, and blue sunshiny sky—and not having a free moment or a free thought left to enjoy them in. The children are constantly with me. As for correcting them, I quickly found that was out of the question; they are to do as they like. A complaint to Mrs Sidgwick only brings black looks on myself, and unjust, partial excuses to screen the children. I have tried that plan once, and succeeded so notably, I shall try no more. I said in my last letter that Mrs Sidgwick did not know me. I now begin to find she does not intend to know me; that she cares nothing about me, except to contrive how the greatest possible quantity of labour may be squeezed out of me; and to that end she overwhelms me with oceans of needlework; yards of cambric to hem, muslin nightcaps to make, and, above all things, dolls to dress. I do not think she likes me at all, because I can't help being shy in such an entirely novel scene, surrounded as I have hitherto been by strange and constantly changing faces. . . . I used to think I should like to be in the stir of grand folks' society; but I have had enough of it—it is dreary work to look on and listen. I see more clearly than I have ever done before, that a private governess has no existence, is not considered as a living rational being, except as connected with the wearisome duties she has to fulfil . . . One of the pleasantest afternoons I have spent here—indeed, the only one at all pleasant—was when Mr Sidgwick walked out with his children; and I had orders to follow a little behind. As he strolled on through his fields, with his magnificent Newfoundland dog at his side, he looked very like what a frank, wealthy, Conservative gentleman ought to be. He spoke freely and unaffectedly to the people he met, and, though he indulged his children and allowed them to tease himself far too much, he would not suffer them grossly to insult others. . . . Don't,' she adds, 'show this letter to papa or aunt, only to Branwell.'

In this connection it is interesting to hear the Sidgwicks' version from the recollections of A. C. Benson, son of Archbishop Benson and one of the Sidgwicks' many cousins, who was often at Stonegappe. 'She was, according to her own account, very unkindly treated, but it is clear that she had no gifts for the management of children, and was also in a very morbid condition the whole time. My cousin Benson Sidgwick, now vicar of Ashby Parva, certainly on one occasion threw a Bible at Miss Brontë! and all that another cousin can recollect of her is that if she was invited to walk to church with them, she thought she was being ordered about like a slave; if she was not invited, she imagined she was excluded from the family circle.' Clearly a prickly and difficult person to have in the house, miserably lacking that serviceable outer skin with which the more resilient extrovert is provided. 'If you were near me,' she told Ellen, 'perhaps I might be tempted to tell you all, to grow egotistical, and pour out the long history of a private governess's trials and crosses in her first situation. As it is, I will only ask you to imagine the miseries of a reserved wretch like me, thrown at once into the midst of a large family—proud as peacocks and wealthy as Jews—at a time when they were particularly gay—when the house was filled with company—all strangers—people whose faces I had never seen before. In this state I had charge given me of a set of pampered, spoilt, turbulent children, whom I was expected constantly to amuse, as well as to instruct. I soon found that the constant demand on my stock of animal spirits reduced them to the lowest state of exhaustion; at times I felt—and, I suppose, seemed—depressed. To my astonishment, I was taken to task on the subject by Mrs Sidgwick with a sternness of manner and a harshness of language scarcely credible; like a fool, I cried most bitterly. I could not help it; my spirits quite failed me at first. I thought I had done my best—strained every nerve to please her; and to be treated in that way, merely because I was shy and sometimes melancholy, was too bad. At first I was for giving all up and going home. But, after a little reflection, I determined to summon what energy I had, and to weather the storm. I said to myself, 'I have never yet quitted a place without gaining a friend; adversity is a good school; the poor are born to labour, and the dependent to endure.' I resolved to be patient, to command my feelings, and to take what came; the ordeal, I reflected, would not last many weeks, and I trusted it would do me good. . . . Mrs Sidgwick is generally considered an agreeable woman; so she is, I doubt not, in general society. Her health is sound, her animal spirits good, consequently she is cheerful in company; but, oh! does this compensate for the absence of every fine feeling—of every gentle and delicate sentiment? She behaves somewhat more civilly to me now than she did at first, and the children are a little more manageable; but she does not know my character, and she does not wish to know it. . . . If I were talking to you I could tell you much more.'

Anne's situation was rather better, though she, too, had her trials. It is clear that Anne, less gifted and more pliable, was having more success as a governess than her sister. 'We have had one letter from her since she went—she expresses herself very well satisfied, and says that Mrs. Ingham is extremely kind; the two eldest children alone are under her care, the rest are confined to the nursery, with which and its occupants she has nothing to do. Both her pupils are desperate little dunces—neither of them can read and sometimes they even profess a profound ignorance of their alphabet; the worst of it is the little monkies are excessively indulged and she is not empowered to inflict any punishment; she is requested when they misbehave themselves to inform their Mamma—which she says is utterly out of the question as in that case she might be making complaints from morning till night. So she alternately scolds, coaxes and threatens, sticks always to her first word and gets on as well as she can. I hope she'll do. . . . It is only the talking part that I fear; but I do seriously apprehend that Mrs Ingham will sometimes consider that she has a natural impediment of speech.'

Branwell too, about this time, having finally given up painting as a career, got a job as tutor in the family of a Mr Postlethwaite at Broughton-in-Furness, where he remained for six months. He seems to have satisfied his employers, since there is no record of trouble or complaint; and he gave up the job after half a year only, apparently, because his father decided—for what reason we do not know—to recall him to Haworth. It is possible that Mr Brontë was uneasy; Branwell was just twenty-three and already had a reputation in the village as a drinker; and certainly the one letter that survives from his period at the Postlethwaites', even when allowance had been made for a youthful desire to amuse and show off to his friends, leaves a disagreeable impression. 'If you saw me now,' he wrote to John Brown the sexton, 'you would not know me, and you would laugh to hear the character the people give me. Oh, the falsehood and hypocrisy of this world! . . . My employer is a retired County magistrate, a large landowner, and of a right hearty and generous disposition. His wife is a quiet, silent and amiable woman, and his sons are two fine, spirited lads. My landlord is a respectable surgeon, is two days out of seven as drunk as a lord! . . . and his daughter! oh! death and damnation! Well, what am I? That is, what do they think I am? A most calm, sedate, sober, abstemious, patient, mild-hearted, virtuous, gentlemanly philosopher—the picture of good works, and the treasure-house of righteous thoughts. Cards are shuffled under the table-cloth, glasses are thrust into the cupboard if I enter the room. I take neither spirits, wine, nor malt liquors. I dress in black, and smile like a saint or martyr. Everybody says, "What a good young gentleman is Mr Postlethwaite's tutor!" This is a fact, as I am a living soul, and right comfortably do I laugh at them. I mean to continue in their good opinion. I took a half-year's farewell of old friend whisky at Kendal on the night after I left.' He goes on to describe an evening of drinking in the Royal Hotel at Kendal, on 'whisky toddy as hot as hell', which ended with finding himself 'in bed next morning, with a bottle of porter, a glass, and a corkscrew beside me. Since then I have not tasted anything stronger than milk-and-water, nor, I hope, shall, till I return at Mid-summer; when we will see about it. . . . My hand shakes no longer. I ride to the banker's at Ulverston with Mr Postlethwaite, and sit drinking tea and talking scandal with old ladies. As to the young ones! I have one sitting by me just now—fair-faced, blue-eyed, dark-haired, sweet eighteen—she little thinks the devil is so near her!' A sober afterthought caused him to add, 'Of course you won't show this letter; and, for Heaven's sake, blot out all the lines scored with red ink.'

As little suited as his sisters, though for rather different reasons, to the exacting tasks of teaching and looking after children, Branwell, like Charlotte, still clung passionately to the idea of literary success; and during the time that he was with the Postlethwaites both were still trying hopefully for encouragement, Branwell by sending poems to Hartley Coleridge, and Charlotte submitting the beginnings and plan of a story to Wordsworth. Coleridge, second son of his famous father, had a temperament curiously similar to Branwell's. The fabulous promise of his youth had come to little; drink, despondency and irresolution had sapped his poetic genius and destroyed his strength. Frail and white-haired at forty, he was living out his last years in aimlessness and self-reproach when Branwell had the ecstasy of meeting him at Ambleside, and sent him an original poem and some translations from Horace, with letters at once egregious, bombastic and pathetic, of the kind we already know. What Coleridge thought of them we cannot be sure; Mrs Gaskell was told that he sent a favourable answer. Charlotte certainly had a 'kind and candid' letter from Wordsworth when he returned her story. Unfortunately this letter has not survived, but from Charlotte's reply we must suppose that he formed no very high opinion of her work, since he had not been able to decide whether the misleading initials under which she concealed herself were those of 'an attorney's clerk or a novel-reading dressmaker'. 'Seriously, sir,' she told him, after several paragraphs of defensive flippancy, 'I am very much obliged to you . . . and on the whole I wonder you took the trouble to read and notice the demi-serious novelette of an anonymous scribe, who had not even the manners to tell you whether he was a man or a woman.'

In the summer of this year, 1839, her short engagement with the Sidgwicks being at an end ('I never was so glad to get out of a house in my life') Charlotte was suddenly excited by a daring suggestion from Ellen that they should spend a seaside holiday together. She had never seen the sea, and had deeply romantic and emotional ideas about it. Ellen had friends who lived within reach of Bridlington, and who had offered to have them both for a prolonged visit; it was a wonderful opportunity of freedom and change. The proposal, however, was received without enthusiasm by Mr Brontë and Miss Branwell, who apprehended heaven knows what undesirable results from such an adventure; and anxious letters were exchanged between Ellen and Charlotte as they tried every means to disperse their disapproval. 'Aunt exclaims against the weather, and the roads, and the four winds of heaven. . . . The elders of the house have never cordially acquiesced in the measure; and now that impediments seem to start up at every step, opposition grows more open. Papa, indeed, would willingly indulge me, but this very kindness of his makes me doubt whether I ought to draw upon it; so, though I could battle out aunt's discontent, I yield to papa's indulgence. He does not say so, but I know he would rather I stayed at home. . . . Reckon on me no more; leave me out in your calculations; perhaps I ought, in the beginning, to have had prudence sufficient to shut my eyes against such a prospect of pleasure, so as to deny myself the hope of it.'

However, Ellen resourcefully solved all the difficulties involved in getting Charlotte and her luggage to Leeds by coming to fetch her, in a friend's carriage. This stratagem, as she afterwards recalled, 'proved to be the very best thing possible; the surprise was so good in its effect, there was nothing to combat—everybody rose into high good humour; Branwell was grandiloquent, he declared "it was a brave defeat, that the doubters were fairly taken aback".' The two friends drove together to Leeds, where Charlotte had her first experience of railway travel. She was in a state of deep excitement, and when they had their first 'distant glimpses of the German Ocean', which she could not really see without her spectacles, she begged Ellen, 'Don't tell me any more. Let me wait.' Two days after their arrival at Easton, where Ellen's friends lived, they walked three miles to Bridlington and she experienced all the emotion she had expected to feel at her first sight of the sea. 'As soon as they were near enough for Charlotte to see it in its expanse, she was quite overpowered; she could not speak until she had shed some tears— she signed to her friend to leave her and walk on; this she did for a few steps, knowing full well what Charlotte was passing through, and the stern efforts she was making to subdue her emotions. Her friend turned to her as soon as she thought she might without inflicting pain; her eyes were red and swollen, she was still trembling, but submitted to be led onwards where the view was less impressive. For the remainder of the day she was very quiet, subdued, and exhausted.'

A whole month was spent at Easton with Ellen's friends,

Mr and Mrs Hudson, and Charlotte painted at least one charming water-colour of the long, low farmhouse, with her host and hostess sitting on a rustic seat, in a romantic profusion of flowers. She and Ellen then went into lodgings for a final week at Bridlington itself, and found it expensive. 'Moderate appetites,' Ellen complained, 'and modest demands for attendance were of no avail as regarded the demands made upon our small finances.' Still, they had amused themselves with the evening parade on the pier—'packed like a ballroom,' Ellen said, 'people had to march round and round in regular file to secure any movement whatever'—and had pleased themselves even better with the cliffs by moonlight; and came home at last well satisfied with their holiday. Charlotte's strong impression of the sea never wore off, and her first sight of it was remembered to the end of her life as a profound experience. 'Have you forgot the sea by this time, Ellen?' she wrote the following October, 'is it grown dim in your mind? . . . If we both live,' she added, with a sad cautiousness already characteristic, 'this period of our lives will long be a theme of pleasant recollection.'

It now became a pressing matter for Charlotte to find another situation. Anne had left Mirfield, having finally confessed that Mrs Blake's children were too much for her; it was 'one long struggle of life-wearing exertion to keep them in anything like decent order'. All three sisters were at home. They were busy enough, for Tabby, recovered from the broken leg, had now become so lame from an ulcer that she had had to give up work and go to live with her sister in the village; except for a little girl who ran errands they were without a servant. 'I manage the ironing,' Charlotte wrote to Ellen, 'and keep the rooms clean; Emily does the baking, and attends to the kitchen. We are such odd animals, that we prefer this mode of contrivance to having a new face amongst us. Besides, we do not despair of Tabby's return, and she shall not be supplanted by a stranger in her absence. I excited aunt's wrath very much by burning the clothes, the first time I attempted to iron; but I do better now. Human feelings are queer things; I am much happier black-leading the stoves, making the beds, and sweeping the floors at home, than I should be living like a fine lady anywhere else . . . I intend to force myself to take another situation when I can get one, though I *hate* and *abhor* the very thoughts of governess-ship. But I must do it; and, therefore, I heartily wish I could hear of a family where they need such a commodity as a governess.'

As the months passed she heard of several, but an exchange of letters proved them all unsuitable. She was privately advised against one employer; another wanted music and singing, which she could not teach. 'I am miserable when I allow myself to dwell on the necessity of spending my life as a governess. The chief requisite for that station seems to me to be the power of taking things easily as they come, and of making oneself comfortable and at home wherever we may chance to be—qualities in which all our family are singularly deficient.' All their family were, on the contrary, singularly well equipped for being happy at home, and the girls found it not at all impossible to combine their own kind of intellectual life with housework, since the strictness of Aunt Branwell's early training had made the conscientious performance of domestic tasks almost automatic. 'They were,' said Mrs Gaskell, who set proper store by a well conducted household, 'grateful to her for many habits she had enforced upon them, and which in time had become second nature : order, method, neatness in everything; a perfect knowledge of all kinds of household work; an exact punctuality, and obedience to the laws of time and place, of which no one but themselves, I have heard Charlotte say, could tell the value in after-life; with their impulsive natures, it was positive repose to have learnt implicit obedience to external laws. People in Haworth have assured me that, according to the hour of day—nay, the very minute—could they have told what the inhabitants of the parsonage were about. At certain times the girls would be sewing in their aunt's bedroom—the chamber which, in former days, before they had outstripped her in their learning, had served them as a schoolroom; at certain (early) hours they had their meals; from six to eight, Miss Branwell read aloud to Mr Brontë; at punctual eight, the household assembled to evening prayers in his study; and by nine he, the aunt, and Tabby were all in bed,—the girls free to pace up and down (like restless wild animals) in the parlour, talking over plans and projects, and thoughts of what was to be their future life.'

It was particularly difficult to resolve on leaving Haworth at this time, when the sisters and Branwell were all at home together, and life was being made unexpectedly gay by the presence of Mr Brontë's new curate. Charlotte looked with disfavour on the general run of curates; those who had so far appeared at Haworth had been unprepossessing, wrapped up in their own importance and in the bigoted war they waged on all dissenters; but the Rev William Weightman was gay and agreeable and altogether charming, a creature from a different world. He was curly-haired, good-looking, and a shocking flirt. They pretended to find him absurd, and among themselves called him Miss Celia Amelia; but there were moments when they found him irresistible. Even Emily was not unfriendly, and it is difficult to resist the impression that Anne may even have been a little in love with him. He seems to have been, in his light way, a charming fellow, and one likes the story of his walking ten miles to post anonymous valentines to the three girls when he learned that none of them, not even Anne, had ever received one. But he was certainly a philanderer, and when he made eyes at Ellen, Charlotte felt bound, though tolerantly, to warn her. 'Don't set your heart on him. He is very fickle—not to you in particular but to half a dozen other ladies; he has just cut his enamorata at Swansea, and sent her back all her letters. His present object of devotion is Caroline Dury, to whom he has just despatched a most passionate copy of verses. Poor lad, his sanguine temperament bothers him grievously.'

Ellen was going through a susceptible phase; Charlotte's letters at this time are full of enquiries and advice concerning the different young men who were making a tender impression, and Mr Weightman had certainly left his mark. 'I am fully convinced, Ellen, that he is a thorough male-flirt, his sighs are deeper than ever and his treading on toes more assiduous. . . . I find he is perfectly conscious of his irresistibleness and is as vain as a peacock on the subject. I am not at all surprised at all this—it is perfectly natural; a handsome, clean, prepossessing, good-humoured young man will never want troops of victims amongst young ladies. So long as you are not among the number it is all right.' And again, 'He pleases so easily that he soon gets weary of pleasing at all. He ought not to have been a parson. Certainly he ought not.' William Weightman lacked the seriousness of character which could have appealed to Charlotte, but in spite of this, and her disapproval of his philandering, she was fond of him, as they all were. 'I know many of his faulty actions, many of his weak points; yet, where I am, he shall always find rather a defender than an accuser.' A little later, when Mr Weightman began to sigh for Anne, and also to show signs of the consumption which was soon to carry him off, Charlotte's sympathy almost brought her to the point where she could wish him comfortably settled, and married to Ellen. 'When he is well and fat and jolly I never think of him—but when anything ails him I am always sorry. He sits opposite to Anne at Church sighing softly and looking out of the corners of his eyes to attract her attention; and Anne is so quiet, her look so downcast, they are a picture. He would be the better of a comfortable wife to settle him; you would settle him, I believe—nobody else would.'

Ellen, who as things turned out never married, seemed designed by nature to become the wife of some young clergyman, and her hopes and susceptibilities are the subject of many of the letters passing between them. It is interesting to see that Charlotte's advice on marriage, given with all the earnest conviction of twenty-four, conflicts with every impulse of her own temperament, which her passionate daydreams had already taught her to distrust. 'I hope,' she told Ellen, who had written to consult her about a possible suitor, 'you will not have the romantic folly to wait for the awakening of what the French call "une grande *passion*". My good girl, "une grande passion" is "une grande *folie*". I have told you so before, and I tell it you again. Mediocrity in all things is wisdom—mediocrity in the sensations is superlative wisdom. . . . No young lady should fall in love till the offer has been made, accepted—the marriage ceremony performed and the first half-year of wedded life passed away. A woman may then begin to love, but with great precaution—very coolly, very moderately, very rationally. If she ever loves so much that a harsh word or a cold look from her husband cuts her to the heart—she is a fool.' Sage advice from one whose secret concern was with the ardent life and loves of the Marquis of Douro! 'I am tolerably convinced,' she added in another letter, 'that I shall never marry at all. Reason tells me so, and I am not so utterly the slave of feeling but that I can *occasionally* hear her voice.'

Of the four of them, Branwell was now the first to leave, having taken the rather surprising job of booking clerk at Sowerby Bridge railway station. 'A distant relation of mine,' wrote Charlotte, forestalling any raising of eyebrows with a joke, 'one Patrick Boanerges, has set off to seek his fortune in the wild, wandering, adventurous, romantic, knight-errant-like capacity of clerk on the Leeds and Manchester railroad.' Branwell's friend, F. A. Leyland, brother of the sculptor whom he had occasionally met in Bradford, tells us that Branwell had tried for this job 'with a perseverance amounting to anxiety', and suggests that he found his six months with the Postlethwaites dull, and considered it a banishment from all cheerful society. Sowerby Bridge is near Halifax, where the Leylands lived; the railway was new, and a subject of general interest, so that the job was evidently, if not brilliant, at least a sufficiently respectable one for Branwell, who was bored at home and anxious to return to his old circle.

It is from this point that we are able to watch the gradual, and saddening, deterioration of Branwell. 'There are always,' said Mrs Gaskell, who had a shrewder idea of Branwell's case than she has sometimes been credited with, 'peculiar trials in the life of an only boy in a family of girls. He is expected to act a part in life; to *do*, while they are only to *be*; and the necessity of their giving way to him in some things is too often exaggerated into their giving way to him in all, and thus rendering him utterly selfish. In the family about whom I am writing, while the rest were almost ascetic in their habits, Branwell was allowed to grow up self-indulgent; but, in early youth, his power of attracting and attaching people was so great, that few came in contact with him who were not so much dazzled by him as to be desirous of gratifying whatever wishes he expressed. Of course, he was careful enough not to reveal anything before his father and sisters of the pleasures he indulged in; but his tone of thought and conversation became gradually coarser, and for a time his sisters tried to persuade themselves that such coarseness was a part of manliness, and to blind themselves by love to the fact that Branwell was worse than other young men.' 'Worse' is a relative term; personal charm, and the facility in conversation which had won him a small but dangerous celebrity, were as much against him as his volatile character. He began to take refuge from failure in showy talk He also, away from censorious eyes, found renewed opportunities of drinking, and both at Sowerby Bridge and at the smaller station of Luddenden Foot, where he was soon transferred, comforted his boredom and disappointment with whisky. There is no evidence that he was taking laudanum at this time, though F. H. Grundy, the railway engineer who became his friend, says that he was; and that it was through his, Grundy's influence that he temporarily gave up the habit; but Grundy, though an interesting witness, is so inaccurate on other points that he may well be so in the matter of Branwell's opium. That dangerous comforter was not, at least, habitually appealed to until later, when he found himself unable to deal with his unhappiness. The first step towards that unhappiness was at this very moment taken for him by Anne, who had found a new post as governess and gone into the household of the Rev Edmund Robinson at Thorp Green.

Charlotte too, 'after a world of trouble in the way of correspondence and interviews', had found a new employer and left home.

§ This time she esteemed herself fortunate in becoming a member of a kind-hearted and friendly household. The master of it she especially regarded as a valuable friend, whose advice helped to guide her in one very important step of her life. But as her definite acquirements were few, she had to eke them out by employing her leisure time in needlework; and altogether her position was that of 'bonne' or nursery governess, liable to repeated and never-ending calls upon her time. This description of uncertain, yet perpetual employment, subject to the exercise of another person's will at all hours of the day, was peculiarly trying to one whose life at home had been full of abundant leisure. *Idle* she never was in any place, but of the multitude of small talks, plans, duties, pleasures, &c., that make up most people's days, her home life was nearly destitute. This made it possible for her to go through long and deep histories of feeling and imagination, for which others, odd as it sounds, have rarely time. This made it inevitable that—later on, in her too short career—the intensity of her feeling should wear out her physical health. The habit of 'making out', which had grown with her growth, and strengthened with her strength, had become a part of her nature. Yet all exercise of her strongest and most characteristic faculties was now out of the question. She could not (as while she was at Miss Wooler's) feel amidst the occupations of the day, that when evening came she might employ herself in more congenial ways. No doubt, all who enter upon the career of a governess have to relinquish much; no doubt, it must ever be a life of sacrifice; but to Charlotte Brontë it was a perpetual attempt to force all her faculties into a direction for which the whole of her previous life had unfitted them. Moreover, the little Brontës had been brought up motherless; and from knowing nothing of the gaiety and the sportiveness of childhood—from never having experienced caresses or fond attentions themselves—they were ignorant of the very nature of infancy, or how to call out its engaging qualities. Children were to them the troublesome necessities of humanity; they had never been drawn into contact with them in any other way. Years afterwards, when Miss Brontë came to stay with us, she watched our little girls perpetually; and I could not persuade her that they were only average specimens of well brought up children. She was surprised and touched by any sign of thoughtfulness for others, of kindness to animals, or of unselfishness on their part; and constantly maintained that she was in the right, and I in the wrong, when we differed on the point of their unusual excellence. §

Her new employers were Mr and Mrs White of Upperwood House, Rawdon, near Bradford. 'The house is not very large, but exceedingly comfortable and well regulated; the grounds are fine and extensive. In taking the place, I have made a large sacrifice in the way of salary, in the hope of securing comfort, —by which word I do not mean to express good eating and drinking, or warm fire, or a soft bed, but the society of cheerful faces, and minds and hearts not dug out of a leadmine, or cut from a marble quarry. My salary is not really more than 16*l.* per annum, though it is nominally 20*l.*, but the expense of washing will be deducted therefrom. My pupils are two in number, a girl of eight, and a boy of six. As to my employers, you will not expect me to say much about their characters when I tell you that I only arrived here yesterday. I have not the faculty of telling an individual's disposition at first sight. Before I can venture to pronounce on a character, I must see it first under various lights and from various points of view. All I can say therefore is, both Mr and Mrs White seem to me good sort of people. I have as yet had no cause to complain of want of considerateness or civility. My pupils are wild and unbroken, but apparently well-disposed. I wish I may be able to say as much next time I write to you. My earnest wish and endeavour will be to please them. If I can but feel that I am giving satisfaction, and if at the same time I can keep my health, I shall, I hope, be moderately happy. But no one but myself can tell how hard a governess's work is to me—for no one but myself is aware how utterly averse my whole mind and nature are for the employment. Do not think that I fail to blame myself for this, or that I leave any means unemployed to conquer this feeling. Some of my greatest difficulties lie in things that would appear to you comparatively trivial. I find it so hard to repel the rude familiarity of children. I find it so difficult to ask either servants or mistress for anything I want, however much I want it. It is less pain for me to endure the greatest inconvenience than to go into the kitchen to request its removal. I am a fool. Heaven knows I cannot help it!' Her departure had been enlivened by yet another valentine from Willie Weightman; 'but I knew better how to treat it than I did those we received a year ago. I am up to the dodges and artifices of his lordship's character. He knows I know him, and you cannot conceive how quiet and respectful he has long been. Mind, I am not writing against him—I never *will* do that. I like him very much. I honour and admire his generous, open disposition, and sweet temper—but for all the tricks, wiles and insincerities of love, the gentleman has not his match for twenty miles round. He would fain persuade every woman under thirty whom he sees that he is desperately in love with her.'

But at Upperwood House there was little gaiety for the governess, and after a fairly promising beginning, the Whites failed to improve on closer acquaintance. 'Mrs White expects a good deal of sewing from me. I cannot sew much during the day, on account of the children, who require the closest attention. I am obliged, therefore, to devote the evenings to this business. . . . This place is far better than Stonegappe, but, God knows, I have enough to do to keep a good heart in the matter. Home-sickness afflicts me sorely. I like Mr White extremely. Respecting Mrs White I am for the present silent. I am trying hard to like her. The children are not such little devils incarnate as the Sidgwicks', but they are over-indulged, and at times hard to manage.' Soon she was writing to Emily, 'I have got up my courage so far as to ask Mrs White to grant me a day's holiday to go to Birstall to see Ellen Nussey, who has offered to send a gig for me. My request was granted, but so coldly and slowly.' And a month later, 'Well can I believe that Mrs W. has been an exciseman's daughter, and I am convinced also that Mr W.'s extraction is very low; yet Mrs W. talks in an amusing strain of pomposity about his and her family and connections and affects to look down with wondrous hauteur on the whole race of "Tradesfolk" as she terms men of business.' (Mr White was a Bradford wool merchant.) 'I was beginning to think Mrs W. a good sort of body in spite of all her bouncing and boasting, her bad grammar and worse orthography; but I have had experience of one little trait in her character which condemns her a long way with me. After treating a person on the most familiar terms of equality for a long time, if any little thing goes wrong she does not scruple to give way to anger in a very coarse unladylike manner. . . . Mrs W. when put out of her way is highly offensive. She must not give me any more of the same sort—or I shall ask for my wages and go.'

She longed for home, and as her distaste for governess life increased with experience, dwelt more and more on the idea of some means of earning a living which the sisters could pursue in private together. 'My home,' she wrote to Henry Nussey, with whom she still exchanged occasional letters, 'is humble and unattractive to strangers, but to me it contains what I shall find nowhere else in the world—the profound, the intense affection which brothers and sisters feel for each other when their minds are cast in the same mould, their ideas drawn from the same source—when they have clung to each other from childhood, and when disputes have never sprung up to divide them.' The best, perhaps the only, solution of the problem lay in a private school, of the very small unpretentious sort which was making a modest living for spinsters all over England. They could not take many girls, and where they would put even a few to sleep is a mystery to anyone who has explored the parsonage; but Miss Wooler's more ambitious establishment had never had more than ten while Charlotte was there, and she decided that room could be found for several pupils.

§ They thought that, by a little contrivance, and a very little additional building, a small number of pupils, four or six, might be accommodated in the parsonage. As teaching seemed the only profession open to them, and as it appeared that Emily at least could not live away from home, while the others also suffered much from the same cause, this plan of school-keeping presented itself as most desirable. But it involved some outlay; and to this their aunt was averse. Yet there was no one to whom they could apply for a loan of the requisite means, except Miss Branwell, who had made a small store out of her savings, which she intended for her nephew and nieces eventually, but which she did not like to risk. §

Risk there certainly was, for such schools were legion and

many of them failed; yet the idea persisted, and had even been cautiously discussed with Mr Brontë and Miss Branwell. Charlotte wrote privately to Ellen for advice. 'I have often, you know, said how much I wished such a thing; but I never could conceive where the capital was to come from for making such a speculation. I was well aware, indeed, that aunt had money, but I always considered that she was the last person who would offer a loan for the purpose in question. A loan, however, she *has* offered, or rather intimates that she perhaps *will* offer in case pupils can be secured, an eligible situation obtained, &c. This sounds very fair, but still there are matters to be considered which throw something of a damp upon the scheme. I do not expect that aunt will sink more than £150 in such a venture; and would it be possible to establish a respectable (not by any means a *showy*) school, and to commence housekeeping with a capital of only that amount? . . . As to getting into debt, that is a thing we could none of us reconcile our mind to for a moment. We do not care how modest, how humble our commencement be, so it be made on sure grounds, and have a safe foundation.'

Emily at Haworth, and Anne in her new situation with the Robinsons, were as eagerly concerned as Charlotte with the scheme, and described it hopefully in two little private papers which, by an odd arrangement of their own, they had decided to write on their birthdays every four years, on each occasion opening and reading the previous diary. 'This is Emily's birthday,' wrote Anne. 'She has now completed her twenty-third year, and is, I believe, at home. Charlotte is a governess in the family of Mr White. Branwell is a clerk in the railroad station at Luddenden Foot, and I am a governess in the family of Mr Robinson. I dislike the situation and wish to change it for another. . . . We are thinking of setting up a school of our own, but nothing definite about it is settled yet, and we do not know whether we shall be able to or not. I hope we shall.' Emily, in excellent health and spirits at home and writing her Gondal chronicles as busily as ever— 'I have a good many books on hand, but I am sorry to say as usual I make small progress with any'—was more optimistic. 'I guess that at the time appointed for the opening of this paper we, i.e. Charlotte, Anne and I, shall be all merrily seated in our own sitting-room in some pleasant and flourishing seminary, having just gathered in for the midsummer holyday. Our debts will be paid off, and we shall have cash in hand to a considerable amount. Papa, aunt and Branwell will either have been or be coming to visit us. It will be a fine warm summer evening, very different from this bleak look-out, and Anne and I will perchance slip out into the garden for a few minutes to peruse our papers. I hope either this or something better will be the case.'

There was another difficulty, beside money, which discouraged their growing ambition for a school. They had no qualifications to show, no diplomas in languages or music, or any other accomplishment to attract pupils. Charlotte had read innumerable French novels to gain proficiency, and Emily and Anne could play the piano a little; but they were aware that all they could offer was not enough. It was at this very moment that something happened which seemed to have a direct bearing on the problem, and which set Charlotte's ambition racing in another direction.

Mary Taylor, the friend who was as intimate as Ellen Nussey, but who contributes so much less to our knowledge of Charlotte because she unfortunately thought it prudent to destroy her letters, had gone with her sister Martha to a finishing school in Brussels, and from there sent such an account of her experiences that Charlotte's imagination took fire, and showed her what seemed a solution of all their difficulties. 'Mary's letters spoke of some of the pictures and cathedrals she had seen—pictures the most exquisite, cathedrals the most venerable. I hardly know what swelled to my throat as I read her letter: such a vehement impatience of restraint and steady work; such a strong wish for wings—wings such as wealth can furnish; such an urgent thirst to see, to know, to learn; something internal seemed to expand bodily for a minute. I was tantalised by the consciousness of faculties unexercised,—then all collapsed, and I despaired.'

At first she was conscious only of a desperate yearning, but soon the thought presented itself—if she and her sisters could have even a few months' foreign schooling, might that not give them advantages which would make their projected school a certain success? The excitement of the idea carried her away, and she dismissed the only plan which had so far been considered, which was that she should take over Miss Wooler's school at Dewsbury Moor and try to revive it from its unprofitable condition. Miss Wooler's sister had retired, the school had dwindled; and the proposal was that Charlotte (without Emily or Anne, whom Miss Wooler would not consider) should take over, giving her old headmistress board and lodging in return for the use of the furniture. Charlotte had been inclined to agree to this arrangement, though without enthusiasm, since 'Dewsbury Moor is a poisoned place to me', and her sisters were excluded. She was worrying, as she often did, about Anne, and could not cheerfully embrace a scheme which offered no escape to this youngest sister. 'I have one aching feeling at my heart . . . it is about Anne. She has so much to endure, far far more than I have. When my thoughts turn to her, they see her always as a patient persecuted stranger, amongst people more grossly insolent, proud and tyrannical than your imagination unassisted can readily depict. I know what concealed susceptibility is in her nature. . . . She is more lonely, less gifted with the power of making friends even than I am.' If Charlotte and Emily could go to Brussels, Anne could perhaps be allowed to stay at home, to mind her health while the plans for the school ripened. Exalted with excitement, but compelling herself to be calm, Charlotte took her courage in both hands and wrote to Aunt Branwell.

'My friends recommend me, if I desire to secure permanent success, to delay commencing the school for six months longer, and by all means to contrive, by hook or by crook, to spend the intervening time in some school on the Continent. They say schools in England are so numerous, competition so great, that without some such step towards attaining superiority, we shall probably have a very hard struggle, and may fail in the end. They say, moreover, that the loan of £100, which you have been so kind as to offer us, will perhaps, not be all required now, as Miss Wooler will lend us the furniture; and that, if the speculation is intended to be a good and successful one, half the sum, at least, ought to be laid out in the manner I have mentioned, thereby insuring a more speedy repayment both of interest and principal.

'I would not go to France or to Paris. I would go to Brussels, in Belgium. The cost of the journey there, at the dearest rate of travelling, would be £5; living is there little more than half as dear as it is in England, and the facilities for education are equal or superior to any other place in Europe. In half a year I could acquire a thorough familiarity with French. I could improve greatly in Italian, and even get a dash of German; i.e. providing my health continued as good as it is now. Mary is now staying at Brussels, at a first-rate establishment there. I should not think of going to the Château de Kockleberg, where she is resident, as the terms are much too high; but if I wrote to her, she, with the assistance of Mrs Jenkins, the wife of the British Chaplain, would be able to secure me a cheap decent residence and respectable protection. I should have the opportunity of seeing her frequently; she would make me acquainted with the city; and, with the assistance of her cousins, I should probably be introduced to connections far more improving, polished, and cultivated, than any I have yet known.

'These are advantages which would turn to real account, when we actually commenced a school; and, if Emily could share them with me, we could take a footing in the world afterwards which we can never do now. I say Emily instead of Anne; for Anne might take her turn at some future period, if our school answered. I feel certain, while I am writing, that you will see the propriety of what I say. You always like to use your money to the best advantage. You are not fond of making shabby purchases; when you do confer a favour, it is often done in style; and, depend upon it, £50, or £100, thus laid out, would be well employed. Of course, I know no other friend in the world to whom I could apply, on this subject, except yourself. I feel an absolute conviction that, if this advantage were allowed us, it would be the making of us for life. Papa will perhaps, think it a wild and ambitious scheme; but who ever rose in the world without ambition? When he left Ireland to go to Cambridge University, he was as ambitious as I am now. I want us *all* to get on. I know we have talents, and I want them to be turned to account. I look to you, aunt, to help us. I think you will not refuse. I know, if you consent, it shall not be my fault if you ever repent your kindness.'

Won by this eloquent appeal, Miss Branwell agreed. She would lend enough to enable Charlotte and Emily to study in Brussels for six months; where, it was not yet settled; and Charlotte's private resolve was to stay longer if she could. 'Before our half-year in Brussels is completed,' she wrote confidentially to Emily, 'you and I will have to seek employment abroad. It is not my intention to retrace my steps home until twelve months, if all continues well.' She had joyfully given notice to Mrs White (who now behaved with such kindness that Charlotte was half ashamed of past criticisms), Anne had with equal relief given warning to the Robinsons, Branwell had asked for leave, and they all hoped to be home together for Christmas. Anne, however, when she left Thorp Green, was persuaded into a half-promise to return. 'Anne has rendered herself so valuable in her difficult situation that they have entreated her to return to them, if it be but for a short time. I almost think she will go back, if we can get a good servant who will do all our work.'

The Christmas holiday was spent in feverish correspondence and enquiry, the Taylors eagerly enlisting their friends to find a suitable school which was less expensive than their own. The French schools at Brussels were poorly thought of, and for a time they proposed to go to another at Lille; but in the end the wife of the British Chaplain in Brussels heard of a school of which nothing but good was spoken, and application was made to the Pensionnat Heger, Rue d'Isabelle. Monsieur Heger told Mrs Gaskell that 'on receipt of a letter from Charlotte, making very particular enquiries as to the possible amount of what are usually termed "extras", he and his wife were so much struck by the simple earnest tone of the letter, that they said to each other:—"These are the daughters of an English pastor, of moderate means, anxious to learn with an ulterior view of instructing others, and to whom the risk of additional expense is of great consequence. Let us name a specific sum, within which all expenses shall be included." '

The sum was named, and found reasonable. Mr Brontë expressed approval, and Charlotte plunged—happily, this time—into an ocean of needlework. 'I have lots of chemises, night-gowns, pocket handkerchiefs, and pockets to make; besides clothes to repair.' The last weeks were passed in a frenzy of preparation, the only thing to mar them being Branwell's dismissal from Luddenden Foot for carelessness and neglect of duty, and his coming home despondent. In February 1842 Mr Brontë took Charlotte and Emily to Brussels.

IX : BRUSSELS

Mary Taylor and her brother travelled with the Brontës to
Brussels. The party stayed for several days in London at the
Chapter Coffee House in Paternoster Row, a small old-
fashioned hotel chosen by Mr Brontë because it was much
frequented by clergymen. The party spent their time in
strenuous sight-seeing. 'Charlotte,' said Mary, 'seemed to think
our business was, and ought to be, to see all the pictures and
statues we could. She knew the artists, and knew where other
productions of theirs were to be found.' Charlotte had evidently
studied guide-books before the journey, as Mr Brontë, so like
his children in many ways, had attended to his French. With
characteristic care he had made himself a little phrase-book of
thirty-six pages, stitched into a leather cover; and knowing
the family, one is not surprised to find that the first section is

headed 'Of the Mind', and that there are careful notes of his expenditure on the journey, which he was pleased to find slightly less than if he had been travelling at home.

Arrived in Brussels the party separated, Mary returning to the Château de Kockleberg, and the Brontës presenting themselves at the Pensionnat Heger. They were shown into a 'cold, glittering salon, with porcelain stove unlit, and gilded ornaments, and polished floor', and were presently received by Madame Heger, who proved to be a small, plump, well-dressed woman in her middle thirties, of pleasant appearance and a correct, reserved manner. After an exchange of civilities Mr Brontë left his daughters in her charge and went to the house of Mr Jenkins, the British chaplain, where he spent the night before returning to Haworth.

The school in which Charlotte and Emily now found themselves was very different from anything they had known in England. The house itself was a large, cold, seventeenth-century building of some pretensions, facing the narrow street and with a formal enclosed garden at the back; and the school was conducted with quietly strict efficiency by the proprietress, whose system was based on perpetual supervision. The house and street have long since disappeared, but the place was unchanged when Mrs Gaskell visited it and was shown round by M Heger, and she was able to describe it in great detail.

§ The school was divided into three classes. In the first were from fifteen to twenty pupils; in the second, sixty was about the average number—all foreigners, excepting the two Brontës and one other; in the third there were from twenty to thirty pupils. The first and second classes occupied a long room, divided by a wooden partition; in each division were four long ranges of desks; and at the end was the *estrade*, or platform for the presiding instructor. On the last row, in the quietest corner, sat Charlotte and Emily, side by side, so deeply absorbed in their studies as to be insensible to any noise or movement around them. The school-hours were from nine to twelve (the luncheon hour), when the boarders and half-boarders—perhaps two-and-thirty girls—went to the refectoire (a room with two long tables, having an oil-lamp suspended over each), to partake of bread and fruit; the *externes*, or morning pupils, who had brought their own refreshment with them, adjourning to eat it in the garden. From one to two, there was fancy work—a pupil reading aloud some light literature in each room; from two to four, lessons again. At four, the *externes* left; and the remaining girls dined in the refectoire, M and Madame Heger presiding. From five to six there was recreation; from six to seven preparation for lessons; and after that succeeded the *lecture pieuse*—Charlotte's nightmare. On rare occasions, M Heger himself would come in, and substitute a book of a different and more interesting kind. At eight, there was a slight meal of water and *pistolets* (the delicious little Brussels rolls), which was immediately followed by prayers, and then to bed.

The principal bedroom was over the long classe, or schoolroom. There were six or eight narrow beds on each side of the apartment, every one enveloped in its white draping curtain; a long drawer, beneath each, served for a wardrobe, and between each was a stand for ewer, basin, and looking-glass. The beds of the two Miss Brontës were at the extreme end of the room, almost as private and retired as if they had been in a separate apartment. §

The régime was one of seriousness, quiet and study, and in spite of their extreme shyness, which from the first kept them awkwardly apart from the other pupils, Charlotte at least was happy in her new surroundings, even if the same cannot be said of the *farouche* Emily.

§ They wanted learning. They came for learning. They would learn. Where they had a distinct purpose to be achieved in intercourse with their fellows, they forgot themselves; at all other times they were miserably shy. Mrs Jenkins told me that she used to ask them to spend Sundays and holidays with her, until she found that they felt more pain than pleasure from such visits. Emily hardly ever uttered more than a monosyllable. Charlotte was sometimes excited sufficiently to speak eloquently and well—on certain subjects; but before her tongue was thus loosened, she had a habit of gradually wheeling round on her chair, so as almost to conceal her face from the person to whom she was speaking. §

'I was twenty-six years old a week or two since,' Charlotte wrote to Ellen, 'and at this ripe time of life I am a schoolgirl, a complete schoolgirl, and on the whole very happy in that capacity. It felt very strange at first to submit to authority instead of exercising it—to obey orders instead of giving them; but I like that state of things.'

What she did not like, however, was her fellow pupils, nor, with the exception of Mme Heger and her husband, any of the teachers; and her response, no less than Emily's, to nearly everything they saw was a censorious and insular hostility. Mary Taylor in her letters home was expressing exactly the same provincial antipathy to the foreigner, so that one cannot resist the impression that Yorkshire narrowness strongly reinforced the already painful reserve of Charlotte and Emily; nor can one feel surprised that they were not popular. 'If the national character of the Belgians,' Charlotte decided, 'is to be measured by the character of most of the girls in the school, it is a character singularly cold, selfish, animal and inferior. They are besides very mutinous and difficult for the teachers to manage, and their principles are rotten to the core. We avoid them.'

There was, in particular, one feature of life in the pensionnat to which their tolerance and good manners were unequal, and this was the circumstance of finding themselves among Catholics. Charlotte and Emily were the children of an Ulster Protestant and a Methodist, and had grown up among people who knew for certain that the Church of Rome was the Whore of Babylon, and who would have been shocked by any other view. They knew, of course, that they were going into a Catholic country, but they seem to have been unprepared for the emotional hostility which Catholic practice aroused in them when they came in contact with it. Years later, in writing of Emily, Charlotte was to speak of the 'strong recoil of her upright heretic and English spirit from the gentle Jesuitry of the foreign and Romish system', but she seems never to have noticed that at the time her own recoil was certainly as violent. 'People talk of the danger which Protestants expose themselves to in going to reside in Catholic countries, and thereby running the chance of changing their faith. My advice to all Protestants who are tempted to anything so besotted as turn Catholic—is to walk over the sea on to the continent, to attend mass regularly for a time, to note well the mummeries thereof, also the idiotic, mercenary aspect of *all* the priests, and *then* if they are still disposed to consider Papistry in any other light than a most feeble childish piece of humbug, let them turn Papists at once, that's all.'

Their hostility to the Catholic religion, which surrounded and isolated them as disgusted Protestants, ever on the watch for duplicity and hypocrisy ('a falsehood you can never get to the bottom of', Mary Taylor called it) did not, however, prevent their being happy during the first months. 'Charlotte and Emily are well,' Mary wrote home to Ellen, 'not only in health but in mind and hope. They are content with their present position and even gay.' To Charlotte, the stimulus of working under a first-class teacher was experience enough for the present; and there seems no doubt that M Heger was a teacher of genius. He was of that ardent and dynamic temperament which insists on an emotional *rapport* between master and pupil; he felt obliged to dominate and control, or he could not teach; and he took an artist's pleasure in playing and extending his pupils intellectually through half-angry, half-loving demands on the emotions. To this method Charlotte responded at once, and with complete success. Emily, as one might expect, was as immediately antagonised. 'Emily and he don't draw well together at all,' Charlotte reported, and this in spite of the fact that Emily worked 'like a horse' and was as fully determined on learning as her sister. M Heger thought her the more gifted of the two, but her self-willed and secret nature was not to be coerced by his explosive and highly personal methods of instruction.

§ M Heger's account is that they knew nothing of French. I suspect they knew as much (or as little), for all conversational purposes, as any English girls do, who have never been abroad, and have only learnt the idioms and pronunciation from an Englishwoman. The two sisters clung together, and kept apart from the herd of happy, boisterous, well-befriended Belgian girls, who, in their turn, thought the new English pupils wild and scared-looking, with strange, odd, insular ideas about dress; for Emily had taken a fancy to the fashion, ugly and preposterous even during its reign, of gigot sleeves, and persisted in wearing them long after they were 'gone out'. Her petticoats, too, had not a curve or a wave in them, but hung down straight and long, clinging to her lank figure. The sisters spoke to no one but from necessity. They were too full of earnest thought, and of the exile's sick yearning, to be ready for careless conversation, or merry game. M Heger, who had done little but observe, during the few first weeks of their residence in the Rue d'Isabelle, perceived that with their unusual characters, and extraordinary talents, a different mode must be adopted from that in which he generally taught French to English girls. He seems to have rated Emily's genius as something even higher than Charlotte's; and her estimation of their relative powers was the same. Emily had a head for logic, and a capability of argument, unusual in a man, and rare indeed in a woman, according to M Heger. Impairing the force of this gift, was a stubborn tenacity of will, which rendered her obtuse to all reasoning where her own wishes, or her own sense of right, was concerned. 'She should have been a man—a great navigator,' said M Heger in speaking of her. 'Her powerful reason would have deduced new spheres of discovery from the knowledge of the old; and her strong imperious will would never have been daunted by opposition or difficulty; never have given way but with life.' And yet, moreover, her faculty of imagination was such that, if she had written a history, her view of scenes and characters would have been so vivid, and so powerfully expressed, and supported by such a show of argument, that it would have dominated over the reader, whatever might have been his previous opinions, or his cooler perceptions of its truth. But she appeared egotistical and exacting compared to Charlotte, who was always unselfish (this is M Heger's testimony); and in the anxiety of the elder to make her younger sister contented she allowed her to exercise a kind of unconscious tyranny over her. §

They settled down to pass the *grandes vacances* in Brussels, continuing their studies in the empty schoolroom and meeting the Taylors for expeditions into the surrounding country. They were not too solitary. Mary and Martha Taylor had cousins in Brussels, to whose house they were often invited; the wife of the English chaplain made efforts to be kind; and a family of English girls, daughters of a Dr Wheelwright who was living in Brussels, came daily to the pensionnat for lessons during the holidays. Besides these, there was a handful of Belgian boarders, to the youngest of whom Emily gave piano lessons. Yet with all these possibilities of company, their 'overpowering shyness' drove them back as relentlessly as ever into their own company, and Emily remained, as Mrs Gaskell said, 'as impenetrable to friendly advances as at the beginning'. At length the school reassembled, and to her own work as pupil Charlotte now added that of English teacher.

§ During the hours of recreation, which were always spent in the garden, they invariably walked together, and generally kept a profound silence; Emily, though so much the taller, leaning on her sister. Charlotte would always answer when spoken to, taking the lead in replying to any remark addressed to both; Emily rarely spoke to any one. Charlotte's quiet, gentle manner never changed. She was never seen out of temper for a moment; and occasionally, when she herself had assumed the post of English teacher, and the impertinence or inattention of her pupils was most irritating, a slight increase of colour, a momentary sparkling of the eye, and more decided energy of manner, were the only outward tokens she gave of being conscious of the annoyance to which she was subjected. But this dignified endurance of hers subdued her pupils, in the long run, far more than the voluble tirades of the other mistresses. §

Mme Heger had offered to be present during these English lessons, with a view to keeping order, but Charlotte preferred to wrestle with difficulties in her own way, and the offer was refused. This evidence of character was noted and approved by M Heger, who wrote encouragingly to Mr Brontë that his daughter was already acquiring 'cette assurance, cet aplomb si nécessaire dans l'enseignement'. Alas, this calm season of progress did not last. A shadow had already reached them from Haworth with Willie Weightman's death, and in the following month Martha Taylor mysteriously sickened, and died in Brussels after a few days' illness. No sooner had Charlotte and Emily visited her grave in the Protestant cemetery with Mary than news came that Aunt Branwell was seriously ill. Mr Brontë summoned his daughters home. They prepared to leave Brussels at once, but the next morning a second letter arrived with news of her death. 'We sailed from Antwerp on Sunday; we travelled day and night and got home on Tuesday morning—and of course the funeral and all was over. We shall see her no more.' Branwell and Anne were at home with Mr Brontë, Anne having been summoned from Thorp Green, Branwell much shaken by having attended with his father at these two death-beds. 'I am incoherent, I fear,' he wrote to F. H. Grundy, 'but I have been waking two nights witnessing such agonising suffering as I would not wish my worst enemy to endure; and I have now lost the guide and director of all the happy days connected with my childhood.' It seemed, indeed, as though Aunt Branwell's death had put a melancholy period to the childish and hopeful part of all their lives.

Miss Branwell's small property was bequeathed to her nieces. 'Branwell, her darling,' said Mrs Gaskell, 'was to have had his share; but his reckless expenditure had distressed the good old lady, and his name was omitted from her will.' This interpretation is unjustified. The will had been made when Branwell was a boy of fiftten and in full favour with every member of the family; and the fact that she left him no money was no doubt due to her belief that, being a boy, and a brilliant one at that, he would earn a good living. It was for the girls that Miss Branwell, experienced in lifelong spinsterhood, was careful to provide. Her little personal belongings she divided fairly enough between the four of them—a workbox to Charlotte, a workbox and ivory fan to Emily, her watch to Anne, her 'Japan dressing-box' to Branwell, and her jewellery, silver spoons, books and clothes between the girls.

The legacies to her nieces, though small, were of great importance: they would provide the means for starting their own school. They did not, however, propose to make the necessary alterations to the parsonage immediately. M Heger had written a long, charming and sympathetic letter to Mr Brontë, urging the desirability of a further period in Brussels for Charlotte and Emily. 'Only another year and the work would have been completed. . . . Then we should have been able, if convenient to you, to offer to your daughters, or at least to one of them, a position according to her taste, and that pleasant independence so difficult for a young person to achieve.' What was to be done? Charlotte was frankly eager to return, Emily was not. Finally it was decided that Charlotte should go back to Brussels for another year, while Anne continued with the Robinsons, who, appreciating her upright and gentle character, were now prepared to take Branwell as tutor to their son. It remained for Emily to stay at home with Mr Brontë, who could not be left alone. His eyesight was rapidly deteriorating, and there was gossip in the village that he was drinking too much. (A letter from Mr Brontë still exists, in which he sternly repudiates these 'false reports', and maintains that it is the smell of his eye lotion which the slanderers have mistaken for 'a smell of a more exceptionable character'.) Emily was well content to stay at home, and so, at the beginning of 1843, they once again separated.

Charlotte returned to Brussels alone, and to a period which, in contrast to the first, was to become increasingly unhappy. There is no doubt that her emotional response to M Heger played its part in her determination to return; it is equally clear that she had no idea where her feelings were taking her. She sincerely believed that her sole reason for going back was to complete her training for the profession she had chosen, and it was not for many months that she began to suspect the true nature of her emotional predicament.

§ Towards the end of January, the time came for Charlotte to return to Brussels. Her journey thither was rather disastrous. She had to make her way alone; and the train from Leeds to London, which should have reached Euston Square early in the afternoon, was so much delayed that it did not get in till ten at night. She had intended to seek out the Chapter Coffee-house, where she had stayed before, and which would have been near the place where the steamboats lay; but she appears to have been frightened by the idea of arriving at an hour which, to Yorkshire notions, was so late and unseemly; and taking a cab, therefore, at the station, she drove straight to the London Bridge Wharf, and desired a waterman to row her to the Ostend packet, which was to sail the next morning. She described to me, pretty much as she had since described it in *Villette*, her sense of loneliness, and yet her strange pleasure in the excitement of the situation, as in the dead of that winter's night she went swiftly over the dark river to the black hull's side, and was at first refused leave to ascend to the deck. 'No passengers might sleep on board,' they said, with some appearance of disrespect. She looked back to the lights and subdued noises of London—that 'Mighty Heart' in which she had no place—and, standing up in the rocking boat, she asked to speak to some one in authority on board the packet. He came, and her quiet simple statement of her wish, and her reason for it, quelled the feeling of sneering distrust in those who had first heard her request; and impressed the authority so favourably that he allowed her to come on board, and take possession of a berth. The next morning she sailed; and at seven on Sunday evening she reached the Rue d'Isabelle once more; having only left Haworth on Friday morning at an early hour.

Her salary was 16*l.* a year; out of which she had to pay for her German lessons, for which she was charged as much (the lessons being probably rated by time) as when Emily learnt with her and divided the expense; viz., ten francs a month. By Miss Brontë's own desire, she gave her English lessons in the *classe*, or schoolroom, without the supervision of Madame or M Heger. They offered to be present, with a view to maintain order among the unruly Belgian girls; but she declined this, saying that she would rather enforce discipline by her own manner and character than be indebted for obedience to the presence of a *gendarme*. She ruled over a new schoolroom, which had been built on the space in the play-ground adjoining the house. Over that First Class she was *surveillante* at all hours; and henceforward she was called *Mademoiselle* Charlotte by M Heger's orders. She continued her own studies, principally attending to German, and to Literature; and every Sunday she went alone to the German and English chapels. Her walks too were solitary, and principally taken in the allée défendue, where she was secure from intrusion. This solitude was a perilous luxury to one of her temperament; so liable as she was to morbid and acute mental suffering. §

'I am settled by this time, of course,' she wrote in March. 'I am not too much overloaded with occupation; and besides teaching English, I have time to improve myself in German. I ought to consider myself well off, and to be thankful for my good fortunes. I hope I am thankful; and if I could always keep up my spirits and never feel lonely, or long for companionship, or friendship, or whatever they call it, I should do very well. As I told you before, M and Madame Heger are the only two persons in the house for whom I really experience regard and esteem, and of course, I cannot be always with them, nor even very often. They told me, when I first returned, that I was to consider their sitting-room my sitting-room also, and to go there whenever I was not engaged in the schoolroom. This, however, I cannot do. In the daytime it is a public room, where music-masters and mistresses are constantly passing in and out; and in the evening, I will not, and ought not to intrude on M and Madame Heger and their children. Thus I am a good deal by myself, out of school-hours; but that does not signify. I now regularly give English lessons to M Heger and his brother-in-law. They get on with wonderful rapidity; especially the first. He already begins to speak English very decently. If you could see and hear the efforts I make to teach them to pronounce like Englishmen, and their unavailing attempts to imitate, you would laugh to all eternity.'

The atmosphere of Brussels was subtly changed. She had not Emily's company to support her, and Mme Heger, she fancied, looked on her with an eye less kindly than before. At first she was at a loss to account for this sudden coolness, and told herself that it was imagination. But the impression persisted, and as the months went by she had to admit that

Mme Heger, though polite and correct as ever, was no longer friendly. Mrs Gaskell, who knew more on this subject than she cared to say, accounted for it by Charlotte's tactlessness in religious matters.

§ One of the reasons for the silent estrangement between Madame Heger and Miss Brontë, in the second year of her residence at Brussels, is to be found in the fact, that the English Protestant's dislike of Romanism increased with her knowledge of it, and its effects upon those who professed it; and when occasion called for an expression of opinion from Charlotte Brontë, she was uncompromising truth. Madame Heger, on the opposite side, was not merely a Roman Catholic, she was dévote. Not of a warm or impulsive temperament, she was naturally governed by her conscience, rather than by her affections; and her conscience was in the hands of her religious guides. She considered any slight thrown upon her church as blasphemy against the Holy Truth; and though she was not given to open expression of her thoughts and feelings, yet her increasing coolness of behaviour showed how much her most cherished opinions had been wounded. Thus, although there was never any explanation of Madame Heger's change of manner, this may be given as one great reason why, about this time, Charlotte was made painfully conscious of a silent estrangement between them; an estrangement of which, perhaps, the former was hardly aware. §

But there was another 'great reason why'; Mme Heger had been quick to notice the English *gouvernante's* too spontaneous, too emotional response to the professor. She disliked enthusiasm, and no doubt had had sufficient experience of this kind of hysteria. If she did not know that Charlotte was absorbed in writing long love poems on the master and pupil theme, she may well have guessed it; and she decided that the tiresome creature should be discouraged. There is no doubt, too, that unexpressed and unconscious jealousy between the two women played its part. Charlotte was as ready to suspect coldness as Mme Heger to suspect unseemly warmth. It did not make for happiness.

Left to herself, without even the bracing presence of Mary

Taylor, who had now left the Château de Kockleberg and gone to Germany to study, Charlotte began to suffer a new loneliness. 'There is a constant sense of solitude in the midst of numbers; the Protestant, the foreigner is a solitary being whether as teacher or pupil. . . .' She was sensitive to the rumours that reached her that some tender interest had taken her back to Brussels. 'If these charitable people knew the total seclusion of the life I lead—that I never exchange a word with any other man than Monsieur Heger and seldom indeed with him—they would perhaps cease to suppose that any such chimerical and groundless notion influenced my proceedings. . . . Not that it is a crime to marry, or a crime to wish to be married; but it is an imbecility which I reject with contempt, for women who have neither fortune nor beauty to make marriage the principal object of their wishes . . . not to be able to convince themselves that they are unattractive, and that they had better be quiet and think of other things than wedlock.' To Branwell she admitted 'one wearies from day to day of caring nothing, fearing nothing, liking nothing, hating nothing, being nothing, doing nothing—yes, I teach, and sometimes get red in the face with impatience at their stupidity. But don't think I ever scold or fly into a passion. . . . Nobody ever gets into a passion here. Such a thing is not known. . . . They are very false in their relations with each other, but they rarely quarrel, and friendship is a folly they are unacquainted with. The black Swan, M Heger, is the only sole veritable exception to this rule—for Madame, always cool and reasoning, is not quite an exception. But I rarely speak to Monsieur now, for not being a pupil I have little or nothing to do with him. From time to time he shows his kindheartedness by loading me with books, so that I am still indebted to him for all the pleasure or amusement I have. . . . It is a curious metaphysical fact,' she added, 'that always in the evening when I am in the great dormitory alone, having no other company than a number of beds with white curtains, I always recur as fanatically as ever to the old ideas, the old faces, and the old scenes in the world below.' Even at twenty-seven, the best drug and the best refuge was to be found in Angria.

The *grandes vacances* of this second year, when they approached, found her in a low and neurasthenic condition. She slept badly and was troubled by evil dreams. Mme Heger remained cold and disapproving—'I am convinced she does not like me'—and Monsieur was 'wondrously influenced by Madame' and had 'withdrawn the light of his countenance'. The big empty house oppressed her, and she took refuge from it in long exhausting walks about the city, returning at night in a state of misery and fatigue which drove away sleep. She was home-sick, perpetually trembling and uneasy, haunted by morbid fancies. 'My heart almost died within me . . .' she wrote later in *Villette*, recalling those unhappy months with a poignancy she dared not quite express even in her unhappy letters to Ellen and Emily. 'How long were the September days! How silent, how lifeless! How vast and void seemed the desolate premises! How gloomy the forsaken garden—grey now with the dust of a town summer departed. Looking forward at the commencement of those eight weeks, I hardly knew how I was to live to the end.' Her dreams became frightful beyond bearing, and the nightmares of her waking and sick imagination rose up to engulf her, bringing with them 'a nameless experience that had the hue, the mien, the terror, the very tone of a visitation from eternity'.

She was on the verge, one might say now, of a nervous breakdown; health and sanity trembled on a perilous edge. In this strange state, hysterical with loneliness and depression, feeling that 'the trial God had appointed me was gaining its climax, and must now be turned by my own hands', she sought relief in a fashion which at any other time would have repelled and shocked her. She went into the cathedral of Ste Gudule and confessed her shaken state of mind to a priest. 'In a solitary part of the Cathedral,' she told Emily, 'six or seven people remained kneeling by the confessionals. In two confessionals I saw a priest. I felt I did not care what I did, provided it was not absolutely wrong, and that it served to vary my life and yield a moment's interest. I took a fancy to change myself into a Catholic and go and make a real confession to see what it was like. Knowing me as you do, you will think this odd, but when people are by themselves they have singular fancies. A penitent was occupied in confessing. . . . After I had watched two or three penitents go and return, I approached at last and knelt down in a niche which was just vacated. I had to kneel there ten minutes waiting, for on the other side was another penitent invisible to me. At last that went away and a little wooden door inside the grating opened, and I saw the priest leaning his ear towards me. I was obliged to begin, and yet I did not know a word of the formula with which they always commence their confessions. It was a funny position. I felt precisely as I did when alone on the Thames at midnight. I commenced by saying I was a foreigner and had been brought up a Protestant. The priest asked if I was a Protestant then. I somehow could not tell a lie, and said "yes". He replied that in that case I could not "jouir du bonheur de la confesse"; but I was determined to confess, and at last he said he would allow me because it might be the first step towards returning to the true church. I actually did confess—a real confession. When I had done he told me his address, and said that every morning I was to go to the rue du Parc—to his house—and he would reason with me and try to convince me of the error and enormity of being a Protestant!!! I promised faithfully to go. Of course, however, the adventure stops there, and I hope I shall never see the priest again. I think you had better not tell papa of this.'

Better not, indeed! Even for Emily the incident is presented in a light very different from the real tone of the experience. 'I was perishing,' she wrote in *Villette*, describing Lucy Snowe's identical confession, 'for a word of advice or an accent of comfort. I had been living for some weeks quite alone; I had been ill; I had a pressure of affliction on my mind of which it would hardly any longer endure the weight.'

Mrs Gaskell, wisely, left this incident alone. It has a not altogether agreeable flavour, and can be accounted for only by a state of mind which Mrs Gaskell was reluctant to explore. Later biographers, however, have been less timid, and have willingly supposed that the matter of Charlotte's confession, the 'pressure of affliction' almost impossible to endure, was her love for M Heger. This is to put an interpretation on the adventure, mysteriously out of character though it was, which

175

it cannot bear. That Charlotte's mind, sick with loneliness and depression, was already dangerously occupied with this fascinating man cannot be denied; but there is nothing to suggest that she was yet awake to the true nature of her predicament. Her falling in love seems to have followed a devious, gradual and subterranean course, unrecognised (except, perhaps, by Mme Heger) until she had said good-bye to the professor for ever. She saw herself in all innocence as a devoted pupil who owed gratitude, loyalty, friendship—every emotion short of love—to the teacher who had provided her first intellectual satisfactions. To the fact that he was also a man of compelling personality, only a few years older than herself, she seems at this time to have been curiously blind. When she awoke, at Haworth, to her real plight, it was too late to change. The damage had been done.

Meanwhile the last dreary months in Brussels had to be lived through. She was determined not to give up the struggle before she had gained proficiency in German, and she forced herself to study, though by this time any form of concentration was difficult. At last, in October, feeling that the long-drawn misery was more than she could bear, she sought out Mme Heger and gave notice. 'If it had depended on her,' she told Ellen, 'I should certainly have soon been at liberty, but M. Heger, having heard of what was in agitation, sent for me the day after, and pronounced with vehemence his decision that I should not leave. I could not at that time have persevered in my intention without exciting him to passion, so I promised to stay a while longer; how long that while will be I do not know. . . . I have much to say, Ellen,' she added cautiously, 'many little odd things queer and puzzling enough, which I do not like to trust to a letter, but which one day perhaps or rather one evening, if ever we should find ourselves again at the fireside at Haworth or at Brookroyd with our feet on the fender, curling our hair, I may communicate to you. . . .' On one of those impulses which she shared with Emily and Anne, to preserve a given moment of experience, she wrote next day on a blank leaf of her school atlas, 'I am very cold—there is no fire—I wish I were at home with Papa, Branwell, Emily, Anne and Tabby—I am tired of being among foreigners

—it is a dreary life—especially as there is only one person in this house worthy of being liked—also another, who seems a rosy sugar plum but I know her to be coloured chalk.'

In December the news that Mr Brontë was fast becoming blind, and wished to have her home again, brought her to a decision. The Hegers, respecting so filial a reason for departure, no longer opposed her. M Heger presented her with a sort of diploma, certifying her proficiency in the French language and her ability to teach it. His kindness, his well-meant but too stirring sympathy, his parting advice, made the last few days an ordeal of struggle and tears. 'I suffered much,' she told Ellen, 'before I left Brussels. I think, however long I live, I shall not forget what the parting with M Heger cost me; it grieved me so much to grieve him, who has been so true, kind and disinterested a friend.' She hardly knew, even then, the bitter truth of what she had just written.

X: CHARLOTTE AND BRANWELL
IN LOVE

When Mrs Gaskell reached this point in her story she paused, and considered the dangerous pitfalls opening before her. In the period following Charlotte's return from Brussels there lay not only a secret, but a scandal. The unhappy secret she had already divined, when M Heger had shown her Charlotte's letters and Mme Heger had strangely refused to see her. The scandal of Branwell's disgrace she had learned, too, partly from what Charlotte had told her—'About Mr Branwell Brontë the less said the better—poor fellow,' she had written to a friend after staying with Charlotte at Haworth— but chiefly from Charlotte's candid letters to Ellen. It was a shocking story, and Mrs Gaskell's moral fastidiousness made her particularly sensitive to its undertones. How were these two matters to be dealt with? Both were of great importance in Charlotte's life; both, since other people concerned were still alive, were dangerous. 'I did so try to tell the truth,' she wrote, after the book was published and the scandalous parts had yielded their harvest of trouble. 'I weighed every line with my whole power and heart.' The conclusion she reached after this heart-searching was that M Heger's story must never be told, but that Branwell's downfall was known to many and could not be disguised.

These difficult matters, however, lay still ahead. The parsonage, after Charlotte's return, was quiet. Charlotte's and Branwell's troubles had begun, but were unsuspected; nobody knew but themselves that there was anything amiss. Branwell and Anne were with the Robinsons at Thorp Green; only Emily and Charlotte were at home.

At first their plans for starting a school of their own hung fire, on account of Mr Brontë's blindness. It was for his sake that Charlotte had left Brussels, and now, seeing how helpless he was becoming and how despondent, she felt that any scheme which involved her leaving him was out of the question. The three sisters still occasionally dreamed of setting up a school in some place more suitable than Haworth, but this was now impossible. Charlotte refused the offer of a teacher's post in Manchester at £100 a year, and accepted the fact that if they were to have a school at all it must be managed at home. 'Our parsonage,' she told M Heger, to whom she had been writing at regular intervals ever since she parted from him, 'is rather a large house—with a few alterations there will be room for five or six boarders. If I could find this number of children of good family, I should devote myself to their education. Emily does not care much for teaching, but she would look after the housekeeping, and, although something of a recluse, she is too good-hearted not to do all she could for the well-being of the children.' The scheme was particularly desirable for Anne's sake; she had already been at Thorp Green for three years, and was unhappy. The Robinsons were pleased with her, she now had Branwell's company and she uttered no complaint; but she hated her life as a governess, perpetually struggling with spoiled and difficult children, and she was sustained only by the hope that soon she would be able to support herself at home. Charlotte set to work to obtain pupils—'As soon as I can get an assurance of only *one* pupil, I will have cards of terms printed, and will commence the repairs necessary in the house'—but everywhere met with a chilling absence of response. One lady had just sent her daughters away to school, a second feared that the climate of Haworth might be damp, a third regretted the remoteness of the situation. Dismayed, Charlotte made efforts to turn the disadvantages of the parsonage into recommendations: its remoteness meant that she could offer cheaper terms than if the school were in a town, its smallness meant that extra attention could be given to a limited number of pupils . . . but all to no avail. She had cards of terms printed without waiting for the promise of a pupil, and sent them out in dozens to everyone she knew.

The prospectuses looked professional, but failed to produce a single letter of enquiry. 'We had prospectuses printed,' wrote Emily in her diary, 'despatched letters to all our acquaintances imparting our plans, and did our little all; but it was found no go.' Gradually the cherished plan was given up— by Anne with painful disappointment, by Emily (one suspects) with secret relief, and by Charlotte with a crushing sense of defeat. With this project gone, Haworth seemed dead indeed, and she felt it closing round her like a prison. There was no future, now, that she could see for any of them; only a slow withering away in dry obscurity. The expense, the time and the pain of the Brussels experiment had borne not the smallest profitable fruit.

There were other things, besides, to fret and worry her. Her eyesight during the past few months had become so bad that she was no longer able to read, and even the powerful solace of writing was denied her. The days dragged by in a kind of dreadful vacancy. 'There is nothing I fear so much as idleness,' she wrote to M Heger, 'the want of occupation, inactivity, the lethargy of faculties . . . I should not know this lethargy if I could write. Formerly I passed whole days and weeks and months in writing, not wholly without result . . . but now my sight is too weak to write. Were I to write much I should become blind.' Anxiety kept creeping into her letters to him, however much she tried to force a cheerful tone. Anxiety that he would not reply, anxiety that he would scold her when he did; the things she longed to say must never be said. In the course of a few months' separation from him a mysterious process of the mind had taken place in her; her feelings had increased with absence and with vacancy; his image had become more powerful and obsessive than when she had left Brussels. She waited for his letters with the troubled longing of a woman who knows at last that she is in love.

At first M Heger replied—sensible, bracing letters at long intervals, intended to do her good. He was eager, later, that Mrs Gaskell should see these letters—as an antidote, perhaps, to Charlotte's own. They had contained, he told her, advice on her character and life, her work and future; they were letters, evidently, which would show beyond doubt his unexceptionable attitude. But they were not to be found; either Charlotte herself or Mr. Nicholls had destroyed them. Only four of Charlotte's letters survived, and from these he allowed Mrs. Gaskell to make extracts—not wholly grasping, perhaps, the naked misery of the passages she was too discreet to quote. These four letters cover a period of sixteen months, in which he had bidden her write to him not more than twice a year, and in which he himself had been sparing of his answers. 'Once more goodbye, Monsieur,' Charlotte had written; 'it hurts to say goodbye even in a letter. Oh, it is certain that I shall see you again one day—it must be so —for as soon as I shall have earned enough money to go to Brussels I shall go there—and I shall see you again if only for a moment.' Six months of silence on his part had followed this indiscretion, and when next she wrote it was with an urgency of appeal which convinced him of the wisdom of not answering. 'Day and night I find neither rest nor peace. If I sleep I am disturbed by tormenting dreams in which I see you, always severe, always grave, always incensed against me. Forgive me then, Monsieur, if I adopt the course of writing to you again. How can I endure life if I make no effort to ease its sufferings?'

The suffering, now, was not concealed. For all her efforts at control, for all her attempts to keep to everyday matters which could not displease him, her letters are so bursting with anguish that one cannot read them, even now, without wincing. 'Monsieur, the poor have not need of much to sustain them—they ask only for the crumbs that fall from the rich men's table. But if they are refused they die of hunger. Nor do I, either, need much affection from those I love. I should not know what to do with a friendship entire and complete—I am not used to it. But you showed me of yore a *little* interest, when I was your pupil in Brussels, and I hold on to the maintenance of that *little* interest—I hold on to it as I would hold on to life.' Nearly a year later, still compelling herself to the long six-monthly intervals, the cry was still the same. 'I tell you frankly that I have tried meanwhile to forget you . . . I have done everything; I have sought occupations; I have denied myself absolutely the pleasure of speaking about you—even to Emily; but I have been able to conquer neither my regrets nor my impatience. . . . Why cannot I have just as much friendship for you, as you for me—neither more nor less? Then should I be so tranquil, so free—I could keep silence then for ten years without an effort. . . . To write to an old pupil cannot be a very interesting occupation for you, I know; but for me it is life. Your last letter was stay and prop to me—nourishment to me for half a year. Now I need another and you will give it me; not because you bear me friendship—you cannot have much—but because you are compassionate of soul and you would condemn no-one to prolonged suffering to save yourself a few moments' trouble. To forbid me to write to you, to refuse to answer me, would be to tear from me my only joy on earth, to deprive me of my last privilege. . . . So long as I believe you are pleased with me, so long as I have hope of receiving news from you, I can be at rest and not too sad. But when a prolonged and gloomy silence seems to threaten me with the estrangement of my master—when day by day I await a letter, and when day by day disappointment comes to fling me back into overwhelming sorrow, and the sweet delight of seeing your handwriting and reading your counsel escapes me as a vision that is vain, then fever claims me— I lose appetite and sleep—I pine away.' To this last letter, written, like all the others, in French, she added in English, 'Farewell, my dear Master—may God protect you with special care and crown you with peculiar blessings.' To this his answer appears to have been a bored silence.

The history of these four letters of Charlotte's is very curious. Mlle Louise Heger, who with her brother presented them to the British Museum in 1913, seventeen years after their father's death, stated that he had torn up all Charlotte's letters as he received them and thrown them in the waste-paper basket. Here, the four of them that survive were found and retrieved by Mme Heger, who pasted the pieces together and hid them in her jewel case, where M Heger found them many years later, after his wife's death. Surprised by the discovery, he threw them away again, and this time they were rescued by his daughter, who eventually in her old age decided they were of interest to posterity. There is only one flaw in this peculiarly interesting story. How, if M Heger threw the letters away as he received them, could he show them to Mrs Gaskell ten years later? Either he kept them, or he must have shown them in the patchwork condition to which his wife had restored them. It is not perhaps a point of much importance, but is interesting for the light it throws on Mme Heger, who in this episode plays a part so perfectly in the character of Mme Beck.

However M Heger regarded the letters, Mrs Gaskell saw at once that they were dangerous; of great significance to the biographer, but impossible to quote. 'I believed him to be too good to publish those letters,' she wrote to Ellen Nussey, '—but I felt that his friends might really with some justice urge him to do so.' For herself, of course, working under the watchful eye of Mr Nicholls, any reference was out of the question. She wisely decided on silence, and contented herself with quoting two harmless paragraphs which gave no clue to the underlying conflict.

For Charlotte, however, the experience was agonising and prolonged, and had to be endured, like all histories of unrequited love, until time and suffering wore it out at last. She told no-one. Only in the four letters concealed in Mme Heger's jewel case, and in one or two scraps of verse that she omitted to destroy, is there any clue to the painful and maturing experience from which her imagination purged itself at last with the writing of *Villette*.

He saw my heart's woe, discovered my soul's anguish,
    How in fever, in thirst, in atrophy it pined;
Knew he could heal, yet looked and let it languish,—
    To its moans spirit-deaf, to its pangs spirit-blind.

But once a year he heard a whisper low and dreary
    Appealing for aid, entreating some reply;
Only when sick, soul-worn and torture-weary,
    Breathed I that prayer, heaved I that sigh.

He was mute as in the grave, he stood stirless as a tower
    At last I looked up and saw I prayed to stone:
I asked help of that which to help had no power,
    I sought love where love was utterly unknown.

The parsonage was not an auspicious place for anyone trying to forget an unhappy love affair. It was deathly quiet; the days were all the same. Emily was more withdrawn than ever, cheerful enough but impersonal and detached, absorbed in her chosen discipline of retreat from the world, turning her extraordinary mind inward upon a region where it fed on endless dramas of her own imagining, on copious prose and poetry which she wrote in secret and kept locked up in a little folding desk. The year in Brussels had not made her any more communicative. The only tenderness she ever showed, as someone told Mrs Gaskell, was not to her own kind. 'She never showed regard to any human creature; all her love was reserved for animals.' This is a familiar phenomenon in those who feel themselves incapable of ordinary contacts, or for some other reason rejected by their fellows; and Mrs Gaskell was aware of it, in some degree, in Charlotte.

§ Charlotte was more than commonly tender in her treatment of all dumb creatures, and they, with that fine instinct so often noticed, were invariably attracted towards her. The deep and exaggerated consciousness of her personal defects—the constitutional absence of hope, which made her slow to trust in human affection, and consequently slow to respond to any manifestation of it—made her manner shy and constrained to men and women, and even to children. We have seen something of this trembling distrust of her own capability of inspiring affection, in the grateful surprise she expresses at the regret felt by her Belgian pupils at her departure. But not merely were her actions kind, her words and tones were ever gentle and caressing, towards animals; and she quickly noticed the least want of care or tenderness on the part of others towards any poor brute creature. . . .

The feeling, which in Charlotte partook of something of the nature of an affection, was, with Emily, more of a passion. . . . The helplessness of an animal was its passport to Charlotte's heart; the fierce, wild, intractability of its nature was what often recommended it to Emily. Speaking of her dead sister, the former told me that from her many traits in Shirley's character were taken; her way of sitting on the rug reading, with her arm round her rough bull-dog's neck; her calling to a strange dog, running past, with hanging head and lolling tongue, to give it a merciful draught of water, its maddened snap at her, her nobly stern presence of mind, going right into the kitchen, and taking up one of Tabby's red-hot Italian irons to sear the bitten place, and telling no one, till the danger was well-nigh over, for fear of the terrors that might beset their weaker minds. All this, looked upon as a well-invented fiction in *Shirley*, was written down by Charlotte with streaming eyes; it was the literal true account of what Emily had done. The same tawny bull-dog (with his 'strangled whistle'), called 'Tartar' in *Shirley*, was 'Keeper' in Haworth parsonage; a gift to Emily. With the gift came a warning. Keeper was faithful to the depths of his nature as long as he was with friends; but he who struck him with a stick or whip, roused the relentless nature of the brute, who flew at his throat forthwith, and held him there till one or the other was at the point of death. Now Keeper's household fault was this. He loved to steal upstairs, and stretch his square, tawny limbs, on the comfortable beds, covered over with delicate white counterpanes. But the cleanliness of the parsonage arrangements was perfect; and this habit of Keeper's was so objectionable, that Emily, in reply to Tabby's remonstrances, declared that, if he was found again transgressing, she herself, in defiance of warning and his well-known ferocity of nature, would beat him so severely that he would never offend again. In the gathering dusk of an autumn evening, Tabby came, half-triumphantly, half-tremblingly, but in great wrath, to tell Emily that Keeper was lying on the best bed, in drowsy voluptuousness. Charlotte saw Emily's whitening face, and set mouth, but dared not speak to interfere; no one dared when Emily's eyes glowed in that manner out of the paleness of her face, and when her lips were so compressed into stone. She went upstairs, and Tabby and Charlotte stood in the gloomy passage below, full of the dark shadows of coming night. Down-stairs came Emily, dragging after her the unwilling Keeper, his hind legs set in a heavy attitude of resistance, held by the 'scruff of his neck', but growling low and savagely all the time. The watchers would fain have spoken, but durst not, for fear of taking off Emily's attention, and causing her to avert her head for a moment from the enraged brute. She let him go, planted in a dark corner at the bottom of the stairs; no time was there to fetch stick or rod, for fear of the strangling clutch at her throat —her bare clenched fist struck against his red fierce eyes, before he had time to make his spring, and, in the language of the turf, she 'punished him' till his eyes were swelled up, and the half-blind, stupefied beast was led to his accustomed lair, to have his swollen head fomented and cared for by the very Emily herself. The generous dog owed her no grudge; he loved her dearly ever after; he walked first among the mourners at her funeral; he slept moaning for nights at the door of her empty room, and never, so to speak, rejoiced, dog fashion, after her death. §

It is an unattractive anecdote, but it shows us something of Emily's unyielding nature. Charlotte would not have been capable of such a thing, and between the two sisters, deep though their attachment was, this harshness, and other mysterious aspects of Emily's personality, prevented that complete sympathy which would have meant much to Charlotte.

'I can hardly tell you,' she wrote to Ellen, 'how time gets on at Haworth. There is no event whatever to mark its progress. One day resembles another; and all have heavy, lifeless physiognomies. Sunday, baking-day and Saturday are the only ones that have any distinctive mark. Meantime, life wears away. I shall soon be thirty; and I have done nothing yet. Sometimes I get melancholy at the prospect before and behind me. Yet it is wrong and foolish to repine. Undoubtedly, my duty directs me to stay at home for the present. There was a time when Haworth was a very pleasant place to me; it is not so now. I feel as if we were all buried here.' Failure and frustration, both in ambition and in love, were slowly numbing her sense of the freshness of life. 'I do not know whether you feel as I do,' she told Ellen, 'but there are times now when it appears to me as if all my ideas and feelings, except a few friendships and affections, are changed from what they used to be; something in me, which used to be enthusiasm, is tamed down and broken.' Mary Taylor, herself on the point of leaving England for ever in the seemingly wild hope of earning her living in New Zealand, made a characteristic effort to induce Charlotte to escape. 'I told her very warmly that she ought not to stay at home; that to spend the next five years at home, in solitude and weak health, would ruin her; that she would never recover it. Such a dark shadow came over her face when I said "Think of what you'll be five years hence!" then I stopped and said, "Don't cry, Charlotte!" She did not cry, but went on walking up and down the room, and said in a little while, "But I intend to stay, Polly." '

Soon it appeared that Mr Brontë's failing eyesight was not the only thing to cause anxiety. Branwell had been very strange of late. He was drinking a good deal when he came home for the holidays, but this alone could not explain his behaviour. He was unaccountably irritable and quarrelsome; sometimes in noisy high spirits and sometimes in moods of suicidal gloom. He made no complaint of his situation at Thorp Green, which he had held successfully now for close on three years; on the contrary, he professed himself more than satisfied, and was even impatient for the holidays to be over.

Nobody knew (though Anne must surely have suspected) what was producing this unwelcome change, but at the end of July 1845, when she and Branwell came home while the Robinson family took their holidays at Scarborough, the truth came suddenly and scandalously out.

Charlotte was from home at the time, having gone to spend three weeks with Ellen at Hathersage in Derbyshire, where Henry Nussey had been appointed vicar, and where Ellen was preparing the vicarage for the wife whom he had at last managed to secure. Charlotte came home to find the parsonage in a state of stunned confusion. 'It was ten o'clock at night,' she told Ellen, 'when I got home. I found Branwell ill; he is so very often owing to his own fault. I was not therefore shocked at first'—his sisters by this time being used to drunkenness—'but when Anne informed me of the immediate cause of his present illness, I was very greatly shocked. He had last Thursday received a note from Mr Robinson sternly dismissing him, intimating that he had discovered his proceedings, which he characterised as bad beyond expression, and charging him on pain of exposure to break off instantly and for ever all communication with every member of his family. We have had sad work with Branwell since. He thought of nothing but stunning or drowning his distress of mind. No one in the house could have rest. At last we have been obliged to send him from home for a week, with someone to look after him. He has written to me this morning, and expresses some sense of contrition for his frantic folly; he promises amendment on his return, but so long as he remains at home I scarce dare hope for peace in the house. We must all, I fear, prepare for a season of distress and disquietude. So Branwell's strange behaviour was at last explained. He was in the throes of a passionate love affair with Mrs. Robinson.

Much has been written and argued about this miserable episode, and it seems likely that, at this distance, we can never know the truth. Was Branwell really Mrs, Robinson's lover, or did his infatuation for her, and his drink and opium-muddled grief, delude him into imagining it? His father and sisters believed his story, and Mrs. Gaskell, accepting the evidence of Charlotte's letters and Ellen's recollections, took Mrs Robinson's misconduct for granted, and told the tale in such sepulchral tones that her readers were left without a possibility of doubt.

§ The story must be told. If I could, I would have avoided it; but not merely is it so well-known to many living as to be, in a manner, public property, but it is possible that, by revealing the misery, the gnawing, life-long misery, the degrading habits, the early death of her partner in guilt —the acute and long-enduring agony of his family—to the wretched woman, who not only survives, but passes about in the gay circles of London society, as a vivacious, well-dressed, flourishing widow, there may be awakened in her some feelings of repentance.

Branwell, I have mentioned, had obtained a situation as a private tutor. Full of available talent, a brilliant talker, a good writer, apt at drawing, ready of appreciation, and with a not unhandsome person, he took the fancy of a married woman, nearly twenty years older than himself. It is no excuse for him to say that she began the first advances, and 'made love' to him. She was so bold and hardened, that she did it in the very presence of her children, fast approaching to maturity; and they would threaten her that, if she did not grant them such and such indulgences, they would tell their bed-ridden father 'how she went on with Mr. Brontë'. He was so beguiled by this mature and wicked woman, that he went home for his holidays reluctantly, stayed there as short a time as possible, perplexing and distressing them all by his extraordinary conduct—at one time in the highest spirits, at another, in the deepest depression—accusing himself of blackest guilt and treachery, without specifying what they were; and altogether evincing an irritability of disposition bordering on insanity. . . .

All the disgraceful details came out. Branwell was in no state to conceal his agony of remorse, or, strange to say, his agony of guilty love, from any dread of shame. He gave passionate way to his feelings; he shocked and distressed those loving sisters inexpressibly; the blind father sat stunned, sorely tempted to curse the profligate woman, who had tempted his boy—his only son—into the deep disgrace of deadly crime.

All the variations of spirits and of temper—the reckless gaiety, the moping gloom of many months, were now explained. There was a reason deeper than any mere indulgence of appetite, to account for his intemperance; he began his career as an habitual drunkard to drown remorse. §

Mrs Gaskell's indignation with Mrs Robinson (an indignation inspired, it must be said, by all she had heard from Charlotte and Mr Brontë) moved her to a denunciation in the righteous and ringing tones of melodrama. 'The man became the victim; the man's life was blighted, and crushed out of him by suffering, and guilt entailed by guilt; the man's family were stung by keenest shame. The woman . . . she goes flaunting about to this day in respectable society; a showy woman for her age; kept afloat by her reputed wealth. I see her name in county papers, as one of those who patronise the Christmas balls; and I hear of her in London drawing-rooms. Now let us read, not merely of the suffering of her guilty accomplice, but of the misery she caused to innocent victims, whose premature deaths may, in part, be laid at her door.'

The libel action with which Mrs Robinson's solicitors threatened Mrs Gaskell, and which caused the offending passages to be suppressed, has intimidated later biographers into believing that the whole thing existed only in Branwell's imagination. We can never, perhaps, be sure; but considering the evidence from our safer distance, we find the whole tone and detail of the episode suggesting that there *was* a love affair, and that Mrs Robinson's denials covered a skilful retreat from a dangerous position.

Mr Robinson, that vaguely threatening clerical figure in the background, was an elderly man and an invalid. Branwell was twenty-five when he first came to Thorp Green, Mrs Robinson a handsome woman of forty-two. She was at an age when the admiration of youth is singularly attractive, and Branwell, having more than his share of the ardent Brontë temperament, was bound to respond to the smallest flicker of encouragement. It is not by any means an unheard-of situation, and might well have gone undiscovered until it wore itself out, like many unsuspected Victorian dramas. But Branwell was unlucky. Either Mr Robinson found out, or else his wife, wishing to put an end to an affair which in its third year was growing irksome, made some complaint or accusation against Branwell, with the result that he was forbidden to return. Whichever happened, the last thing the Robinsons wanted was a scandal, which was exactly what Branwell's frantic behaviour eventually achieved.

Mrs. Robinson's real attitude to Branwell we shall never know; but once the affair was known, or Mrs Robinson's accusation made, we can readily see that it was in her interest to keep him at a distance. It seems likely that she sent him letters and money on occasion, and it is said that they even met in secret at Harrogate; but it is hard to believe the melodramatic picture of her sufferings that we find in Branwell's letters. We can only suppose that it was at this point that the opium dreams began to colour his experience. Mr Robinson's death, which occurred about twelve months after Branwell's dismissal, allowed him at first a deluded hope, soon extinguished by the news (brought to him at Haworth by her coachman) that the terms of her husband's will forbade her to remarry. This was not strictly true, as an examination of the will makes clear. She was to enjoy her husband's estate only during her widowhood (a quite usual condition at that time), but would not be much impoverished by marrying again, since she possessed a comfortable fortune of her own. The misleading message about the will, however, serves to make plain her attitude to Branwell, who in spite of this and other rebuffs continued to believe that she loved him, and that only 'difficulties placed in my way by powerful and wealthy men' kept him from the marriage.

His confidants during these wretched months were John Brown the sexton, who was sent with him to Liverpool when he was in *delirium tremens,* and J. B. Leyland the sculptor, to whom he described the successive stages of the affair in a curious and often pathetic correspondence. It eased him to describe his sufferings to Leyland (for his sisters, and particularly Charlotte, were unresponsive) and to talk and daydream on paper about Mrs Robinson. After her husband's death he claimed to have received a 'long, kind and faithful' letter from her physician, which would be extremely interesting to read if it had survived. 'He knows me *well*,' he told Leyland, 'and he pities my case most sincerely, for he declared that though used to the rough ups and downs of this weary world, he shed tears from his heart when he saw the state of that lady and knew what I should feel. When he mentioned my name— she stared at him and fainted. When she recovered she in turns dwelt on her inextinguishable love for me—her horror at having been the first to delude me into wretchedness, and her agony at having been the cause of the death of her husband, who, in his last hours, bitterly repented of his treatment of her. Her sensitive mind was totally wrecked. She wandered into talking of entering a nunnery. . . .' It is somehow difficult to believe in this affecting scene. If Mrs Robinson really suffered as Branwell believed, she also showed an admirable resilience, for it was not long before she became the wife of Sir Edward Scott and was reported by her daughters to be in the highest spirits. What is certain, however, is that Branwell believed in her, and brooded on his vision of her misery, and on his own torments, until he was sunk in a swamp of morbid melancholy from which nothing could save him.

Charlotte has been much blamed for her evident lack of sympathy with Branwell's woe, but it must be remembered that during the three years that he now spent at home, in a state of gradual decline both physical and moral, he must have become a distasteful burden to them all. Mr Brontë confided in no-one about his son's collapse, and Emily and Anne made only cryptic references to it in their diaries. Charlotte was the only one of the family who wrote constantly and freely to an intimate friend, and in her letters to Ellen we find bitter words that the others left unsaid. This has given rise to a legend, passionately sponsored without evidence by the biographers of Emily, that while gentle Anne grieved over her brother and stalwart Emily befriended him, Charlotte alone rejected him with impatience. There was, it is true, an element of acerbity in Charlotte's nature, but it is unreasonable to assume that she alone was sickened by Branwell's deterioration because she alone has left any record of it.

The three years which followed Branwell's dismissal from Thorp Green provide a pitiful last chapter to the history of an only son of whom too much was expected. Mysteriously lacking in the Brontë strength of character, he was unable to face performance or to withstand failure. Only in drink and opium in these last years could he recover his illusions, and he turned to both as to his only friends. From time to time, in that quiet household where often the only sounds were the tick of the clock and the scratch of pen on paper, he tried to recapture the old excitement of writing, to prove to himself that all was as before. 'I have, since I saw you at Halifax', he told Leyland, 'devoted my hours of time snatched from downright illness, to the composition of a three-volume *Novel*—one volume of which is completed—and along with the two forthcoming ones, has been really the result of half a dozen by-past years of thoughts about, and experience in, this crooked path of Life.' But even this resource failed him, since any kind of sustained effort was impossible, and all power of self-discipline was gone. 'I suffer very much from that mental exhaustion which arises from brooding on matters useless at present to think of,' he excused himself; and later, 'Constant and unavoidable depression of mind and body sadly shackle me in even trying to go on with any mental effort.' Only with laudanum could he recapture the old serenity and confidence; sober, he knew his mental bankruptcy, and was capable, still, of flashes of bitter truth. 'Noble writings, works of art, music or poetry now instead of rousing my imagination, cause a whirlwind of blighting sorrow that sweeps over my mind with unspeakable dreariness, and if I sit down and try to write, all ideas that used to come clothed in sunlight now press round me in funeral black. . . . I shall never be able to realise the too sanguine hopes of my friends, for at 28 I am a thoroughly *old man*.' The only refuge from such appalling knowledge was in opium, and the compensations of its visionary world.

XI : CURRER, ELLIS AND ACTON BELL

It was in this dull, anxious and frustrated period—the least propitious, one would have thought, for such a development—that the genius of Charlotte and Emily began to ripen. It was perhaps the very circumstances of failure and anxiety that quickened the growth, for they were now once more united in their old seclusion, as dependent on themselves as when they were children, and with no resource or interest but in writing. Charlotte's eyesight was still deplorable, but she now ignored it, preferring the risk of blindness to being idle; and had turned to her Brussels experience for material. Anne, too, beside her Gondal chronicles, was trying her hand on a story of governess life; she had begun this at Thorp Green, and now quietly worked at her sober theme in the evenings. She had had, indeed, a modest success already, for *Chambers's Journal* had printed one of her poems.

Nobody knew very clearly what Emily was doing. The Gondals still flourished 'bright as ever', and she was writing a great deal of prose as well as poetry; but she was wonderfully uncommunicative, and no one but Anne knew what she kept in her desk. Emily alone in the family seems at this time to have been cheerful and content. 'We have cash enough for our present wants,' she wrote in her diary paper of 1845, '. . . we are all in decent health, only that papa has a complaint in his eyes, and with the exception of B., who, I hope, will be better and do better hereafter. I am quite contented for myself : not as idle as formerly, altogether as hearty, and having learnt to make the most of the present and long for the future with less fidgetiness that I cannot do all I wish; seldom or never troubled with nothing to do, and merely desiring that everybody could be as comfortable as myself and as undesponding, and then we should have a very tolerable world of it . . . I have plenty of work on hands, and writing, and am altogether full of business.'

This writing might have remained a secret for ever if Charlotte had not one day come across a little manuscript book of poems which Emily had forgotten to hide. 'One day in the autumn of 1845, I accidentally lighted on a MS. volume of verse, in my sister Emily's hand-writing. Of course, I was not surprised, knowing that she could and did write verse : I looked it over, and something more than surprise seized me— a deep conviction that these were not common effusions, nor at all like the poetry women generally write. I thought them condensed and terse, vigorous and genuine. To my ear they had also a peculiar music, wild, melancholy, and elevating. My sister Emily was not a person of demonstrative character, nor one, on the recesses of whose mind and feelings, even those nearest and dearest to her could, with impunity, intrude unlicensed : it took hours to reconcile her to the discovery I had made, and days to persuade her that such poems merited publication. . . . Meantime, my younger sister quietly produced some of her own compositions, intimating that since Emily's had given me pleasure, I might like to look at hers. I could not but be a partial judge, yet I thought that these verses too had a sweet sincere pathos of their own. We had very early cherished the dream of one day becoming authors. This dream, never relinquished even when distance divided and absorbing tasks occupied us, now suddenly acquired strength and consistency : *it took the character of a resolve.*'

In this, as in most of their undertakings, the resolve was Charlotte's. She caught eagerly at the idea that the three of them should publish a book of poems, and was prepared to break down Emily's resistance and to shoulder the correspondence and business herself. She had apparently never thought that her own verses merited this effort; unlike Anne, she had had no original poem published, and her only appearance in any periodical had been some anonymous translations of French verse; but she saw at once that Emily's poems were on a different level. Emily herself, it seems, had had no thought of publication, and violently resisted. Her poetry was a part of her daydream life, and intensely private. It was the expression of that uncensored experience that filled her solitary hours with 'mute music', and gave her the freedom of many imaginary lives. Whatever was real or personal in the poems was doubly disguised under Gondal names and identities. She neither wished nor cared to share it with anyone.

If Emily, however, was the nearly immovable object, Charlotte was the irresistible force, and gradually Charlotte's enthusiasm prevailed. Even Emily cannot have been quite insensible to the attractions of a possible success, and when it was suggested that they should conceal their own names under pseudonyms she was finally won. After much discussion, and keeping their own initials, they chose the names Currer, Ellis and Acton Bell—'the ambiguous choice,' Charlotte afterwards explained, 'being dictated by a sort of conscientious scruple at assuming Christian names positively masculine, while we did not like to declare ourselves women, because—without at the time suspecting that our mode of writing and thinking was not what is called "feminine"—we had a vague impression that authoresses are liable to be looked on with prejudice.' They hoped, without actually wishing to deceive, that the publisher would suppose them to be men.

Charlotte now with her sisters copied out a selection of the poems, and made some tentative applications to publishers. At first she was unsuccessful, but eventually, having written to Messrs. Chambers of Edinburgh for advice, she applied to Aylott and Jones of Paternoster Row, a firm of booksellers and stationers who as a side-line published occasional classical and theological works, and who were willing to accept the not very formidable risk of publishing a book of poems at the authors' expense. The sum required by this firm was thirty guineas, which the sisters made up between them from their savings. The poems, Charlotte felt obliged to warn the publishers, 'are not the production of a clergyman, nor are they exclusively of a religious character'. Finding herself ignorant of the technical details of book production, she bought a manual of the subject and studied it, and was soon writing to Paternoster Row with instructions on the choice of type and format.

Not a word was breathed at home about the undertaking. Neither Mr Brontë nor Branwell, nor even Ellen, was allowed to guess that anything was afoot. The sisters had the intoxicating experience of receiving proofs to correct, but this was done in secret. They were determined that no one should know of this reckless venture until there was at least a hope of some success. In the meantime, the excitement of preparing the poems for the press led to the discussion of a more ambitious plan: Charlotte's and Anne's novels were making progress, and Emily too had turned aside from Gondal to a prose tale: why should they not follow the poems with these works of fiction? Accordingly Charlotte wrote once more to Aylott and Jones, asking whether they might be disposed to consider 'a work of fiction, consisting of three distinct and unconnected tales', which the authors did not wish to publish at their own expense. This, however, the firm refused to do, since Mr Aylott's religious views precluded any dealings with light literature. Disappointed but not discouraged, the sisters worked steadily on through the spring of 1846—Charlotte with *The Professor*, Anne with *Agnes Grey*, and Emily—extraordinary and unpredictable first work—with *Wuthering Heights*.

As the publication date for the poems approached, Charlotte kept anxiously in touch with Paternoster Row. How many review copies should be sent out, and to which periodicals? The costs of printing had proved to be £5 in excess of the estimate, and she was frightened to spend more. 'I should think,' she wrote cautiously, 'the success of a work depends more on the notice it receives from periodicals than on the quantity of advertisements.' The publishers seem to have thought the £2 meagre, but Charlotte, already nervous over the cost of the adventure, was not to be tempted. 'Should the poems be remarked upon favourably, it is my intention to appropriate a further sum for advertisement. If, on the other hand, they should pass unnoticed or be condemned, I consider it would be quite useless to advertise, as there is nothing either in the title of the work, or the names of the authors, to attract attention from a single individual.'

Clearly, for all their hidden excitement, the sisters felt there were no good grounds for optimism, but they cannot have been quite prepared for the almost total silence which greeted the book. It received only a few indifferent reviews and sold only two copies. 'Our book,' Charlotte wrote a year later, 'is found to be a drug; no man needs it or heeds it. In the space of a year our publisher has disposed but of two copies, and by what painful efforts he succeeded in getting rid of these two, himself only knows.' There was nothing for it but to swallow the pill, say nothing, and work on with quiet persistence at their novels.

This they continued to do, in silence and in secret, undisturbed by anything more agreeable than Branwell's drinking bouts, or more interesting that the ordination of their father's latest curate, Arthur Nicholls. This apparently dull and unpromising young man had been appointed to Haworth two years before, at the age of twenty-six. Mr Brontë was reasonably pleased with him, but he had not made a favourable impression in the parish, and Charlotte in particular regarded him with dislike. He was an Irishman, of that forbidding, serious and unsupple kind that is bred in the north of hardworking Scottish ancestry. He had been born in Antrim, orphaned in childhood, and brought up by an uncle and aunt at Banagher, where his uncle, Dr Alan Bell, was headmaster of the Royal High School. He had achieved a second class in Divinity at Trinity College, Dublin, and had taken his degree the year before coming to Haworth. He seemed solid, safe, sensible and not at all brilliant. 'Papa has got a new curate lately,' Charlotte had written to Ellen, a few days after he arrived, 'a Mr Nicholls from Ireland—he did duty for the first time on Sunday—he appears a respectable young man, reads well, and I hope will give satisfaction.' His appearance was not arresting, but it was by no means disagreeable. Of middle height, with a pale, serious face framed in a long oval by thick dark hair and whiskers, he made an impression of rather dull sobriety. He was unprepossessingly reserved in manner, but anyone who took his calm demeanour for passivity would have been mistaken; his level gaze could have a startling intensity. It had proved an immense relief to Mr. Brontë, blind as he now was and dreading an inevitable operation for cataract, to have a satisfactory curate, however dull, who could take over most of the burdens of his office, attend every morning at the village school, visit the sick and take a good many of the services; and we may picture Mr Nicholls rising early and donning his surplice with sober regularity, tramping about Haworth in stout boots, and spending his evenings alone in his lodgings at the sexton's, where he ate in solitude, read religious works of a Puseyite flavour, and presumably went to bed early. We may also, perhaps, suppose that that level gaze of his had been turned more often than was absolutely necessary towards Charlotte; often enough, at least, for some lively gossiping glance to intercept it. 'Who,' she had enquired rather tartly of Ellen, 'gravely asked you whether Miss Brontë was not going to be married to her Papa's curate? I scarcely need say that never was rumour more unfounded. It puzzles me to think how it could possibly have originated. A cold far-away sort of civility are the only terms on which I have ever been with Mr. Nicholls. I could by no means think of mentioning such a rumour to him even as a joke. It would make me the laughing-stock of himself and his fellow curates for half a year to come. They regard me as an old maid, and I regard them, one and all, as highly uninteresting specimens of the coarser sex.'

Charlotte's initial indifference, then, was coloured by prejudice. She had already refused offers of marriage from two clergymen, one of whom had been by no means ineligible, and it nettled her that she could be supposed likely to marry this commonplace curate. It was not that she dreamed, by now, of any better match; she had made up her mind, not without bitterness, that she would never marry; if spinsterhood were her lot she must make the best of it. 'I speculate much,' she had written some months earlier to Miss Wooler, 'on the existence of unmarried and never-to-be-married women nowadays, and I have already got to the point of considering that there is no more respectable character on this earth than an unmarried woman who makes her own way through life quietly, perseveringly, without support of husband or brother, and who, having attained the age of 45 or upwards, retains in her possession a well regulated mind, a disposition to enjoy simple pleasures, fortitude to support inevitable pains, sympathy with the sufferings of others, and willingness to relieve want as far as her means extend.' Clearly there was little hope for Mr Nicholls, should he ever conceive the idea of marrying Miss Brontë, and it is probable that he had already, as Mrs Gaskell believed, 'begun his service to her, in the same tender and faithful spirit as that in which Jacob served for Rachel'. She was prejudiced against him, she despised the general run of curates, and his stipend was £100 a year. His ordination as priest, which took place in the September of this disappointing year, raised not the smallest ripple of sympathy or interest.

Charlotte had now finished her novel, *The Professor*, and the parcel of manuscript had started its round of the publishers. She was far from satisfied with the book, which had been written partly as an experiment, partly as an exercise in self-discipline. The experience of the last few years had sobered her; at thirty she had learned to distrust the exuberance of her own imagination, and to believe that the daydreams which had coloured her early work were a dangerous indulgence which conscience compelled her to forgo. In this she was partly right and partly wrong. The luxuriance and violent feeling of the Angrian world lay very near the heart of her inspiration; they were often extravagant and absurd, but they were fertile; needing discipline but not entire suppression. 'I determined to take nature and truth as my sole guides,' she wrote later, when *The Professor* had been finally laid aside as a failure, 'and to follow their very footprints. I restrained imagination, eschewed romance, repressed excitement; overbright colouring, too, I avoided, and sought to produce something which should be soft, grave and true.' The result, though it has charm and value, and though Charlotte herself continued to believe in it, was altogether too quiet for current taste. None of the publishers to whom she sent it considered it worth taking, and the original brown paper of the parcel became complicated with old scored-out addresses, which Charlotte was too innocent to remove. It seemed as though her first novel was to be an even greater failure than the poems.

§ During this summer of 1846, while her literary hopes were waning, an anxiety of another kind was increasing. Her father's eyesight had become seriously impaired by the progress of the cataract which was forming. He was nearly blind. He could grope his way about, and recognise the figures of those he knew well, when they were placed against a strong light; but he could no longer see to read; and thus his eager appetite for knowledge and information of all kinds was severely balked. He continued to preach. I have heard that he was led up into the pulpit, and that his sermons were never so effective as when he stood there, a grey sightless old man, his blind eyes looking out straight before him, while the words that came from his lips had all the vigour and force of his best days. . . . For some time before this autumn, his daughters had been collecting all the information they could respecting the probable success of operations for cataract performed on a person of their father's age. About the end of July, Emily and Charlotte had made a journey to Manchester for the purpose of searching out an operator; and there they heard of the fame of the late Mr Wilson as an oculist. They went to him at once, but he could not tell, from description, whether the eyes were ready for being operated upon or not. It therefore became necessary for Mr Brontë to visit him; and towards the end of August, Charlotte brought her father to him. He determined at once to undertake the operation, and recommended them to comfortable lodgings, kept by an old servant of his. These were in one of numerous similar streets of small monotonous-looking houses, in a suburb of the town. §

A nurse was engaged, and to her anxiety over her father's inevitable suffering Charlotte was obliged to add the worries of an unaccustomed kind of housekeeping, since there were no meals provided in the lodgings, and private nurses, even before the raising of their standard and status by Miss Nightingale, had already a reputation for domestic exigence. 'For ourselves I could contrive—papa's diet is so very simple; but there will be a nurse coming in a day or two, and I am afraid of not having things good enough for her. Papa requires nothing you know but plain beef and mutton, tea and bread and butter; but a nurse will probably expect to live much better.' The morning of the operation was by no means cheered by the arrival of *The Professor* once again in his brown wrapping, accompanied by a curt rejection; but this disappointment passed unnoticed in the general apprehension before the operation, which was necessarily performed without anæsthetic. 'The operation is over,' she wrote finally to Ellen; 'it took place yesterday. . . . The affair lasted precisely a quarter of an hour; it was not the simple operation of couching . . . but the more complicated one of extracting the cataract. . . . Papa displayed extraordinary patience and firmness; the surgeons seemed surprised. I was in the room all the time, as it was his wish that I should be there; of course I neither spoke nor moved till the thing was done, and then I felt that the less I said, either to papa or the surgeons, the better. Papa is now confined to his bed in a dark room, and is not to be stirred for four days; he is to speak and be spoken to as little as possible.'

It was in the little parlour of the Manchester lodgings, with her father lying in a darkened room upstairs, that Charlotte now began to write *Jane Eyre*. The theme had been taking shape in her mind for some time, while *The Professor* was plodding its weary way round London, and now that she found herself in solitude and quiet, with little to distract her, she began to write with all her old imaginative impetus, and at an exhilarating rate. For the whole of the month that was spent in Manchester she worked without pause, oblivious of the outside world, and returned to Haworth with a heavy bundle of manuscript. The absorption and irresistible impetus, this finding herself suddenly and unpredictably 'in the vein', was characteristic of her method of work. She was not a writer who could work daily and steadily, but when the fit was on she could write for long periods at great pressure. Mrs. Gaskell, when she stayed at Haworth, had questioned her with professional curiosity about her working habits, which were very different from her own.

§ She said that it was not every day that she could write. Sometimes weeks or even months elapsed before she felt that she had anything to add to that portion of her story which was already written. Then, some morning she would waken up, and the progress of her tale lay clear and bright before her, in distinct vision. When this was the case, all her care was to discharge her household and filial duties, so as to obtain leisure to sit down and write out the incidents and consequent thoughts, which were, in fact, more present to her mind at such times than her actual life itself. Yet notwithstanding this 'possession' (as it were), those who survive, of her daily and household companions, are clear in their testimony, that never was the claim of any duty, never was the call of another for help, neglected for an instant. It had become necessary to give Tabby—now nearly eighty years of age—the assistance of a girl. Tabby relinquished any of her work with jealous reluctance, and could not bear to be reminded, though ever so delicately, that the acuteness of her senses was dulled by age. The other servant might not interfere with what she chose to consider her exclusive work. Among other things, she reserved to herself the right of peeling the potatoes for dinner; but as she was growing blind, she often left in those black specks, which we in the North call the 'eyes' of the potato. Miss Brontë was too dainty a housekeeper to put up with this; yet she could not bear to hurt the faithful old servant, by bidding the younger maiden go over the potatoes again, and so reminding Tabby that her work was less effectual than formerly. Accordingly she would steal into the kitchen, and quietly carry off the bowl of vegetables, without Tabby's being aware, and, breaking off in the full flow of interest and inspiration in her writing, carefully cut out the specks in the potatoes, and noiselessly carry them back to their place. This little proceeding may show how orderly and fully she accomplished her duties, even at those times when the 'possession' was upon her.

Any one who has studied her writings . . . must have noticed her singular felicity in the choice of words. She herself in writing her books, was solicitous on this point. One set of words was the truthful mirror of her thoughts; no others, however apparently identical in meaning, would do. . . . She would wait patiently searching for the right term, until it presented itself to her. It might be provincial, it might be derived from the Latin; so that it accurately represented her idea, she did not mind whence it came; but this care makes her style present the finish of a piece of mosaic. Each component part, however small, has been dropped into the right place. She never wrote down a sentence until she clearly understood what she wanted to say, had deliberately chosen the words, and arranged them in their right order. Hence it comes that, in the scraps of paper covered with her pencil writing which I have seen, there will occasionally be a sentence scored out, but seldom, if ever, a word or an expression. She wrote on these bits of paper in a minute hand, holding each against a piece of board, such as is used in binding books, for a desk. This plan was necessary for one so short-sighted as she was; and, besides, it enabled her to use pencil and paper, as she sat near the fire in the twilight hours, or if (as was too often the case) she was wakeful for hours in the night. Her finished manuscripts were copied from these pencil scraps, in clear, legible, delicate traced writing, almost as easy to read as print. §
She brought her father home at the end of September. His sight was gradually returning, but it was still uncertain, and he needed constant care. There was little time now for

working on *Jane Eyre*, but the evenings still were long and quiet, and the sisters took possession of the dining-room, as they had in the past, leaving Mr. Brontë to go to bed early and Branwell to his own devices.

§ The sisters retained the old habit, which was begun in their aunt's life-time, of putting away their work at nine o'clock, and beginning their study, pacing up and down the sitting room. At this time, they talked over the stories they were engaged upon, and described their plots. Once or twice a week, each read to the others what she had written, and heard what they had to say about it. Charlotte told me, that the remarks made had seldom any effect in inducing her to alter her work, so possessed was she with the feeling that she had described reality; but the readings were of great and stirring interest to all, taking them out of the gnawing pressure of daily-recurring cares, and setting them in a free place. It was on one of these occasions, that Charlotte determined to make her heroine plain, small, and unattractive, in defiance of the accepted canon. §

In spite of the stimulus of creation, and the new confidence in the work which carried her along, the future still seemed dry and barren, and there was some bitterness in Charlotte's resistance to the temptation (which from time to time now ironically presented itself in the form of teaching offers) to escape from home. 'If I *could* leave home, Ellen, I should not be at Haworth now. I know life is passing away and I am doing nothing—earning nothing—a very bitter knowledge it is at moments; but I see no way out of the mist. More than one very favourable opportunity has now offered which I have been obliged to put aside. Probably when I am free to leave home I shall neither be able to find place nor employment —perhaps too I shall be quite past the prime of life . . . These ideas sting me keenly sometimes—but whenever I consult my conscience it affirms that I am doing right in staying at home. . . . I returned to Brussels after Aunt's death against my conscience—prompted by what then seemed an irresistible impulse; I was punished for my selfish folly by a total withdrawal for more than two years of happiness and peace of mind.' And a little later: 'I shall be thirty-one next birthday. My youth is gone like a dream; and very little use have I ever made of it. What have I done these last thirty years? Precious little.'

The winter of 1846 was bitterly cold. Everyone at the parsonage suffered in turn from colds and influenza. Charlotte and Emily recovered from their various ills as spring approached, but Anne's vitality was visibly diminished. 'Poor Anne has suffered greatly from asthma, but is now, we are glad to say, rather better. She had two nights last week when her cough and difficulty of breathing were painful indeed to hear and witness, and must have been most distressing to suffer; she bore it, as she bears all affliction, without one complaint, only sighing now and then when nearly worn out She has an extraordinary heroism of endurance. I admire, but I certainly could not imitate her.'

The hoped for improvement was short-lived; Anne grew thinner and quieter as the year wore on, and spring was followed by a wet and chilly summer. 'I would fain hope that her health is a little stronger than it was, and her spirits a little better; but she leads much too sedentary a life, and is continually sitting stooping over a book or over her desk. It is with difficulty one can prevail on her to take a walk or induce her to converse. . . .' Nor was Anne's health the only anxiety, for Branwell was being particularly troublesome, owing to the possession of mysterious small sums of money which his sisters believed could come only from Mrs Robinson. The only way to keep him sober was to keep him poor, but he was skilful at wringing sovereigns out of Mr Brontë by threatening suicide; the old man was still weak-minded where Branwell was concerned, and indeed bore most of the burden of his wretched state, sleeping with him in his own bedroom at night, and keeping him with him as far as possible during the day. Branwell had given up all thought of looking for employment, and it was rarely, now, that he attempted to write. He complained to Leyland of spells of 'horror inexpressible, and violent palpitation of the heart. . . . I wish,' he added, 'I could flee to writing as a refuge, but I cannot.' He still persisted in his belief that Mrs Robinson was by now

unk in religious melancholy and withering into a 'patiently
ƿining decline', but he seems no longer to have nursed any
llusions about himself. 'I only know,' he wrote to Leyland,
'that it is time for me to be something when I am nothing.
Then my father cannot have long to live, and that when he
dies, my evening, which is already twilight, will become night.
That I shall then have a constitution still so strong that it will
keep me years in torture and despair when I should every
hour pray that I might die.' Neither he nor anyone else
suspected how drink and opium were preparing the ground
for the seeds of tuberculosis which were in them all. He had
several bad falls about the house and village, occasioned by
fits. 'You must expect to find him weaker in mind,' Charlotte
warned Ellen, who was planning a visit to Haworth, 'and
the complete rake in appearance.' None of them guessed that
he had only a year to live.

In the midst of these anxieties, however, came a heartening
letter. *The Professor,* so often rejected and returned, came
back once more, this time accompanied by a letter so kindly
and encouraging in tone that, as Charlotte afterwards wrote,
'this very refusal cheered the author better than a vulgarly
expressed acceptance would have done.' It came at an auspicious moment. *Jane Eyre* was all but finished, and as the
publishing house in question, Messrs. Smith and Elder, had
expressed an interest in any future work of fiction by Currer
Bell, she made haste to finish it, and sent them the manuscript by rail. Now followed a few days of acute suspense,
concealed with difficulty while Ellen came to stay. Suddenly
everything seemed big with promise. *Wuthering Heights* and
Agnes Grey had, a little before this, and after a long and
weary round, been accepted by the firm of T. C. Newby,
though on rather grudging terms, by which a part of the
expense was to be borne by the authors. Still, it was an
acceptance; and it must have been more than usually difficult to drop no hint of all this hidden excitement. Mr Brontë,
indeed, as he afterwards told Mrs Gaskell, 'had his suspicions of something going on; but, never being spoken to,
he did not speak on the subject, and consequently his ideas
were vague and uncertain, only just prophetic enough to keep

him from being absolutely stunned when, later on, he heard of the success of *Jane Eyre*'.

There was from the beginning no doubt in the minds of the publishers as to the quality of the book. It came first into the hands of Mr W. S. Williams, the firm's reader, who was so vividly impressed that he urged it upon Mr George Smith, the head of the firm, to take home with him for the week-end. Mr Smith began to read it on the Sunday morning, having nothing to do until twelve o'clock, when he had arranged to ride into the country with a friend. 'Before twelve o'clock,' he afterwards recorded, 'my horse came to the door, but I could not put the book down. I scribbled two or three lines to my friend, saying I was very sorry that circumstances had arisen to prevent my meeting him, sent the note off by my groom, and went on reading the MS. Presently the servant came to tell me that luncheon was ready; I asked him to bring me a sandwich and a glass of wine, and still went on with *Jane Eyre*. Dinner came; for me the meal was a very hasty one, and before I went to bed that night I had finished reading the manuscript.' (Since then, countless thousands of readers have gone through this almost hypnotic experience in their first reading of *Jane Eyre*.)

The novel was accepted, and within a month the first bundles of proofs were arriving at the parsonage. Some of these Charlotte was obliged to correct during a brief visit to Ellen, but still nothing was said. The two friends sat on either side of the drawing-room table, the one with her proofs, the other with her needlework, in an exquisite Victorian balance of reticence and discretion. Yet however pleased she was with the prospect of publication, and however warmly the publishers encouraged her, Charlotte's characteristic honesty and caution compelled her to warn them not to expect too much. 'Permit me, Sir,' she wrote to Mr Williams, 'to caution you against forming too favourable an idea of my powers, or too sanguine an expectation of what they can achieve. I am, myself, sensible both of deficiencies of capacity and disadvantages of circumstances which will, I fear, render it somewhat difficult for me to attain popularity as an author. . . . Still, if health be spared and time vouchsafed me, I mean to do my best.'

The printing of *Jane Eyre* went forward while Emily's and Anne's manuscripts lay still in Newby's office, and at length, barely six weeks from the day of its acceptance, the novel appeared. No sign of this tremendous event could be seen at the parsonage. Mr Nicholls came back from his holiday, Branwell got drunk, and nothing seemed changed. 'We are getting on here the same as usual,' Charlotte wrote to Ellen, during this very week, '—only that Branwell has been more than ordinarily troublesome and annoying of late; he leads Papa a wretched life. Mr Nicholls is returned just the same; I cannot for my life see those interesting germs of goodness in him you discovered: his narrowness of mind always strikes me chiefly. I fear he is indebted to your imagination for his hidden treasure.' But in London *Jane Eyre* was already causing excitement, and Thackeray was complaining to Mr Williams that he had lost a whole day in reading it. Like Mr Smith, he felt sure it was a woman's book. 'Who the author can be I can't guess. If a woman she knows her language better than most ladies do, or has had a "classical" education. . . . It is a woman's writing, but whose? Give my respects and thanks to the author, whose novel is the first English one . . . that I've been able to read for many a day.'

The reviewers were more cautious and were slow to commit themselves, being uncertain, as Mrs Gaskell wryly observed, 'as to whether it was safe to praise an unknown author'. But the book's vitality carried it to almost instant success without the critics. Recommendations flew by word of mouth, and in a few weeks the rush began for copies. Speculation as to the identity of the author (for no one believed for a moment in Currer Bell) fanned the flame of interest even higher, and it was gradually borne in on Charlotte that the extraordinary and unexpected had happened at last—she was the author of what would now be called a best-seller.

§ There is little record remaining of the manner in which the first news of its wonderful success reached and affected the one heart of the three sisters. I once asked

Charlotte—we were talking about the description of Lowood school, and she was saying that she was not sure whether she should have written it, if she had been aware how instantaneously it would have been identified with Cowan Bridge—whether the popularity to which the novel attained had taken her by surprise. She hesitated a little, and then said : 'I believed that what had impressed me so forcibly when I wrote it, must make a strong impression on any one who read it. I was not surprised at those who read *Jane Eyre* being deeply interested in it; but I hardly expected that a book by an unknown author could find readers.'

The sisters had kept the knowledge of their literary ventures from their father, fearing to increase their own anxieties and disappointment by witnessing his; for he took an acute interest in all that befell his children, and his own tendency had been towards literature in the days when he was young and hopeful. It was true he did not much manifest his feelings in words; he would have thought that he was prepared for disappointment as the lot of man, and that he could have met it with stoicism; but words are poor and tardy interpreters of feelings to those who love one another, and his daughters knew how he would have borne ill-success worse for them than for himself. So they did not tell him what they were undertaking. He says now that he suspected it all along, but his suspicions could take no exact form, as all he was certain of was, that his children were perpetually writing—and not writing letters. We have seen how the communications from their publishers were received 'under cover to Miss Brontë'. Once, Charlotte told me, they overheard the postman meeting Mr Brontë, as the latter was leaving the house, and inquiring from the parson where one Currer Bell could be living, to which Mr Brontë replied that there was no such person in the parish. . . .

Now, however, when the demand for the work had assured success to *Jane Eyre*, her sisters urged Charlotte to tell their father of its publication. She accordingly went into his study one afternoon after his early dinner, carrying with her a copy of the book, and one or two reviews, taking care to include a notice adverse to it.

She informed me that something like the following conversation took place between her and him. (I wrote down her words the day after I heard them; and I am pretty sure they are quite accurate.)

'Papa, I've been writing a book.'

'Have you, my dear?'

'Yes, and I want you to read it.'

'I am afraid it will try my eyes too much.'

'But it is not in manuscript; it is printed.'

'My dear! you've never thought of the expense it will be! It will be almost sure to be a loss, for how can you get a book sold? No one knows you or your name.'

'But, papa, I don't think it will be a loss; no more will you, if you will just let me read you a review or two, and tell you more about it.'

So she sat down and read some of the reviews to her father; and then, giving him the copy of *Jane Eyre* that she intended for him, she left him to read it. When he came in to tea, he said, 'Girls, do you know Charlotte has been writing a book, and it is much better than likely?' §

XII : THE TASTE OF FAME

From this time, pride in Charlotte's achievement was to be the chief pleasure and solace of Mr Brontë's old age. Of all his brilliant children, she alone was the one to taste success, and he eagerly gathered up every crumb of praise. Mrs Gaskell was touched, when she visited him after Charlotte's death, by his collection of newspaper articles and reviews, of which there was 'hardly any notice, however short and clumsily worded, in any obscure provincial paper, but what has been cut out and carefully ticketed with its date by the poor, bereaved father,—so proud when he first read them—so desolate now'. There were many such trophies to preserve, for the success of *Jane Eyre* went far beyond anything anyone expected, and public interest was further stimulated by the unknown authorship. Mrs Gaskell believed that Charlotte persisted in keeping her secret because she had promised her sisters it should never be revealed through her, and it is certainly true that Emily's resistance to the idea of confiding in anyone was angry and violent. But Charlotte had other reasons for remaining unknown. Anonymity gave her freedom to express the warmth, the poetry, the depth of feeling that were in her, and which were hidden behind the austere front she presented to the world. Besides, her portraits of living people were too recognisable to be safe. 'If I were known,' she wrote to W. S. Williams, 'I should ever be conscious in writing that my book would be read by ordinary acquaintances, and that idea would fetter me intolerably.'

§ Henceforward Charlotte Brontë's existence becomes divided into two parallel currents—her life as Currer Bell, the author; her life as Charlotte Brontë, the woman. There were separate duties belonging to each character—not opposing each other; not impossible, but difficult to be reconciled. When a man becomes an author, it is probably merely a change of employment to him. He takes a portion of that time which has hitherto been devoted to some other study or pursuit; he gives up something of the legal or medical profession, in which he has hitherto endeavoured to serve others, or relinquishes part of the trade or business by which he has been striving to gain a livelihood; and another merchant or lawyer, or doctor, steps into his vacant place, and probably does as well as he. But no other can take up the quiet, regular duties of the daughter, the wife, or the mother, as well as she whom God has appointed to fill that particular place: a woman's principal work in life is hardly left to her own choice; nor can she drop the domestic charges devolving on her as an individual, for the exercise of the most splendid talents that were ever bestowed. And yet she must not shrink from the extra responsibility implied by the very fact of her possessing such talents. She must not hide her gift in a napkin; it was meant for the use and service of others. In an humble and faithful spirit must she labour to do what is not impossible, or God would not have set her to do it. §

Her life as an author had its practical difficulties, which Mrs Gaskell, who knew what it was to write in the midst of a busy household and in the small leisure snatched from domestic life, very well understood; it brought, however, compensating satisfactions of a sort which Mrs Gaskell had long enjoyed, but which in Charlotte's life were wonderfully new.

First and best of these was the free exchange of ideas with intellectual equals, particularly with W. S. Williams, whose sympathetic and serious intelligence made him the ideal partner in a stimulating and voluminous correspondence; and she was soon exchanging letters as well with G. H. Lewes, Thackeray and other literary men. 'I cannot thank you sufficiently for your letters,' she told Williams, 'and I can give you but a faint idea of the pleasure they afford me; they seem to introduce such light and life to the torpid retirement where we live like dormice.' It is in this new character as an author, discussing with other writers the things that interested her, that we see an aspect of Charlotte's mind that was withheld from Ellen. She was far from being the narrow and sententious prig that her detractors have sometimes represented. Even to Miss Wooler, writing soon after the abdication of Louis Philippe, she was now able to express unorthodox views on the subject of war that are more in tune with present-day moods than with the mid-nineteenth century. 'I have now outlived youth; and, though I dare not say that I have outlived all its illusions . . . yet, certainly, many things are not what they were ten years ago : and, amongst the rest, "the pomp and circumstance of war" have quite lost in my eyes their fictitious glitter. I have still no doubt that the shock of moral earthquakes wakens a vivid sense of life, both in nations and individuals; that the fear of dangers on a broad national scale, diverts men's minds momentarily from brooding over small private perils, and for the time gives them something like largeness of views; but, as little doubt have I, that convulsive revolutions put back the world in all that is good, check civilisation, bring the dregs of society to its surface; in short, it appears to me that insurrections and battles are the acute diseases of nations, and that their tendency is to exhaust, by their violence, the vital energies of the countries where they occur.'

To G. H. Lewes, who had written a valuable appreciation of *Jane Eyre*, but who was apparently disposed to scold her, as an author, privately, she replied with spirit, though without ever abandoning her native diffidence or forgetting for a moment the respect she felt she owed as a beginner to an established novelist. 'I mean to observe your warning about being careful how I undertake new works; my stock of materials is not abundant, but very slender; and, besides, neither my experience, my acquirements, nor my powers, are sufficiently varied to justify my ever becoming a frequent writer. I tell you this, because your article in *Frazer* left in me an uneasy impression that you were disposed to think better of the author of *Jane Eyre* than that individual deserved; and I would rather you had a correct than a flattering opinion of me, even though I should never see you.

'If I ever *do* write another book, I think I will have nothing of what you call "melodrama"; I think so, but I am not sure. I *think*, too, I will endeavour to follow the counsel which shines out of Miss Austen's "mild eyes", "to finish more and be more subdued"; but neither am I sure of that. When authors write best, or, at least, when they write most fluently, an influence seems to waken in them, which becomes their master —which will have its own way—putting out of view all behests but its own, dictating certain words, and insisting on their being used, whether vehement or measured in their nature; new-moulding characters, giving unthought of turns to incidents, rejecting carefully-elaborated old ideas, and suddenly creating and adopting new ones.

'Is it not so? And should we try to counteract this influence? Can we indeed counteract it?'

Lewes's holding up Jane Austen as a model genuinely puzzled her. Her own temperament, warm, poetical, inclining less to restraint than to extravagance, made her curiously unperceptive of the other's genius. 'Why do you like Miss Austen so very much? I am puzzled on that point. . . . I had not seen *Pride and Prejudice* till I read that sentence of yours, and then I got the book. And what did I find? An accurate daguerreotyped portrait of a commonplace face; a carefully-fenced, highly-cultivated garden, with neat borders and delicate flowers; but no glance of a bright vivid physiognomy, no open country, no fresh air, no blue hill, no bonny beck. I should hardly like to live with her ladies and gentlemen, in their elegant but confined houses.' Two temperaments less in harmony than Jane Austen's and Charlotte Brontë's would be difficult to imagine, and try as she might she could not accept Lewes's advice that she should discipline imagination to Miss Austen's exquisite degree. 'Imagination,' she reminded him, 'is a strong, restless faculty, which claims to be heard and exercised : are we to be quite deaf to her cry, and insensate to her struggles? When she shows us bright pictures, are we never to look at them, and try to reproduce them? And when she is eloquent, and speaks rapidly and urgently in our ea., are we not to write to her dictation?' She could not yield, on a point so fundamental, even to Lewes : but to Williams she showed a diffidence, a grasp of her own abilities and a distrust of their success, which reveal a simple but unusual mental honesty. 'I am afraid,' she told him, in a letter discussing Lewes, 'if he knew how much I write from intuition, how little from actual knowledge, he would think me presumptuous ever to have written at all.'

The success of *Jane Eyre*, however, was so plainly demonstrated that she began to feel some confidence, and when early in 1848 a second edition was prepared, took courage to dedicate it to Thackeray. She had had, as yet, no personal contact with him, but she admired him above all other living novelists, and his praise of *Jane Eyre* encouraged her to pay this innocent compliment. The result was unfortunate. Unknown to either Miss Brontë or her publishers, Thackeray's wife had been kept under restraint for some years, and the dedication started excited gossip connecting Thackeray with Mr Rochester, and speculating still more eagerly about Currer Bell, who must clearly have been one of the Thackerays' governesses. This discovery caused acute embarrassment, and Charlotte was horrified by the thought that Thackeray might suppose her to know of his misfortune, or even to have had him in mind when she wrote her novel. His kind letter, however, thanking her for the 'enormous compliment', and exonerating her from any knowledge of his concerns, reassured without entirely comforting her. 'The very fact of his not complaining at all,' she wrote miserably to Williams, 'and addressing me with such kindness, notwithstanding the pain and annoyance I must have caused him, increases my chagrin.

I could not half express my regret to him in my answer, for I was restrained by the consciousness that that regret was just worth nothing at all—quite valueless for healing the mischief I had done.'

Wuthering Heights and *Agnes Grey* had at last been published, after months of irritating delay, and only now, as their authors suspected, because the publishers hoped to reap some benefit from the fame of Currer Bell. They caused no stir. *Agnes Grey* was mildly commended by a few reviewers, but *Wuthering Heights,* though it sold tolerably, affected most of its readers with moral distaste. There can have been few literary reputations which have risen to such posthumous heights as Emily Brontë's, but it was impossible for her to know success during her life. Her spirit was almost totally, though unconsciously, out of tune with her time. Her un-sentimental harshness was condemned, the simple grandeur of her prose unnoticed, her innocence misunderstood. She remains, even after a hundred years, so mysterious a genius that this failure to reach the ear of her contemporaries is not surprising. Mrs Gaskell perfectly reflected early Victorian educated taste when she mentioned in passing that *Wuthering Heights* had 'revolted many readers by the power with which wicked and exceptional characters are depicted.' She was will-ing to concede its genius, but obviously felt it to be an unpleasant and freakish book. Even Charlotte's opinion, based on a far greater depth of understanding and on a recognition of Emily's genius that never wavered, is qualified by doubts that perhaps the book would have been better left unwritten. Charlotte loved Emily, and understood her as far as anyone could; she was unable, it is true, to penetrate her spiritual reserve and grieved over this failure; but she knew her stature as a novelist, essayist and poet, and came nearer than any other critic of their generation to a true guess at the nature of Emily's genius. She never swerved from the opinion that it was far greater than her own, and that she possessed rare qualities as a poet; she was also sufficiently sensitive to Emily's prose, and her clear and logical handling of abstract subjects, to write to W. S. Williams, 'I should say Ellis will not be seen in his full strength till he is seen as an essayist.' Mrs Gaskell, who after all was not writing Emily's biography, contented herself with quoting a passage from Charlotte's preface to the second edition of *Wuthering Heights*, which appeared after Emily's death, and made no further attempt to unravel the mystery surrounding her character and nearly everything she wrote; and in trying to reach some understanding of her curious genius we cannot begin better than by examining Charlotte's considered opinion of her sister's work, since everything that Charlotte wrote on the subject has the value of knowledge, at least a partial understanding, and a great sincerity.

'Had Ellis Bell,' wrote Charlotte in her preface, 'been a lady or a gentleman accustomed to what is called "the world", her view of a remote and unreclaimed region, as well as of the dwellers therein, would have differed greatly from that actually taken by the homebred country girl. Doubtless it would have been wider—more comprehensive : whether it would have been more original or more truthful is not so certain. . . . I am bound to avow that she had scarcely more practical knowledge of the peasantry amongst whom she lived, than a nun has of the country people who sometimes pass her convent gates. My sister's disposition was not naturally gregarious; circumstances favoured and fostered her tendency to seclusion : except to go to church or take a walk on the hills, she rarely crossed the threshold of home. Though her feeling for the people round her was benevolent, intercourse with them she never sought; nor, with very few exceptions, ever experienced. And yet she knew them : knew their ways, their language, their family histories; she could hear of them with interest, and talk of them with detail, minute, graphic, and accurate; but *with* them, she rarely exchanged a word. Hence it ensued that what her mind had gathered of the real concerning them, was too exclusively confined to those tragic and terrible traits of which, in listening to the secret annals of every rude vicinage, the memory is sometimes compelled to receive the impress. Her imagination, which was a spirit more sombre than sunny, more powerful than sportive, found in such traits material whence it wrought creations like Heathcliff, like Earnshaw, like Catherine. Having formed these beings she did not know what she had done. If the auditor of her work when read in manuscript, shuddered under the grinding influence of natures so relentless and implacable, of spirits so lost and fallen; if it was complained that the mere hearing of certain vivid and fearful scenes banished sleep by night, and disturbed mental peace by day, Ellis Bell would wonder what was meant, and suspect the complainant of affectation. Had she but lived, her mind would of itself have grown like a strong tree, loftier, straighter, wider-spreading, and its matured fruits would have attained a mellower ripeness and sunnier bloom; but on that mind time and experience alone could work: *to the influence of other intellects, it was not amenable.*'

Charlotte herself was to some degree horrified by Heathcliff, and by the air of elemental evil which breathes through the wildness and poetry of the tale, and she felt bound to apologise to the public and explain—an act of piety for which she has been laughed at since. Nevertheless her summing up of the emotional effect of *Wuthering Heights* has great imaginative truth, and has scarcely been bettered by the many critics and scholars who have attempted the same task since. '*Wuthering Heights* was hewn in a wild workshop, with simple tools, out of homely materials. The statuary found a granite block on a solitary moor; gazing thereon, he saw how from the crag might be elicited a head, savage, swart, sinister; a form moulded with at least one element of grandeur—power. He wrought with a rude chisel, and from no model but the vision of his meditations. With time and labour, the crag took human shape; and there it stands colossal, dark, and frowning, half statue, half rock: in the former sense, terrible and goblin-like; in the latter, almost beautiful, for its colouring is of mellow grey, and moorland moss clothes it; and heath, with its blooming bells and balmy fragrance, grows faithfully close to the giant's foot.'

There have been innumerable theories about Emily Brontë; most of them would have amazed and some disgusted her.

She has inspired cults as extravagant as the neglect of her contemporaries was blind; yet she founded no school; neither *Wuthering Heights* nor her poetry has had successors. The reason for this lies surely in a fact that Charlotte knew—her material was solely the vision of her meditations. Her concern was less with the world about her than with the abstract and the philosophical, though she would not have expressed it in those terms. Her preoccupation was less with men and women, of whom she knew little, than with God and the soul, with problems of good and evil; and on these she had brooded much. Her poems and few surviving essays reveal a mind extraordinarily innocent and independent, an imagination darkened by an awareness of evil, free alike from sentimentality and optimism. Her view of mandkind was, for some reason that we shall never know, profoundly pessimistic; she saw little good in humanity and she expected little; in life, as in her work, she professed no real allegiance to her own kind; she relied upon herself and on her conception of God. The experiences which formed her unique personality are out of our reach; we can never know what they were, or what it was that so early turned her imagination inwards and caused her to refuse the ordinary demands of life, as no doubt she did refuse them. We can only speculate, believing as we now do that some loss of love in childhood, some sense of inadequacy, some suspicion or fear that love will be refused, are among the commonest causes of that turning inward, that refusal of ordinary life which can take many remarkable neurotic forms, and of which Emily Brontë provides a singular example. Where there is also genius, as in her case, and a capacity for passion, the mind must discover its own satisfactions, on a secure and private level. The escape which Emily found in childhood so perfectly answered her imaginative needs that in time it was made to serve her emotionally as well. Her experience, passionate and innocent, lay in a world which she alone controlled, and which was therefore safe. No rebuff, no loss of love could touch her on this level, where she demanded nothing that she herself could not satisfy. It is from states of mind like this that the recluse, the stoic, and often the hero are made; also the mystic, whose ecstasy lies in sole communion with God; and Emily Brontë contained elements of all these. To the influence of other intellects she was not amenable. She was not one 'on the recesses of whose mind and feelings, even those nearest and dearest to her could, with impunity, intrude unlicensed'. 'Stronger than a man, simpler than a child, her nature stood alone.' This compulsive necessity to rely on herself in everything, on the rest of the world in nothing, was to cause her sisters acute unhappiness at the time of her illness and death; it was also responsible for those mysterious longings which undoubtedly led into some form of mystical experience.

The word 'mystic' is generally so loosely used that it is desirable to know what we mean when we speak specifically of mystical experience. Briefly, it is here taken to mean a sense of direct knowledge of or communion with God—Eternity—the Unseen—the Absolute; a state of mind achieved deliberately, with great difficulty, and only as a result of considerable self-discipline. It is a state of mind impossible to describe except metaphorically, which is perhaps why mystics of all ages and all creeds have been driven to describe their experience in the language of love. It is a process and a means of ecstasy so rare that it has never evolved a language of its own. It is a form of trance; there is a partial suspension of consciousness not unlike that experienced in hypnosis, but it differs from other forms of self-induced trance in that it has a mounting ecstasy and crisis, and there is often considerable distress as consciousness returns. The emotion at its peak is one of spiritual exaltation, usually expressed in terms of union and love; indeed, it cannot be described otherwise, and it is possible to maintain that the experience is closer to that of sexual love than many people are willing to believe.

The mystics who have tried to record their experiences have shown a sufficient similarity in most of their descriptions to make it clear that mystic ecstasy is a valid experience which can be achieved by many types of people. It is not necessarily religious, though the emotions it satisfies are also those that are fed by religious experience, and it is usually associated with it, even among those primitive peoples who achieve their ecstasies through fasting and various drugs. It seems always to follow the same course, through meditation and concentration, and what St Theresa of Avila calls 'the sleep of the mental faculties', to the final ecstasy; and it is illuminating to compare St Theresa's own accounts with Emily Brontë's. 'The soul,' wrote St Theresa, describing the ecstasy, 'seems to leave the organs which she animates. . . . She falls into a sort of swoon. . . . It is only with the greatest effort that she can make the slightest movement with her hands. The eyes close of themselves, and if they are kept open, they see almost nothing. . . . If spoken to, the soul hears the sound of the voice, but no distinct word.' This state is evidently very close to that self-induced hypnotic trance which many types of people are able to attain, either spontaneously or after learning a technique; it implies a degree of physical and mental relaxation so complete that consciousness becomes extremely thin, or is suspended altogether; and if the conscious emotions at the moment of entering trance are concentrated on the idea of spiritual union with God, or with some force greater than self, the adept is occasionally able to reach rapture. There seems no doubt that Emily Brontë, alone at night in the little closet-like bedroom which had once been the children's study and was now her securest retreat, did reach something of the same experience, though her account of it—marvellously expressive and perhaps the closest description of mystical experience that we have—does not precisely identify the union achieved as being with God. The Unseen, the Invisible, a messenger of Hope—she avoids the conventional religious terms, and seems to feel that the spirit of her communion is too huge and abstract to be pinned down by any name.

> He comes with western winds, with evening's wandering
> airs,
> With that clear dusk of heaven that rings the thickest
> stars;
> Winds take a pensive tone, and stars a tender fire,
> And visions rise and change which kill me with desire—

Desire for nothing known in my maturer years,
When joy grew mad with awe at counting future tears;
When, if my spirit's sky was full of flashes warm,
I knew not whence they came, from sun or thunderstorm;

But first a hush of peace, a soundless calm descends;
The struggle of distress and fierce impatience ends;
Mute music soothes my breast—unuttered harmony
That I could never dream till earth was lost to me.

Then dawns the Invisible, the unseen its truth reveals;
My outward sense is gone, my inward essence feels—
Its wings are almost free, its home, its harbour found;
Measuring the gulf it stoops and dares the final bound!

Oh, dreadful is the check, intense the agony
When the ear begins to hear and the eye begins to see;
When the pulse begins to throb, the brain to think again,
The soul to feel the flesh and the flesh to feel the chain!

Yet I would lose no sting, would wish no torture less;
The more that anguish racks the earlier it will bless;
And robed in fires of Hell, or bright with heavenly shine,
If it but herald Death, the vision is divine.

This wonderful poem, like nearly all of Emily's that remain, is embedded in the Gondal mass and does not stand alone. It is part of a longer poem which in Emily's manuscript is headed 'Julian M. and A. G. Rochelle', and the verses quoted above are put into the mouth of a young female prisoner in a dungeon. There is no clue to suggest that they describe Emily's personal experience; none, save the fact that the stanzas leap suddenly to life in the midst of pages of Gondal verse on a very pedestrian level. There is a force and conviction about them, a ring of truth which makes it difficult to accept them as purely invented for one of the Gondal heroines; and the poem describes a spiritual adventure so rare that it seems unlikely to have been inspired by anything less vital than inner knowledge. Yet this method of interpreting Emily's poems by their 'feeling' is a dangerous one. If we accept the mystical poem as to the fruit of personal experience, what right have we to reject the beautiful lyric which in her manuscript is headed 'R. Alcona to J. Brenzaida', and which begins

> Cold in the earth, and the deep snow piled above thee!
> Far, far removed, cold in the dreary grave!
> Have I forgot, my Only Love, to love thee,
> Severed at last by Time's all-wearing wave?"

It is as profoundly moving as the other, and at least one of her biographers has built on it a structure so ambitious that it collapsed finally in laughter; the discovery of Emily's lover, 'Louis Parensell', who in the end turned out to be 'Love's Farewell' in Charlotte's handwriting, has been the nicest of unconscious jests in Brontë research. Yet reject it we must, if we are to demand even the smallest shred of evidence before accepting a poem as autobiographical. Emily, like Charlotte and Branwell, was potentially capable of passion, and to no common degree; but because of the peculiarities of her nature this passion could be liberated only on an imaginative level, on its own terms of primitive freedom and innocence. The griefs of love are more easily imagined by poets, even by the few who have no actual experience, than the stages of mystical ecstasy; which perhaps in the last analysis is our only reason for accepting the mystical stanzas and rejecting the love lament as poems of experience.

There seem to be some grounds for believing that Emily may have begun a second novel after the publication of *Wuthering Heights,* but, as with every other speculation about her, we have no proof. The only scrap of possible evidence is a single letter, found in Emily's little folding writing desk many years after her death, and in two slight references in Charlotte's letters. The letter is from T. C. Newby, and although it was not in its envelope when found, there was an empty envelope in the desk addressed to 'Ellis Bell Esq' in the same hand, and the letter is folded to fit into it. Many people believe that it was addressed to Acton Bell, whose second novel, *The Tenant of Wildfell Hall*, was published by Newby in July 1848, six months after the date of this letter; but nothing else relating to Anne was found in Emily's desk, and the existence of the envelope proves that Emily was at least in communication with her publisher.

'Dear Sir,—

I am much obliged by your kind note and shall have great pleasure in making arrangements for your next novel. I would not hurry its completion for I think you are quite right not to let it go before the world until well satisfied with it, for much depends on your next work. If it be an improvement on your first you will have established yourself as a first-rate novelist, but if it falls short the critics will be too apt to say that you have expended your talent in your first novel. I shall therefore have pleasure in accepting it upon the understanding that its completion be at your own time.

'Believe me, my dear Sir,
Yrs. sincerely,
T. C. Newby.'

Feb. 15. 1848

Nine months later, when Emily was in her last illness, Charlotte wrote to George Smith that Emily was 'too ill to occupy herself with writing', which seems to suggest that if she were *not* ill there was at least writing on hand; and to W. S. Williams, less than two weeks before Emily's death, 'Ellis Bell is at present in no condition to trouble himself with thoughts either of writing or publishing. Should it please Heaven to restore his health and strength, he reserves to himself the right of deciding whether or not Mr Newby has forfeited every claim to his second work.'

These references, though not conclusive, do suggest that Emily was at work on a second novel when she died. What became of the manuscript, if it ever existed, we shall perhaps never know, as we shall probably also never know what happened to the Gondal prose chronicles. Whether Emily herself destroyed them, or laid such an obligation, in the event of her death, upon Anne; whether Charlotte thought it prudent to burn them after the deaths of her sisters (this seems unlikely); or whether they are still lying undiscovered in some forgotten cupboard, we cannot tell. It is just possible that the first part of a second novel by Emily may yet come to light, and one can imagine few more interesting literary discoveries. Hers is so mysterious a genius, so strangely lacking in any bridge across the chasm which divides her work from what we know of her life, that the world would seize with eagerness on such a discovery. Even the five surviving essays which she wrote during her Brussels period for M Heger have recently been translated and published, and minutely examined by scholars for crumbs of knowledge. Nothing that she wrote can be without interest, and these essays give us a further insight into her melancholy, pessimistic, misanthropic, unsentimental, profoundly religious and independent nature. How much more eagerly should we seize on the second work of which Charlotte wrote, and which it is not impossible to believe may still be in existence.

The Tenant of Wildfell Hall, on which Anne had been tenaciously at work for many months, was finished in June 1848 and accepted by T. C. Newby for publication. This time there was no delay, and as well as hurrying the sheets through the press the enterprising publisher made a bargain with an American firm, which announced the book as a successor to *Jane Eyre* and a new work by Currer Bell, Mr Newby having privately passed the word that Currer, Ellis and Acton Bell were really one and the same person. This news was hastily sent back to London by the American house which had genuinely entered into agreement with Smith and Elder for Currer Bell's new novel, with demands for an explanation; and Smith and Elder wrote to Haworth, asking, courteously enough, to have the matter made clear.

Here was a dilemma. Charlotte was still protecting their incognito with a determination that had led her into downright untruthfulness to Ellen. "I have given *no one* a right either to affirm, or to hint, in the most distant manner, that I was "publishing",' she wrote, rather too vehemently, when Ellen had mentioned a local rumour that Miss Brontë had written a novel, and disingenuously assured her friend that 'you are authorised by Miss Brontë to say, that she repels and disowns every accusation of the kind'. Yet she could not allow her kind and honourable publishers to suspect that the three pseudonyms were a cover for any sort of literary chicanery. On this the three sisters were indignantly agreed, and they determined on a personal demonstration to both publishers.

§ With rapid decision, they resolved that Charlotte and Anne should start for London that very day, in order to prove their separate identity to Messrs. Smith and Elder, and demand from the credulous publisher his reasons for a 'belief' so directly at variance with an assurance which had several times been given to him. Having arrived at this determination, they made their preparations with resolute promptness. There were many household duties to be performed that day; but they were all got through. The two sisters each packed up a change of dress in a small box, which they sent down to Keighley by an opportune cart; and after early tea, they set off to walk thither—no doubt in some excitement; for, independently of the cause of their going to London, it was Anne's first visit there. A great thunderstorm overtook them on their way that summer evening to the station; but they had no time to seek shelter. They only just caught the train at Keighley, arrived at Leeds, and were whirled up by the night train to London.

About eight o'clock on the Saturday morning, they arrived at the Chapter Coffee-house, Paternoster Row— a strange place, but they did not well know where else to go. . . . In Mr Brontë's few and brief visits to town, during his residence at Cambridge, and the period of his curacy in Essex, he had stayed at this house; hither he had brought his daughters, when he was convoying them to Brussels; and here they came now, from very ignorance where else to go. It was a place solely frequented by men; I believe there was but one female servant in the house. Few people slept there; some of the stated meetings of the Trade were held in it, as they had been for more than a century; and, occasionally country booksellers, with now and then a clergyman, resorted to it; but it was a strange desolate place for the Miss Brontës' to have gone to, from its purely business and masculine aspect. The old 'grey-haired elderly man', who officiated as waiter, seems to have been touched from the very first with the quiet simplicity of the two ladies, and he tried to make them feel comfortable and at home in the long, low, dingy room up-stairs, where the meetings of the Trade were held. The high narrow windows looked into the gloomy Row; the sisters, clinging together on the most remote window-seat . . . could see nothing of motion, or of change, in the grim, dark houses opposite, so near and close, although the whole breadth of the Row was between. The mighty roar of London was round them, like the sound of an unseen ocean, yet every footfall on the pavement below might be heard distinctly, in that unfrequented street. . . .

When they had been discussing their project in the quiet of Haworth Parsonage the day before, and planning the mode of setting about the business on which they were going to London, they had resolved to take a cab, if they should find it desirable, from their inn to Cornhill; but, amidst the bustle and 'queer state of inward excitement' in which they found themselves, as they sat and considered their position on the Saturday morning, they quite forgot even the possibility of hiring a conveyance; and when they set forth, they became so dismayed by the crowded streets, and the impeded crossings, that they stood still repeatedly, in complete despair of making progress, and were nearly an hour in walking the half-mile they had to go. Neither Mr Smith nor Mr Williams knew that they were coming; they were entirely unknown to the publishers of *Jane Eyre*, who were not, in fact, aware whether the 'Bells' were men or women, but had always written to them as to men. § The bizarre interview which followed was fully described by Charlotte in a letter to Mary Taylor, who, unlike Ellen Nussey, had been taken into confidence about the identity of the Bells (perhaps because she was at a safe enough distance, in New Zealand) and knew that Charlotte was the author of *Jane Eyre*. 'We found 65 to be a large bookseller's shop, in a street almost as bustling as the Strand. We went in, walked up to the counter. There were a great many young men and lads here and there; I said to the first I could accost, "May I see Mr Smith?" He hesitated, looked a little surprised. We sat down and waited a while, looking at some books on the counter. . . . At last we were shown up to Mr Smith. "Is it Mr Smith?" I said, looking up through my spectacles at a tall young man. "It is." I then put his own letter into his hand, directed to Currer Bell. He looked at it and then at me again. "Where did you get this?" he said. I laughed at his perplexity; a recognition took place. I gave my real name: Miss Brontë. We were in a small room, ceiled with a great skylight, and there explanations were rapidly gone into; Mr Newby being anathematised, I fear, with undue vehemence. Mr Smith hurried out and returned quickly with one whom he introduced as Mr Williams, a pale, mild, stooping man of fifty. . . . Another recognition and a long, nervous shaking of hands. Then followed talk—talk—talk.'

Mr Smith also, though later, recorded his impressions. Anne Brontë he saw as a 'gentle, quiet, rather subdued person, by no means pretty, yet of a pleasing appearance. Her manner was curiously expressive of a wish for protection and encouragement, a kind of constant appeal which invited sympathy.' Charlotte's appearance struck him as 'interesting rather than attractive. She was very small, and had a quaint, old-fashioned look. Her head seemed too large for her body. She had fine eyes, but her face was marred by the shape of the mouth and by the complexion. There was but little feminine charm about her; and of this fact she herself was uneasily and perpetually conscious. It may seem strange that the possession of genius did not lift her above the weakness of an excessive anxiety about her personal appearance. But I believe she would have given all her genius and her fame to have been beautiful. Perhaps few women ever existed more anxious to be pretty than she, or more angrily conscious of the circumstance that she was *not* pretty.'

Mr Smith pressed the two ladies to come and stay at his house, but this they declined. 'We returned to our inn, and I paid for the excitement of the interview by a thundering headache and harrassing sickness. Towards evening, as I got no better and expected the Smiths to call, I took a strong dose of sal volatile. It roused me a little; still, I was in grievous bodily case when they were announced. They came in, two elegant young ladies, in full dress, prepared for the Opera—Mr Smith himself in evening costume, white gloves etc. We had by no means understood that it was settled we were to go to the Opera, and were not ready. Moreover, we had no fine, elegant dresses with us, or in the world. However . . . I thought it would be wise to make no objections; I put my headache in my pocket, we attired ourselves in the plain, high-made country garments we possessed, and went with them to their carriage, where we found Mrs Williams. They must have thought us queer, quizzical-looking beings, especially me with my spectacles. I smiled inwardly at the contrast, which must have been apparent, between me and Mr Smith as I walked with him up the crimson-carpeted staircase of the Opera House and stood amongst a brilliant throng at the box door, which was not yet open. Fine ladies and gentlemen glanced at us with a slight, graceful superciliousness quite warranted by the circumstances. Still, I felt pleasantly excited in spite of headache and sickness and conscious clownishness, and I saw Anne was calm and gentle, which she always is.'

The following day, Sunday, Mr Williams took them to church, and in the afternoon Mr Smith called in his carriage with his mother, and took them off to dine at his house in Bayswater. 'The rooms, the drawing-room especially, looked splendid to us. There was no company—only his mother, his two grown-up sisters, and his brother, a lad of twelve or thirteen, and a little sister, the youngest of the family, very like himself. . . . We had a fine dinner, which neither Anne nor I had appetite to eat, and were glad when it was over. I always feel under an awkward constraint at table. Dining out would be hideous to me.' The next day they visited the Royal Academy and the National Gallery, dined again at Mr Smith's and had tea with Mr Williams and his family. They also at some time during the visit saw and reproached Mr Newby, though there is no record of this interview, and one gets the impression that the strain of all these social encounters was so great that by this time they had all but lost sight of the original reason for their visit. 'I was thin when I went,' Charlotte told Mary, 'but was meagre indeed when I returned; my face looked grey and very old, with strange, deep lines ploughed in it; my eyes stared unnaturally.' Nevertheless, they had taken an exciting and important step, and there was much on which they could now look back with pleasure. There was to be little enough that was pleasant in the months to come.

XIII : DEATH OF BRANWELL,
EMILY AND ANNE

If Charlotte found herself feverish and exhausted after the London visit, she was not the only one whose health had suffered. Branwell was noticeably worse. 'His constitution seems much shattered. Papa, and sometimes all of us, have sad nights with him. He sleeps most of the day, and consequently will lie awake at night. But has not every house its trial?' It had been, indeed, with influenza and Charlotte's 'bilious fever', a bad year, and Mr Brontë worried perpetually about the unhealthiness of the place.

§ There is no doubt that the proximity of the crowded churchyard rendered the Parsonage unhealthy, and occasioned much illness to its inmates. Mr Brontë represented the unsanitary state of Haworth pretty forcibly to the Board of Health; and, after the requisite visits from their officers, obtained a recommendation that all future interments in the churchyard should be forbidden, a new graveyard opened on the hillside, and means set on foot for obtaining a water-supply to each house, instead of the weary, hard-worked housewives having to carry every bucketful, from a distance of several hundred yards, up a steep street. But he was baffled by the rate-payers; as, in many a similar instance, quantity carried it against quality, numbers against intelligence. And thus we find that illness often assumed a low typhoid form in Haworth, and fevers of various kinds visited the place with sad frequency. §

It was not, however, the proximity of the graveyard which was destroying Branwell, but the old enemy, tuberculosis, which had now become active in a body weakened by long dissipation, and was making its rapid, easy, unsuspected advance. Nobody seems to have realised quite how ill he was, though he kept to his bed a good deal, saw various doctors from time to time, and talked openly of death; but he had done all these things, at intervals, for so long that they were now ignored. His old friend of the railway days, Francis Grundy, still came occasionally to Haworth, and has left a curiously moving account of his last interview with Branwell, who rose from his bed one evening in order to join his friends at the 'Black Bull'. (Grundy represents the interview as having taken place a few days before Branwell's death, whereas it was really in 1846, fully two years before. In this, as in other matters, Grundy is an interesting, but suspect witness.) 'Presently a door opened cautiously, and a head appeared. It was a mass of red, unkempt, uncut hair, wildly floating round a great, gaunt forehead; the cheeks yellow and hollow, the mouth fallen, the thin white lips not trembling but shaking, the sunken eyes, once small, now glaring with the light of madness—all told the sad tale but too surely. I hastened to my friend, greeted him in my gayest manner, as I knew he best liked, drew him quickly into the room, and forced upon him a stiff glass of hot brandy. Under its influence, and that of the bright, cheerful surroundings, he looked frightened—frightened of himself. He glanced at me for a moment, and muttered something of leaving a warm bed to come out into the cold night. Another glass of brandy, and returning warmth gradually brought him back to something like the Brontë of old. He even ate some dinner, a thing which he said he had not done for long; so our last interview was pleasant, though grave. I never knew his intellect clearer. He described himself as waiting anxiously for death—indeed, longing for it, and happy, in these his sane moments, to think that it was so near. He once again declared that that death would be due to the story I knew, and to nothing else.'

The end, when at last it came, was sudden. Two days before his death he was in the village; the following day he took to his bed, and on Sunday morning, the 24th of September, died after a brief and painful struggle. Mrs Gaskell was told, by 'one who attended Branwell in his last illness', that he insisted on standing up to die, and that his pockets were full of Mrs Robinson's letters. According to Charlotte, however, he was conscious at the moment of death, and for the last two days had returned almost to his old gentle and affectionate character—'the peculiar change which frequently precedes death'. He had joined in the prayers which Mr Brontë offered at his bedside, murmuring a quiet Amen. 'How unusual that word appeared from his lips,' wrote Charlotte to Mr Williams, 'of course you who did not know him, cannot conceive.' The rake and the unbeliever fell away in those last hours, giving the grieving father and sisters a parting glimpse of the Branwell they had lost many years before.

Mr Brontë was prostrated by grief and shock. 'My poor father naturally thought more of his *only* son than of his daughters, and, much and long as he had suffered on his account, he cried out for his loss like David for that of Absalom—my son! my son!—and refused at first to be comforted.' At this very crisis Charlotte, too, failed, being overtaken by that mysterious 'bilious fever' which was her worst enemy, and which now laid her low to such a degree that the doctor was urgently recalled. At length, however, calm succeeded the turmoil of this unhappy week; Mr Brontë summoned his old resolution in the face of loss, and Charlotte slowly recovered. 'It is not permitted us to grieve for him who is gone as others grieve for those they lose,' she wrote. '. . . I do not weep from a sense of bereavement—there is no prop withdrawn, no consolation torn away, no dear companion lost—but for the wreck of talent, the ruin of promise, the untimely dreary extinction of what might have been a burning and a shining light. My brother was a year my junior. I had aspirations and ambitions for him once, long ago—they have perished mournfully. Nothing remains of him but a memory of errors and sufferings. There is such a bitterness of pity for his life and death, such a yearning for the emptiness of his whole existence, as I cannot describe.'

Is there anything else to be said of Branwell, withdrawing at the age of thirty-one from a life which had fallen grotesquely into ruin? Nothing, perhaps, if there had not been an attempt made, nearly twenty years after his death, to acclaim him as the author of *Wuthering Heights*. This claim receives little attention today, since it has been thoroughly examined and discredited;[1] but because it has left a faint miasma of doubt in the minds of many it is perhaps worth while to glance again at the story.

In 1876 a Mr William Dearden (the same who, ten years earlier, had attacked Mrs Gaskell and attempted to discredit her portrait of Mr Brontë, much to Mr Brontë's annoyance) wrote a second letter to *The Halifax Guardian*, this time to make the curious revelation that Branwell, not Emily, had written *Wuthering Heights,* and had once read the first chapters aloud to Dearden and other friends in a public-house. Dearden and Branwell had, according to this tale, each agreed to write a poetic drama, and to meet again in a month's time to compare 'the results of our lucubrations'. At this second meeting Branwell produced some pages of manuscript from his hat, and found that by mistake he had brought the beginnings of a prose work, a novel. He read this instead, and Dearden, after twenty years, felt suddenly sure that what he had read had been the beginning of *Wuthering Heights.* To prove his case he quoted from a doggerel poem of his own, describing the event, which he claimed had been written at the time, but which internal evidence shows to have been written many years later. In short, the story rests on Dearden's evidence alone; that evidence contains contradictions which give it an air of having been twisted or contrived to suit

[1] Notably by Miss Irene Cooper-Willis in *The Brontës* (Duckworth, 1933), and *The Authorship of Wuthering Heights*, which appeared in *The Trollopian* of 1947.

his purpose; and the whole long letter gives an inescapable impression of having been written to draw attention to William Dearden through his old acquaintance with the Brontës, and to an unpublished drama of his own, which he claimed had been written in competition with Branwell.

The only support of Dearden's story comes from another doubtful source, F. H. Grundy. In 1879, after spending twenty years in Australia, he wrote and published his recollections of Branwell in a book called *Pictures of the Past*. It contains many inaccuracies and misrepresentations, so that, knowing already his quality as a witness, one is bound to accept with reserve his statement that at his first visit to the parsonage 'Patrick Brontë declared to me, and what his sister said bore out the assertion, that he wrote a great portion of *Wuthering Heights* himself'. At the time of this visit *Wuthering Heights* was not yet published, and together with *Agnes Grey* was making a discouraging round of the London publishers. Grundy, however, does not mention this, and speaks of the book as though it were already before the public.

Among Branwell's literary remains there is a prose fragment of about 23,000 words which it is useful to compare with *Wuthering Heights*, since it was apparently written at about the same time. This fragment, *And the Weary are at Rest*, has been printed in the Transactions of the Brontë Society, and is available to anyone interested in making the comparison. It provides a contrast which must for ever dispose of Dearden's and Grundy's claims, far more effectually even than the contradictions and inaccuracies of their stories; for Branwell's fragment is a bewildering tangle of bombast, as different from the clear, certain, dramatic prose of *Wuthering Heights* as anything could well be. Yet it is just possible that it was this manuscript which Branwell took out of his hat, since one of the characters in it is a psalm-smiting dialect-speaking Yorkshire manservant whom Dearden's memory, more than twenty years later, may have identified with the Joseph of *Wuthering Heights*.

Neither Dearden nor Grundy was ever able to suggest any reason why Charlotte and Emily should have conspired together to deceive the world, and indeed the texture of their story is very flimsy. Any one of a number of situations may have given rise to it. *Wuthering Heights* may have grown out of an earlier story which Branwell and Emily had planned or discussed together, in the days before disaster had overtaken him. He may equally well have picked up some pages of Emily's manuscript by mistake, and have irresponsibly passed them off as his own. Or he may have claimed, to Grundy, that part of his sister's unpublished novel had been written by himself, rather than make the humiliating confession that he alone of all the family had produced nothing. There are other possibilities of this kind, but that Branwell himself wrote *Wuthering Heights* is not one of them. He must have known that his sisters were writing steadily, and as late as 1847 may even have known something of the contents and themes of their novels; but by the time, late in the same year, that their first books were published, Branwell was so far gone in his *dégringolade* that they are unlikely to have confided their secret to him. (They would in any case have been unwise to do so if they wanted their anonymity preserved.) This theory —that Branwell knew something about their novels in their early stages, but by the time of publication was no longer in his sisters' confidence—perhaps explains an apparent contradiction between Dearden's and Grundy's stories and Charlotte's version of the matter. 'My unhappy brother,' she told Williams, 'never knew what his sisters had done in literature— he was not aware that they had ever published a line. We could not tell him of our efforts for fear of causing him too deep a pang of remorse for his own time misspent, and talents misapplied. Now he will never know.'

A far more dreadful loss had soon to be endured. Emily caught cold at Branwell's funeral, and soon her hard, obstinate cough, her loss of appetite, her restless nights and feverish days began to cause Charlotte and Anne painful anxiety. Charlotte herself was still far from well; her recent illness and the depression following Branwell's death, and now her deep uneasiness about Emily, drained her vitality and made creative work impossible. *Shirley,* the new novel which had been making steady progres, was laid aside. 'Both head and hand,' she told Williams, 'seem to have lost their cunning; imagination is pale, stagnant, mute. This incapacity chagrins me; sometimes I have a feeling of cankering care on the subject, but I combat it as well as I can; it does no good.' It was impossible to free her mind from apprehension.

'Emily's cold and cough are very obstinate. I fear she has pain in her chest, and I sometimes catch a shortness in her breathing, when she has moved at all quickly. She looks very thin and pale. Her reserved nature occasions me great uneasiness of mind. It is useless to question her; you get no answers. It is still more useless to recommend remedies; they are never adopted. Nor can I shut my eyes to Anne's great delicacy of constitution. The late sad event has, I feel, made me more apprehensive than common. I cannot help feeling much depressed sometimes.' The great difficulty, where Emily was concerned, lay in herself. Ruthlessly self-sufficient, incapable of opening her heart or confessing a weakness, she fought her illness with the most dangerous weapon she could find, by disregarding it. Mind, according to her experience, had almost limitless authority over matter. It could create a world in which she moved at ease; induce an exaltation as passionate as love; now it should conjure sickness out of sight. This was the test of power. Every expression of concern, every offer of help she rejected angrily, as a species of betrayal. 'I would fain hope that Emily is a little better this evening, but it is difficult to ascertain this. She is a real stoic in illness; she neither seeks nor will accept sympathy. To put any questions, to offer any aid, is to annoy; she will not yield a step before pain or sickness till forced; not one of her ordinary avocations will she voluntarily renounce. You must look on and see her do what she is unfit to do, and not dare to say a word—a painful necessity for those to whom her health and existence are as precious as the life in their veins. When she is ill there seems to be no sunshine in the world for me. The tie of sister is near and dear indeed, and I think a certain harshness in her powerful and peculiar character only makes me cling to her more.'

'The details of her illness,' Charlotte recorded later, in one of the most moving passages she ever wrote, 'are deep-branded in my memory, but to dwell on them, either in thought or narrative, is not in my power. Never in all her life had she lingered over any task that lay before her, and she did not linger now. She sank rapidly. She made haste to leave us. Yet, while physically she perished, mentally she grew stronger than we had yet known her. Day by day, when I saw with what a front she met suffering, I looked on her with an anguish of wonder and love. I have seen nothing like it; but, indeed, I have never seen her parallel in anything. Stronger than a man, simpler than a child, her nature stood alone. The awful point was, that while full of ruth for others, on herself she had no pity; the spirit was inexorable to the flesh; from the trembling hand, the unnerved limbs, the faded eyes, the same service was exacted as they had rendered in health. To stand by and witness this, and not dare to remonstrate, was a pain no words can render.'

§ In fact, Emily never went out of doors after the Sunday succeeding Branwell's death. She made no complaint; she would not endure questioning; she rejected sympathy and help. Many a time did Charlotte and Anne drop their sewing, or cease from their writing, to listen with wrung hearts to the failing step, the laboured breathing, the frequent pauses, with which their sister climbed the short staircase; yet they dared not notice what they observed, with pangs of suffering even deeper than hers. They dared not notice it in words, far less by the caressing assistance of a helping arm or hand. They sat still and silent. §

In the midst of this miserable anxiety the sisters' little volume of poems was issued again, this time by Smith and Elder, who had somewhat quixotically bought it from the original publisher. It made no stir, and Charlotte, though disappointed, was not surprised that the critics dismissed her own poems; what still amazed her was their blindness to the genius of Emily. 'Blind is he as any bat,' she complained of the *Spectator's* critic, 'insensate as any stone, to the merits of Ellis. He cannot feel or will not acknowledge that the very finish and *labor limae* which Currer wants, Ellis has; he is not aware that the "true essence of poetry" pervades his compositions. Because Ellis's poems are short and abstract, the critics think them comparatively insignificant and dull. They are mistaken.'

Emily said little about the unfavourable reviews, either of her poems or of *Wuthering Heights,* but she cut out four or five from the newspapers and concealed them in her desk. A particularly hostile notice from the *North American Review* provoked no comment but a smile; but Charlotte came to believe that Emily had been more deeply wounded by this type of criticism than she would admit. The *North American Review* is worth reading; there is no mincing the matter there. What a bad set the Bells must be! What appalling books they write! Today, as Emily appeared a little easier, I thought the "Review" would amuse her, so I read it aloud to her and Anne. As I sat between them at our quiet but now somewhat melancholy fireside, I studied the two ferocious authors. Ellis, the "man of uncommon talents, but dogged, brutal and morose", sat leaning back in his easy chair drawing his impeded breath as best he could, and looking, alas! piteously pale and wasted; it is not his wont to laugh, but he smiled half amused and half in scorn as he listened. Acton was sewing, no emotion ever stirs him to loquacity, so he only smiled too, dropping at the same time a single word of calm amazement to hear his character so darkly portrayed. I wonder what the reviewer would have thought of his own sagacity could he have beheld the pair as I did.'

One of the factors which make the death of Emily, and indeed of Anne, such painful reading, is the contemporary ignorance of tuberculosis and its treatment. Today, when the proportion of complete cures is encouragingly high, it is understood that total rest—the complete immobilisation of the patient in bed, with even the smallest unnecessary movement forbidden—is as important a condition as fresh air. A tuberculous lung is 'healed' by the infected part being sealed off from the rest, and the most natural method of bringing this about is by innumerable fine adhesions which are liable to form when the lung has long periods of rest. These adhesions are as fine as the threads of a spider's web; the smallest movement can break them, destroying the work of weeks; and it has been observed that the highest proportion of cures is found among those who are submitted to rigid hospital discipline in this respect. Emily Brontë, involved as she was in her mysterious defiance, refused to lie in bed at all, or even to rest. She would consult no doctor; when one was brought to the house she refused to see him, and the medicines he prescribed she would not take; but had she been less intractable it is unlikely that the Haworth physician could have helped her. So, between ignorance and obstinacy, Emily made her own death tragically certain, and allowed no cry for help to escape her until it was too late.

At Mr Williams's suggestion Charlotte wrote for advice to a homœopathic physician, and gave him an exact description of Emily's symptoms. 'A peculiar reserve of character renders it difficult to draw from her all the symptoms of her malady, but as far as they can be ascertained they are as follows: Her appetite failed; she evinced a continual thirst, with a craving for acids, and required a constant change of beverage. In appearance she grew rapidly emaciated; her pulse —the only time she allowed it to be felt—was found to be 115 per minute. The patient usually appeared worse in the forenoon, she was then frequently exhausted and drowsy; towards evening she often seemed better. Expectoration accompanies the cough. The shortness of breath is aggravated by the slightest exertion. The patient's sleep is supposed to be tolerably good at intervals, but disturbed by paroxysms of coughing. Her resolution to contend against illness being very fixed, she has never consented to lie in bed for a single day —she sits up from 7 in the morning till 10 at night. All medical aid she has rejected, insisting that Nature should be left to take her own course. She has taken no medicine, but occasionally a mild aperient and Locock's cough wafers. . . . Her diet, which she regulates herself, is very simple and light. The patient has hitherto enjoyed pretty good health, though she has never looked strong, and the family constitution is not supposed to be robust. Her temperament is highly nervous. She has been accustomed to a sedentary and studious life.'

While she waited for the physician's answer, Charlotte shrinkingly faced the idea of Emily's death.

§ 'I told you Emily was ill, in my last letter. She has not

rallied yet. She is *very* ill. I believe, if you were to see her, your impression would be that there is no hope. A more hollow, wasted, pallid aspect I have not beheld. The deep tight cough continues; the breathing after the least exertion is a rapid pant; and these symptoms are accompanied by pains in the chest and side. Her pulse, the only time she allowed it to be felt, was found to beat 115 per minute. In this state she resolutely refuses to see a doctor; she will give no explanation of her feelings, she will scarcely allow her feelings to be alluded to. Our position is, and has been for some weeks, exquisitely painful. God only knows how all this is to terminate. More than once, I have been forced boldly to regard the terrible event of her loss as possible, and even probable. But nature shrinks from such thoughts. I think Emily seems the nearest thing to my heart in the world.'

When a doctor had been sent for, and was in the very house, Emily refused to see him. Her sisters could only describe to him what symptoms they had observed; and the medicines which he sent she thrust aside, denying that she was ill.

'I hardly know what to say to you about the subject which now interests me the most keenly of anything in this world, for in truth, I hardly know what to think myself. Hope and fear fluctuate daily. The pain in her side and chest is better; the cough, the shortness of breath, the extreme emaciation continue. I have endured, however, such tortures of uncertainty on this subject that, at length, I could endure it no longer; and as her repugnance to seeing a medical man continues immutable,—as she declares "no poisoning doctor" shall come near her,—I have written unknown to her, to an eminent physician in London, giving as minute a statement of her case and symptoms as I could draw up, and requesting an opinion. I expect an answer in a day or two. . . .'

But Emily was growing rapidly worse. I remember Miss Brontë's shiver at recalling the pang she felt when, after having searched in the little hollows and sheltered crevices of the moors for a lingering spray of heather—just one spray, however withered—to take in to Emily, she saw that the flower was not recognised by the dim and indifferent eyes. Yet, to the last, Emily adhered tenaciously to her habits of independence. She would suffer no one to assist her. Any effort to do so roused the old stern spirit. One Tuesday morning, in December, she arose and dressed herself as usual, making many a pause, but doing everything for herself, and even endeavouring to take up her employment of sewing: the servants looked on, and knew what the catching, rattling breath, and the glazing of the eye too surely foretold; but she kept at her work; and Charlotte and Anne, though full of unspeakable dread, had still the faintest spark of hope. On that morning Charlotte wrote thus,—probably in the very presence of her dying sister:—

'I should have written to you before, if I had had one word of hope to say; but I have not. She grows daily weaker. The physician's opinion was expressed too obscurely to be of use. He sent some medicine, which she would not take. Moments so dark as these I have never known. I pray for God's support to us all. Hitherto He has granted it.'

The morning drew on to noon. Emily was worse: she could only whisper in gasps. Now, when it was too late, she said to Charlotte, 'If you will send for a doctor, I will see him now.' About two o'clock she died.

'Emily suffers no more from pain or weakness now. She never will suffer more in this world. She is gone, after a hard, short conflict. She died on *Tuesday*, the very day I wrote to you. I thought it very possible she might be with us still for weeks; and a few hours afterwards, she was in eternity. Yes; there is no Emily in time or on earth now. Yesterday we put her poor, wasted, mortal frame quietly under the church pavement. We are very calm at present. Why should we be otherwise? The anguish of seeing her suffer is over; the spectacle of the pains of death is gone by; the funeral day is past. We feel she is at peace. No need now to tremble for the hard frost and the keen wind. Emily does not feel them. She died in a time of promise.

We saw her taken from life in its prime. But it is God's will, and the place where she is gone is better than that she has left.

'God has sustained me, in a way that I marvel at, through such agony as I had not conceived. I now look at Anne, and wish she were well and strong; but she is neither, nor is Papa. Could you now come to us for a few days? . . . Try to come. I never so much needed the consolation of a friend's presence. Pleasure, of course, there would be none for you in the visit, except what your kind heart would teach you to find in doing good to others.'

As the old, bereaved father and his two surviving children followed the coffin to the grave, they were joined by Keeper, Emily's fierce, faithful bull-dog. He walked alongside of the mourners, and into the church, and stayed quietly there all the time that the burial service was being read. When he came home, he lay down at Emily's chamber door, and howled pitifully for many days. . . . §

The parsonage was now sad and quiet indeed: a 'dreary calm' lay on everything like a frost. The weather was bitterly cold. 'Some sad comfort I take,' wrote Charlotte on Christmas Day, 'as I hear the wind blow and feel the cutting keenness of the frost, in knowing that the elements bring her no more suffering—their severity cannot reach her grave—her fever is quieted, her restlessness soothed, her deep, hollow cough is hushed for ever; we do not hear it in the night or listen for it in the morning; we have not the conflict of the strangely strong spirit and the fragile frame before us—relentless conflict—once seen, never to be forgotten. . . . My father says to me almost hourly, "Charlotte, you must bear up—I shall sink if you fail me". . . . The sight too of my sister Anne's very still but deep sorrow wakens in me such fear for her that I dare not falter. Somebody *must* cheer the rest.

'So I will not now ask why Emily was torn from us in the fulness of our attachment, rooted up in the prime of her own days, in the promise of her powers—why her existence now lies like a field of green corn trodden down—like a tree in full bearing, struck at the root. I will only say, sweet is rest after labour and calm after tempest, and repeat again and again that Emily knows that now.'

There was no respite from anxiety after Emily's death, for the same symptoms soon revealed themselves in Anne, and with heavy heart Charlotte turned to nursing this last sister. In this struggle, which before long she had to recognise as hopeless, she was at least spared the agony of helplessness which Emily had imposed. Anne was a docile invalid, anxious to do everything that might sensibly be done. She consulted the Haworth doctor, and another more eminent physician who was summoned from Leeds, patiently submitting to the blisters, plasters and nauseous oils that they prescribed.

§ All through this illness of Anne's, Charlotte had the comfort of being able to talk to her about her state; a comfort rendered inexpressibly great by the contrast which it presented to the recollection of Emily's rejection of all sympathy. If a proposal for Anne's benefit was made, Charlotte could speak to her about it, and the nursing and dying sister could consult with each other as to its desirability. §

The physician from Leeds had examined Anne with a stethoscope, and announced the fact that both lungs were affected. He held out little hope. Her decline was gentler and less rapid than Emily's, and her suffering less; yet it was apparent from the beginning what the end must be; and Charlotte, looking into the past, realised with misery that she might even have foreseen it long ago. 'All the days of this winter have gone by darkly and heavily like a funeral train; since September sickness has not quitted the house—it is strange —but I suspect now all this had been coming on for years. Unused any of us to the possession of robust health, we have not noticed the gradual approaches of decay; we did not know its symptoms; the little cough, the small appetite, the tendency to take cold at every variation of atmosphere have been regarded as things of course. I see them in another light now.'

The bitter Yorkshire winter dragged on, and the doctors

refused to sanction Anne's removal to a warmer place. Until the cold weather was past it would be dangerous to travel. Charlotte summoned what patience and fortitude she could, and tried to still her tortured imagination. 'This is not the time to regret, dread, or weep. What I have and ought to do is very distinctly laid out for me; what I want, and pray for, is strength to perform it. The days pass in a slow, dark march; the nights are the test; the sudden wakings from restless sleep, the revived knowledge that one lies in her grave, and another not at my side, but in a separate and sick bed.' She was haunted by the nightmare of Emily's death; it came between her and her daily tasks; it was more terrible even than the fear of losing Anne. 'I cannot forget Emily's death day. It becomes a more fixed—a darker, a more frequently recurring idea than ever. It was very terrible: she was torn conscious, panting, reluctant though resolute out of a happy life. But it *will not do* to dwell on these things.'

In the midst of these painful preoccupations she scarcely felt a wounding attack which appeared in the *Quarterly Review,* in which the writer pronounced that the author of *Jane Eyre,* if a woman, 'must be one who for some sufficient reason has long forfeited the society of her sex'. Smith and Elder were indignant, but she herself was too numbed with misery to care. 'I read the *Quarterly* without a pang—except that I thought there were some sentences disgraceful to the critic.' She was working desultorily, when she had the heart, on *Shirley,* but it was weary work, and she missed the stimulus of Emily's criticism. Her most pressing preoccupation was the question of Anne's being taken to Scarborough for the sea air. Anne longed for this, and believed that it was the one measure that might save her. She even came out of her reserve so far as to write to Ellen Nussey, begging for her company, since it was taken for granted that Charlotte could not leave Mr Brontë. 'The doctors say that change of air or removal to a better climate would hardly ever fail of success in consumptive cases, if the remedy be taken *in time*; but the reason why there are so many disappointments is that it is generally deferred till it is too late. Now I would not commit this error; and to say the truth, though I suffer much less from pain and fever than I did when you were with us, I am decidedly weaker, and very much thinner. . . . Under these circumstances, I think there is no time to be lost. I have no horror of death : if I thought it inevitable, I think I could quietly resign myself to the prospect, in the hope that you, dear Miss Nussey, would give as much of your company as you possibly could to Charlotte, and be a sister to her in my stead. But I wish it would please God to spare me not only for Papa's and Charlotte's sakes, but because I long to do some good in the world before I leave it. I have many schemes in my head for future practice, humble and limited indeed, but still I should not like them all to come to nothing, and myself to have lived to so little purpose.'

It was now April, and still cold; the doctors urged her to wait for warmer weather, but Anne felt herself growing daily weaker, and was impatient of delay. It was difficult to know what to do : Ellen's relations were unwilling to let her go, and their reason was painfully present in everyone's mind : Anne might die at Scarborough. At last, however, the spring weather came, and Ellen obtained permission from her family. Mr Brontë, too, decided that he could be left with the two servants, so that Charlotte could go with them. Charlotte prepared for the journey with a sinking heart, haunted by the knowledge that Anne was dying. 'She wonders, I believe, why I don't talk more about the journey : it grieves me to think she may even be hurt by my seeming tardiness. She is very much emaciated . . . her arms are no thicker than a little child's. The least exertion brings a shortness of breath. She goes out a little every day, but we creep rather than walk.'

§ May had come, and brought the milder weather longed for; but Anne was worse for the very change. A little later on, it became colder, and she rallied, and poor Charlotte began to hope that, if May were once over, she might last for a long time. Miss Brontë wrote to engage the lodgings at Scarborough,—a place which Anne had formerly visited with the family to whom she was governess. They took a good-sized sitting-room, and an airy double-bedded room (both commanding a sea-view), in one of the best situations of the town. Money was as nothing in comparison with life; besides, Anne had a small legacy left to her by her godmother, and they felt that she could not better employ this than in obtaining what might prolong life, if not restore health. . . .

The two sisters left Haworth on Thursday, May 24th. They were to have done so the day before, and had made an appointment with their friend to meet them at the Leeds station, in order that they might all proceed together. But on Wednesday morning Anne was so ill, that it was impossible for the sisters to set out; yet they had no means of letting their friend know of this, and she consequently arrived at the Leeds station at the time specified. There she sate waiting for several hours. . .

The next day she could bear the suspense no longer, and set out for Haworth, reaching there just in time to carry the feeble, fainting invalid into the chaise which was waiting to take them down to Keighley. The servant who stood at the Parsonage gates, saw Death written on her face, and spoke of it. Charlotte saw it and did not speak of it,—it would have been giving the dread too distinct a form; and if this last darling yearned for the change to Scarborough, go she should, however Charlotte's heart might be wrung by impending fear. The lady who accompanied them, Charlotte's beloved friend of more than twenty years, has kindly written out for me the following account of the journey—and of the end. . . .

'The first stage of our journey was to York; and here the dear invalid was so revived, so cheerful, and so happy, we drew consolation, and trusted that at least temporary improvement was to be derived from the change which *she* had so longed for, and her friends had so dreaded for her.

'By her request they went to the Minister, and to her it was an overpowering pleasure; not for its own imposing and impressive grandeur only, but because it brought to her susceptible nature a vital and overwhelming sense of omnipotence. She said, while gazing at the structure, "If finite power can do this, what is the . . .?" and here emotion stayed her speech, and she was hastened to a less exciting scene.

'Her weakness of body was great, but her gratitude for every mercy greater. After such exertion as walking to her bed-room, she would clasp her hands and raise her eyes in silent thanks, and she did this not to the exclusion of wonted prayer, for that too was performed on bended knee, ere she accepted the rest of her couch.

'On the 25th we arrived at Scarborough; our dear invalid having, during the journey, directed our attention to every prospect worthy of notice.

'On the 26th she drove on the sands for an hour; and lest the poor donkey should be urged by its driver to a greater speed than her tender heart thought right, she took the reins, and drove herself. When joined by her friend, she was charging the boy-master of the donkey to treat the poor animal well. She was ever fond of dumb things, and would give up her own comfort for them.

'On Sunday, the 27th, she wished to go to church, and her eye brightened with the thought of once more worshipping her God amongst her fellow-creatures. We thought it prudent to dissuade her from the attempt, though it was evident her heart was longing to join in the public act of devotion and praise.

'She walked a little in the afternoon, and meeting with a sheltered and comfortable seat near the beach, she begged we would leave her, and enjoy the various scenes near at hand, which were new to us but familiar to her. She loved the place, and wished us to share her preference.

'The evening closed in with the most glorious sunset ever witnessed. The castle on the cliff stood in proud glory gilded by the rays of the declining sun. The distant ships glittered like burnished gold; the little boats near the beach heaved on the ebbing tide, inviting occupants. The view was grand beyond description. Anne was drawn in her easy chair to the window, to enjoy the scene with us. Her face became illumined almost as much as the glorious scene she gazed upon. Little was said, for it was plain that her thoughts were driven by the imposing view before her to penetrate forwards to the regions of unfading glory. She again thought of public worship, and wished us to leave her, and join those who were assembled at the House of God. We declined, gently urging the duty and pleasure of staying with her, who was now so dear and so feeble. On returning to her place near the fire, she conversed with her sister upon the propriety of returning to their home. She did not wish it for her own sake, she said: she was fearing others might suffer more if her decease occurred where she was. She probably thought the task of accompanying her lifeless remains on a long journey was more than her sister could bear—more than the bereaved father could bear, were she borne home another, and a third tenant of the family-vault in the short space of nine months.

'The night was passed without any apparent accession of illness. She rose at seven o'clock, and performed most of her toilet herself, by her expressed wish. Her sister always yielded such points, believing it was the truest kindness not to press inability when it was not acknowledged. Nothing occurred to excite alarm till about 11 a.m. She then spoke of feeling a change. She believed she had not long to live. Could she reach home alive, if we prepared immediately for departure? A physician was sent for. Her address to him was made with perfect composure. She begged him to say "How long he thought she might live;—not to fear speaking the truth, for she was not afraid to die". The doctor reluctantly admitted that the angel of death was already arrived, and that life was ebbing fast. She thanked him for his truthfulness, and he departed to come again very soon. She still occupied her easy chair, looking so serene, so reliant: there was no opening for grief as yet, though all knew the separation was at hand. She clasped her hands, and reverently invoked a blessing from on high; first upon her sister, then upon her friend, to whom she said, "Be a sister in my stead. Give Charlotte as much of your company as you can." She then thanked each for her kindness and attention.

'Ere long the restlessness of approaching death appeared, and she was borne to the sofa; on being asked if she were easier, she looked gratefully at her questioner, and said, "It is not *you* who can give me ease, but soon all will be well, through the merits of our Redeemer." Shortly after this, seeing her sister could hardly restrain her grief, she said, "Take courage, Charlotte; take courage." Her faith never failed, and her eye never dimmed till about two o'clock, when she calmly and without a sigh passed from the temporal to the eternal. So still, and so hallowed were her last hours and moments. There was no thought of assistance or of dread. The doctor came and went two or three times. The hostess knew that death was near, yet so little was the house disturbed by the presence of the dying, and the sorrow of those so nearly bereaved, that dinner was announced as ready, through the half-opened door, as the living sister was closing the eyes of the dead one.' §

Crushed though she was by this final loss, it was still not so terrible as the nightmare memory of Emily's death. 'Her quiet, Christian death did not rend my heart as Emily's stern, simple, undemonstrative end did. I let Anne go to God, and felt He had a right to her. I could hardly let Emily go. I wanted to hold her back then, and I want her back now. Anne, from her childhood, seemed preparing for an early death. Emily's spirit seemed strong enough to bear her to fulness of years. They are both gone, and so is poor Branwell, and Papa has now me only—the weakest, puniest, least promising of his six children. Consumption has taken the whole five. For the present Anne's ashes rest apart from the others. I have buried her here at Scarboro', to save Papa the anguish of the return and a third funeral.'

Mr. Brontë wrote urging Charlotte not to come home immediately, but to stay for a while longer at the sea with Ellen. Accordingly they went to Filey, then to Ellen's friends near Bridlington. At the end of June they parted, and Charlotte came home.

'All was clean and bright waiting for me. Papa and the servants were well; and all received me with an affection which should have consoled. The dogs seemed in strange ecstasy. I am certain they regarded me as the harbinger of others. The dumb creatures thought that as I was returned, those who had been so long absent were not far behind.

'I left Papa soon, and went into the dining-room: I shut the door—I tried to be glad that I was come home. I have always been glad before—except once—even then I was cheered. But this time joy was not to be the sensation. I felt that the house was all silent—the rooms were all empty. I remembered where the three were laid—in what narrow dark dwellings—never more to reappear. So the sense of desolation and bitterness took possession of me. The agony that *was to be undergone*, and *was not* to be avoided, came on. I underwent it, and passed a dreary evening and night, and a mournful morrow; to-day I am better.

'I do not know how life will pass, but I certainly do feel confidence in Him who has upheld me hitherto. Solitude may be cheered, and made endurable beyond what I can believe. The great trial is when evening closes and night approaches. At that hour, we used to assemble in the dining-room—we used to talk. Now I sit by myself—necessarily I am silent. I cannot help thinking of their last days, remembering their sufferings, and what they said and did, and how they looked in mortal affliction. Perhaps all this will become less poignant in time. . . .'

July 14th, 1849.

'I do not much like giving an account of myself. I like better to go out of myself, and talk of something more cheerful. My cold, wherever I got it, whether at Easton or elsewhere, is not vanished yet. It began in my head, then I had a sore throat, and then a sore chest, with a cough, but only a trifling cough, which I still have at times. The pain between my shoulders likewise amazed me much Say nothing about it, for I confess I am too much disposed to be nervous. This nervousness is a horrid phantom. I dare communicate no ailment to Papa; his anxiety harasses me inexpressibly.

'My life is what I expected it to be. Sometimes when I wake in the morning, and know that Solitude, Remembrance, and Longing are to be almost my sole companions all day through—that at night I shall go to bed with them, that they will long keep me sleepless—that next morning I shall wake to them again,—sometimes, Nell, I have a heavy heart of it. But crushed I am not, yet; nor robbed of elasticity, nor of hope, nor quite of endeavour. I have some strength to fight the battle of life. I am aware, and can acknowledge, I have many comforts, many mercies. Still I can *get on*. But I do hope and pray, that never may you, or any one I love, be placed as I am. To sit in a lonely room—the clock ticking loud through a still house—and have open before the mind's eye the record of the last year, with its shocks, sufferings, losses—is a trial.

'I write to you freely, because I believe you will hear me with moderation—that you will not take alarm or think me in any way worse off than I am.'

XIV: CHARLOTTE ALONE

Fame as a writer, the golden dream of youth to all the Brontës, came to Charlotte in those years of her life which were laid waste by loneliness. The five years which followed her sisters' deaths were her years of celebrity; her liveliest years, in which she tasted success and experienced a little of the pleasures of the world; but they are also years in which solitude, sickness and despair recur like a refrain. Success could no longer give her the pleasure she had dreamed of; the most it could do was to nourish the will to survive.

§ She went on with her work steadily. But it was dreary to write without any one to listen to the progress of her tale, —to find fault or to sympathise,—while pacing the length of the parlour in the evenings, as in the days that were no more. Three sisters had done this,—then two, the other sister dropping off from the walk,—and now one was left desolate, to listen for echoing steps that never came,—and to hear the wind sobbing at the windows, with an almost articulate sound. §

The novel which had been begun while Anne and Emily were alive was now the only interest she had, and she drove herself to it with the desperation of a mind which dares not be idle. *Shirley* is her least attractive work, being built on a foundation of acquired fact rather than springing from the warmer source of personal emotion. Charlotte's imagination was not one that could be nourished on social history. For perhaps this very reason, however, the writing of *Shirley* sustained her now, when a more emotional theme might have failed her. The idea of *Shirley* had not been spontaneously generated; she had deliberately, as she told Mrs Gaskell, 'sought a subject for her next work', and had found it in the recent history of industrial rioting which had still been matter for stirring anecdote when she was a schoolgirl at Roe Head.

§ She was anxious to write of things she had known and seen; and among the number was the West Yorkshire character, for which any tale laid among the Luddites would afford full scope. In *Shirley* she took the idea of most of her characters from life, although the incidents and situations were, of course, fictitious. She thought that if these last were purely imaginary, she might draw from the real without detection, but in this she was mistaken; her studies were too closely accurate. This occasionally led her into difficulties. People recognised themselves, or were recognised by others, in her graphic descriptions of their personal appearance, and modes of action and turns of thought; though they were placed in new positions, and figured away in scenes far different to those in which their actual life had been passed. . . . The 'three curates' were real living men, haunting Haworth and the neighbouring district; and so obtuse in perception that, after the first burst of anger at having their ways and habits chronicled was over, they rather enjoyed the joke of calling each other by the names she had given them. 'Mrs Pryor' was well known to many who loved the original dearly. The whole family of the Yorkes were, I have been assured, almost daguerreotypes. Indeed, Miss Brontë told me that before publication, she had sent those parts of the novel in which these remarkable persons are introduced, to one of the sons; and his reply, after reading it, was simply that 'she had not drawn them strong enough'. From those many-sided sons, I suspect, she drew all that there was of truth in the characters of the heroes of her first two works. They, indeed, were almost the only young men she knew intimately, besides her brother.

The character of Shirley herself, is Charlotte's representation of Emily. I mention this, because all that I, a stranger, have been able to learn about her has not tended to give either me, or my readers, a pleasant impression of her. But we must remember how little we are acquainted with her, compared to that sister, who, out of her more intimate knowledge, says that she 'was genuinely good, and truly great', and who tried to depict her character in Shirley Keeldar, as what Emily Brontë would have been, had she been placed in health and prosperity. §

It is, indeed, difficult to relate the character of Shirley to what we know of Emily; and 'representation' is not, perhaps, the word. Shirley is less a portrait than a romantic figure in which Emily's outline has played a determining part. She is the shell of Emily, carefully polished and lovingly made presentable, with all powerful and peculiar qualities left out. It comforted Charlotte to fashion this dashing heroine as a concept of her sister, but as a *portrait* she carries no more conviction than a graceful Byronic figure on a tomb.

The strains and griefs of the last year had reduced Charlotte's physical vitality to a low ebb, and her work was constantly interrupted by illness. It was not a robust age; consumption was commonplace, and carried off countless young women far more resistant physically than Charlotte Brontë. Fears, symptoms and reassurances were an everyday topic of correspondence between friends; the emphasis was on thankfulness for survival. Charlotte had good reason for the anxiety so often reflected in her letters to Ellen, for as well as chronic sleeplessness and a disorder of the liver, she suffered from a soreness in the chest and from pains in the side which hinted at the beginnings of consumption. With the deaths of her brother and sisters always vividly before her she became morbidly nervous about her own health, and Mr Brontë's watchful anxiety increased her apprehensions.

§ It may easily be conceived that two people living together as Mr Brontë and his daughter did, almost entirely dependent on each other for society, and loving each other deeply (although not demonstratively)—that these two last members of a family would have their moments of keen anxiety respecting each other's health. There is not one letter of hers which I have read, that does not contain some mention of her father's state in this respect. Either she thanks God with simple earnestness that he is well, or some infirmities of age beset him, and she mentions the fact, and then winces away from it, as from a sore that will not bear to be touched. He, in his turn, noted every indisposition of his one remaining child's, exaggerated its nature, and sometimes worked himself up into a miserable state of anxiety. . . . §

'I have had to entreat Papa's consideration on this point,' she wrote to Ellen; '—indeed I have had to *command* it. My nervous system is soon wrought on.' To Mr Williams, who had suggested that she should engage a companion, she replied with sad decision: 'I should not like to see youth thus immured. The hush and gloom of our house would be more oppressive to a buoyant than to a subdued spirit. The fact is,' she concluded, 'my work is my best companion.' Imagination had always been her anodyne, and now, bereft of nearly everything else, she turned to it with a kind of passionate loyalty. 'The loss of what we possess nearest and dearest to us in this world, produces an effect upon the character: we search out what we have yet left that can support, and when found, we cling to it with a hold of new-strung tenacity. The faculty of imagination lifted me when I was sinking, three months ago; its active exercise has kept my head above water since; its results cheer me now.'

Shirley was finished at last, and James Taylor, a partner in the firm of Smith Elder whom she now saw for the first time, called at Haworth on his way back from Scotland, and carried the manuscript to London. 'Whatever now becomes of the work,' wrote Charlotte, 'the occupation of writing it has been a boon to me. It took me out of dark and desolate reality into an unreal but happier region.' Her publishers, to her relief, sent a favourable report, though they could not fail to see that this second novel was not quite what they had hoped for after *Jane Eyre*. They were uneasy about the mockery of the curates, and several other points, and suggested alterations; but Charlotte as a writer was incapable of changing or modifying a book once she had finished it. 'I can work indefatigably at the correction of a work before it leaves my hands, but when once I have looked on it as completed and submitted to the inspection of others, it becomes next to impossible to alter or amend. With the heavy suspicion on my mind that all may not be right, I yet feel forced to put up with the inevitably wrong.'

She received £500 for the copyright, as she had done for *Jane Eyre*, and as she was later to do for her third novel. The sum of £1,500 was therefore the whole of the earnings of her literary life—a modest total, which she did not question. She received the money with particular gratitude at this moment, for the railway shares she had bought with her inheritance from Miss Branwell, and which she had relied on to provide a 'small competency' for life, had disastrously dropped, so that almost nothing was left. Her success as a writer was undoubtedly profitable to her publishers, but it made little difference to the economy of her own life; even during the months of *Shirley*'s greatest success we find her regretting, to Ellen, her inability to afford five shillings a yard for material for a dress. 'Papa says he would have lent me a sovereign if he had known'—but she had thought it better to make do with cheaper stuff.

Shirley was published in October 1849, and the following months, having made up her mind to consult a London doctor and learn the truth about her health, she went to London and stayed for several weeks as the guest of George Smith's mother in Westbourne Place. 'At first it was sad; it recalled the last time I went and with whom, and to whom I came home, and in what dear companionship I again and again narrated all that had been seen, heard and uttered in that visit. Emily would never go into any sort of society herself, and whenever I went I could on my return communicate to her a pleasure that suited her, by giving her the distinct faithful impression of each scene I had witnessed. When pressed to go she would sometimes say, "What is the use? Charlotte will bring it all home to me." . . . My occupation is gone now.' The Smiths, it seems, found her a difficult guest, never quite at ease with the mother and daughters, though she could be natural and friendly with George Smith himself. 'Strangers,' he remembered afterwards, 'used to say that they were afraid of her. She was very quiet and self-absorbed, and gave the impression that she was always engaged in observing and analysing the people she met'— an uncomfortable quality in a guest. No effort was spared, however, to please and entertain her, and once the physician she consulted had pronounced (one wonders how accurately) that her lungs were sound, she began, very quietly, to enjoy the visit. *Shirley* was having mixed reviews, but there was already no doubt of its popular success. Mrs Gaskell and Harriet Martineau, still in the dark as to the identity of Currer Bell, wrote admiring letters; Thackeray expressed a wish to meet her. It was all a great pleasure and a great strain; she was anxious about the suitability of her clothes, and dinner parties were spoiled by bilious headaches. She called on Harriet Martineau, out of gratitude for her letter, and made a friend. Miss Martineau had guessed that Currer Bell was a woman, and though she had addressed a letter to 'Currer Bell Esq.', the note inside had begun, without apology, 'Dear Madam'. Charlotte went rather nervously to the interview, and impressed Miss Martineau as being young-looking, almost childlike, 'in a deep mourning dress, neat as a Quaker's, with her beautiful hair smooth and brown, her fine eyes blazing with meaning, and her sensible face indicating a habit of self-control'. In spite of their differences of mind and temperament they found themselves in unexpected sympathy, and Charlotte was able to throw off her reserve and talk to Miss Martineau about her sisters.

The first meeting with Thackeray was less happy. She was overwhelmed by his personality, by his celebrity, by her own admiration for his genius, and found herself 'fearfully stupid'. Thackeray for his part was touched by her appearance, by the 'trembling little frame, the little hand, the great honest eyes'; but at dinner he found her a solemn and difficult neighbour. She took everything he said with earnest seriousness, and was nonplussed when she sometimes suspected he was speaking in jest. The pleasant, easy, often frivolous conversation of men like Thackeray was a foreign language; it puzzled and disappointed her, and the more earnestly she listened for memorable words the more mischievously was Thackeray tempted to tease her. The truth was, as George Smith shrewdly recognised, that 'Charlotte Brontë's heroics roused Thackeray's antagonism. He declined to pose on a pedestal for her admiration, and with characteristic contrariety of nature he seemed to be tempted to say the very things that set Charlotte Brontë's teeth, so to speak, on edge, and affronted all her ideals. He insisted on discussing his books very much as a clerk in a bank would discuss the ledgers he had to keep for a salary. . . . Miss Brontë wanted to persuade him that he was a great man with a "mission" and Thackeray, with many wicked jests, declined to recognise the "mission".'

Still, these were wonderful things to report to Mr Brontë, who was hungry for news and eagerly watched the post for Charlotte's letters. With no Emily now to interest or amuse, it is touching to see how assiduously she collected experiences for her father—the National Gallery, Macready's *Macbeth*, an exhibition of Turner's paintings, even a visit to the Zoo, where she observed for him 'lions, tigers, leopards, elephants, numberless monkeys, camels, five or six camelopards, a young hippopotamus with an Egyptian for its keeper, birds of all kinds. . . .'

§ Her father had quite enough of the spirit of hero-worship in him to make him take a vivid pleasure in the accounts of what she had heard and whom she had seen. It was on the occasion of one of her visits to London that he had desired her to obtain a sight of Prince Albert's armoury, if possible. I am not aware whether she managed to do this; but she went to one or two of the great national armouries in order that she might describe the stern steel harness and glittering swords to her father, whose imagination was forcibly struck by the idea of such things; and often afterwards, when his spirits flagged and the languor of old age for a time got the better of his indomitable nature, she would again strike on the measure wild, and speak about the armies of strange weapons she had seen in London, till he resumed his interest in the old subject, and was his own keen, warlike, intelligent self again. §

The visit over, she returned once more to the noiseless life of the parsonage, determined that the contrast with London should not make Haworth seem more desolate, but that she would comfort the long quiet of winter evenings with pleasant memories. She had brought home with her, as a present from George Smith to Mr Brontë, a crayon portrait of herself by George Richmond; and this was received with pleasure and hung proudly in the parlour. But the quiet was almost unbroken, and became oppressive. With *Shirley* finished, she had not even the old solace of work, and found herself depending from day to day on the arrival of the post. She was quick to see the danger of this dependence, and made heroic efforts to free herself from it, deliberately limiting the number of letters she wrote and urging her friends at Cornhill to write less often. She believed herself now destined to a life of loneliness, and that her only hope of peace was to come to terms with it. The boxes of books from Cornhill were her only resource. 'What, I sometimes ask, could I do without them? I have recourse to them as to friends; they shorten and cheer many an hour that would be too long and too desolate otherwise; even when my tired sight will not permit me to continue reading, it is pleasant to see them on the shelf, or on the table.' She shared the books, now, with Mr Brontë; he was able to take pleasure in some that were sent, and she was thankful for any interest they could pursue together.

§ Owing to Mr Brontë's great age, and long-formed habits of solitary occupation when in the house, his daughter was left to herself for the greater part of the day. Ever since his serious attacks of illness, he had dined alone; a portion of her dinner, regulated by strict attention to the diet most suitable for him, being taken into his room by herself. After dinner she read to him for an hour or so, as his sight was too weak to allow of his reading long to himself. He was out of doors among his parishioners for a good part of each day; often for a longer time than his strength would permit. Yet he always liked to go alone, and consequently her affectionate care could be no check upon the length of his walks to the more distant hamlets which were in his care. He would come back occasionally utterly fatigued; and be obliged to go to bed, questioning himself sadly as to where all his former strength of body had gone to. His strength of will was the same as ever. That which he resolved to do he did, at whatever cost of weariness; but his daughter was all the more anxious from seeing him so regardless of himself and his health. The hours of retiring for the night had always been early in the Parsonage; now family prayers were at eight o'clock; directly after which Mr Brontë and old Tabby went to bed, and Martha was not long in following. But Charlotte could not have slept if she had gone,—could not have rested on her desolate couch. She stopped up,—it was very tempting,—later and later; striving to beguile the lonely night with some employment, till her weak eyes failed to read or to sew, and could only weep in solitude over the dead that were not. No one on earth can even imagine what those hours were to her. All the grim superstitions of the North had been implanted in her during her childhood by the servants, who believed in them. They recurred to her now,—with no shrinking from the spirits of the Dead, but with such an intense longing once more to stand face to face with the souls of her sisters, as no one but she could have felt. It seemed as if the very strength of her yearning should have compelled them to appear. On windy nights, cries, and sobs, and wailings seemed to go round the house, as of the dearly-beloved striving to force their way to her. Some one conversing with her once objected, in my presence, to that part of *Jane Eyre* in which she hears Rochester's voice crying out to her in a great crisis of her life, he being many, many miles distant at the time. I do not know what incident was in Miss Brontë's recollection when she replied, in a low voice, drawing in her breath, 'But it is a true thing; it really happened.' §

The winter of 1849 was hard and cold, and there were many weeks when her own health, and the bitter weather, kept her a prisoner. Even when the slow northern spring began to appear, and the moors invited her as they had done in the past, she found their empty solitude intolerable. 'When I go out there alone everything reminds me of the times when others were with me, and then the moors seem a wilderness, featureless, solitary, saddening. My sister Emily had a particular love for them, and there is not a knoll of heather, not a branch of fern, not a young bilberry leaf, not a fluttering lark or linnet, but reminds me of her. The distant prospects were Anne's delight, and when I look round she is in the blue tints, the pale mists, the waves and shadows of the horizon. In the hill-country their poetry comes by lines and stanzas into my mind: once I loved it; now I dare not read it.' During these dreary months Charlotte and her father drew closer together than they had ever done. Their relations were, as always, undemonstrative, but Mr. Brontë now made occasional efforts to overcome his reserve.

'A few days since, a little incident happened which curiously touched me. Papa put into my hands a little packet of letters and papers,—telling me that they were Mamma's, and that I might read them. I did read them, in a frame of mind I cannot describe. The papers were yellow with time, all having been written before I was born: it was strange now to peruse, for the first time, the records of a mind whence my own sprang; and most strange, and at once sad and sweet, to find that mind of a truly fine, pure, and elevated order. They were written to Papa before they were married. There is a rectitude, a refinement, a constancy, a modesty, a sense, a gentleness about them indescribable. I wished that she had lived, and that I had known her. . . .'

There was one sense in which Charlotte's seclusion was becoming less complete: the anonymity of Currer Bell was wearing thin. It had been more or less tacitly abandoned during the London visit, much against her wish, because of the awkwardness of keeping up the pretence, to friends of the Smiths, that Miss Brontë had nothing to do with Currer Bell. Now, even in Haworth itself, the secret had been told.

§ The publication of *Shirley* seemed to fix the conviction that the writer was an inhabitant of the district where the story was laid. And a clever Haworth man, who had somewhat risen in the world, and gone to settle in Liverpool, read the novel, and was struck with some of the names of places mentioned, and knew the dialect in which parts of it were written. He became convinced that it was the production of some one in Haworth. But he could not imagine who in that village could have written such a work except Miss Brontë. Proud of his conjecture, he divulged the suspicion (which was almost certainty) in the columns of a Liverpool paper; thus the heart of the mystery came slowly creeping out. §

Once known as a local production, *Shirley* was read with excitement in the village. 'The Haworth people have been making great fools of themselves over *Shirley*; they have taken it in an enthusiastic light. When they got the volumes at the Mechanics' Institute, all the members wanted them. They cast lots for the whole three, and whoever got a volume was only allowed to keep it two days, and was to be fined a shilling per diem for longer detention. It would be mere nonsense and vanity to tell you what they say.' Even the pilloried curates bore no malice—'each characteristically finds solace for his own wounds in crowing over his brethren'—and Mr. Nicholls, who now learned for the first time that Miss Brontë had written a novel and 'came in cold and disapproving one day to ask her if the report he had heard at Keighley was true', was unexpectedly pleased with his own character. 'Mr Nicholls,' she told Ellen, 'has finished reading *Shirley*, he is delighted with it. John Brown's wife seriously thought he had gone wrong in the head as she heard him giving vent to roars of laughter as he sat alone, clapping his hands and stamping on the floor. He would read all the scenes about the curates aloud to Papa, he triumphed in his own character.' Mr Nicholls was no doubt agreeably surprised to find himself, in the person of Mr Macarthey, drawn with less venom than

the others, and described even as 'decent, decorous and conscientious'. Charlotte, however, was impatient when she found
her portrait of the bigoted Macarthey taken as a compliment.
'Much good may it do him,' she wrote with some asperity to
Ellen.

The local enthusiasm spread beyond the parish, and a few
cautious sightseers began to arrive, peering curiously over the
parsonage wall and joining Mr Brontë's congregation. John
Brown the sexton, Branwell's old friend, began to earn
occasional half-crowns by pointing out Miss Brontë as she
went into church. Letters, too, were delivered at the parsonage,
letters from strangers who wanted to meet her and who
sent embarrassing manuscripts for her opinion. 'They are most
difficult to answer, put off, and appease without offending, for
such characters are excessively touchy and when affronted
turn malignant. Their books are too often deplorable.'

Shirley itself was selling steadily, to the great satisfaction of
Cornhill, and in spite of a few unfavourable reviews. The
most savage of these had appeared in *The Times*, which devoted nearly three columns to ridiculing the novel as 'at once
the most high flown and stalest of fictions'. This attack had
appeared while Charlotte was staying with the Smiths; they
had tried to hide the newspaper, but she had seen it at last
and it had cost her some quiet tears. She had guessed,
when Thackeray called that afternoon, that he had come out
of curiosity to see how she had taken it. The blow had been
unjust as well as cruel, and its violence had defeated its own
ends; Charlotte soon found that common sense and others'
sympathy helped her to withstand it. An article by G. H.
Lewes in the *Edinburgh Review* wounded her far more deeply.
Lewes had written to her on the publication of *Shirley*, telling
her that he intended to review it; and she had replied with
an earnest request that he should judge the novel on its
merits, not by any standard that he should think applicable
only to a woman. This provoked a long review headed 'Mental
Equality of the Sexes?—Female Literature', stressing the
author's sex in almost every line. Charlotte was always sensitive
on this point, and it must be remembered that the critical temper of the time was very different from our own. A woman's

production was commonly judged according to the popular idea of the sentiments proper to a lady. This criterion was all very well for 'Keepsake' literature, but could not without damage be applied to the work of a serious writer. Charlotte resented Lewes's mischievous condescension, and sent him an angry one-lined note: 'I can be on my guard against my enemies, but God deliver me from my friends!' He protested against her touchiness, and she wrote again, this time in a calmer and more friendly mood; but he was never quite forgiven.

One of the proofs of her new celebrity, which pleased Mr Brontë more than it did Charlotte, was the benevolent attention of Sir James Kay-Shuttleworth, that same wealthy physician who had already secured the acquaintance of Mrs Gaskell, and who now wished to be known as the friend of Charlotte Brontë. He called at the parsonage; he invited her to stay; and because Mr Brontë so eagerly pressed her to accept she paid a reluctant visit. The few days spent at Gawthorpe Hall, on the borders of Lancashire, were precisely what she least cared for—the company of self-important strangers with whom she had not the smallest spontaneous sympathy. Still, Sir James was immensely talkative and kind, and so transparently pleased with his new capture that she felt half ashamed of not enjoying herself. 'On the whole, now that the visit is over, I do not regret having paid it. The worst of it is, that there is now some menace hanging over my head of an invitation to go to them in London during the season. This, which would be a great enjoyment to some people, is a perfect terror to me. . . . I tremble at the thought of the price I must necessarily pay in mental distress and physical wear and tear.' As the season approached, Sir James renewed his attentions, comfortably unaware that Charlotte was steeling herself for the ordeal with the desperate reflection that 'he who shuns suffering will never win victory'. She cast about for excuses, but 'Papa is eager and restless for me to go; the idea of a refusal quite hurts him'. However, when the time came, Mr Brontë was having a touch of his spring bronchitis, and she was able to make this a reason for staying at home. A little later, with Mr Brontë better

266

and Sir James himself now conveniently unwell, she rather guiltily accepted a more congenial invitation from Mrs. Smith, and went quietly up to London at the beginning of June.

This visit was chiefly memorable for an interview with Thackeray, when Charlotte, finding herself once more in the presence of her hero, took the opportunity of scolding him for that levity of outlook which she found unworthy. 'The giant sat before me: I was moved to speak to him of some of his shortcomings (literary of course); one by one the faults came into my mind, and one by one I brought them out and sought some explanation or defence. He did defend himself, like a great Turk and heathen—that is to say, the excuses were often worse than the crime itself.' It was an uneasy and rather ludicrous situation: their admiration for one another could never reconcile the differences of temperament. She could not come to terms with Thackeray's mocking spirit, nor he with her solemnity. At a dinner party at Thackeray's house she entered 'in mittens, in silence, in seriousness', and cast such a constraint over the evening that Thackeray's daughter, who was still a girl, long remembered the occasion as one of social horror. 'She sat gazing at him with kindling eyes of interest, lighting up with a sort of illumination now and then as she answered him. I can see her bending forward over the table, not eating, but listening to what he said as he carved the dish before him.' While dinner lasted and Thackeray had the courage of his conversation, things were not too bad; but the exodus to the drawing-room brought disaster. 'Everyone waited for the brilliant conversation which never began at all. . . . The room looked very dark, the lamp began to smoke a little, the conversation grew dimmer and more dim, the ladies sat round still expectant, my father was too much perturbed by the gloom and the silence to be able to cope with it at all.' He solved the difficulty, with shocking cowardice, by leaving the drawing-room on some excuse and spending the rest of the evening at his club; leaving Miss Brontë to reflect, perhaps, on the overrated joys of London society.

With George Smith, however, handsome and easy and agreeable, Charlotte's relations were now on a delightful footing. 'George and I understand each other very well,' she wrote confidently to Ellen, 'and respect each other very sincerely. We both know the wide breach time has made between us; we do not embarrass each other, or very rarely; my six or eight years of seniority, to say nothing of lack of all pretension to beauty, etc., are a perfect safeguard. I should not in the least fear to go with him to China.' Mrs Smith, however, whose maternal watchfulness Charlotte had remarked before, was less confident, and seems to have suspected a growing warmth between them. She was opposed to her son's plan for taking Charlotte on a two-day jaunt to Edinburgh, when he went with his sister to fetch his younger brother home from school; and gave way only, reluctantly, when George insisted. ('His mother is master of the house, but he is master of his mother.') One suspects that Mrs Smith showed more shrewdness here than Charlotte, and was hostile to the idea of this subdued spinster as a wife for her attractive son, however profitable she might be to him as an author. A few months later we find Charlotte glancing (though without expectation) at the possibility of marriage. 'Were there no vast barrier of age, fortune, etc.,' she confided to Ellen, 'there is perhaps enough personal regard to make things possible which now are impossible. If men and women married because they liked each other's temper, look, conversation, nature and so on—and if, besides, years were more nearly equal—the chance you allude to might be admitted as a chance. But other reasons regulate matrimony, reasons of convenience, of connection, of money. Meantime I am content to have him as a friend, and pray God to continue to me the commonsense to look on one so young, so rising and so hopeful in no other light.' By this time George Smith was talking of a trip with Charlotte and his sisters to the Rhine, and Charlotte was fully aware of emotional danger. 'That hint about the Rhine disturbs me; I am not made of stone; and what is mere excitement to him, is fever to me. . . . I cannot conceive either his mother or his sisters relishing it, and all London would gabble. . . .'

This, however, was still some months ahead, and the Scottish jaunt was undertaken in a sufficiently light-hearted spirit, without misgiving. It yielded unalloyed pleasure. The journey in charming company, the romantic sight-seeing, the stern beauty of Edinburgh itself, seemed like a glimpse of another life, far happier than her own. She had always had a poetic idea of Scotland, 'but now, as a reality, I like it far better; it furnished me with some hours as happy almost as any I ever spent'.

In the August of 1850, to please her father, she accepted another invitation from the Kay-Shuttleworths, this time to Windermere, where Sir James had taken a furnished house for the summer. This week proved to be unexpectedly pleasant, for Mrs Gaskell was staying there as well, and the two ladies met for the first time. Mrs Gaskell's charm and evident sweetness of character put Charlotte at her ease; she forgot her shyness and felt she had made a friend. Mrs Gaskell for her part was at once passionately interested, and wrote a long description of Miss Brontë as soon as she got home. 'She is,' she told her friend Catherine Winkworth, '. . . *undeveloped*; thin and more than half a head shorter than I; soft brown hair, not so dark as mine; eyes (very good and expressive, looking straight and open at you) of the same colour, a reddish face; large mouth and many teeth gone; altogether *plain*; the forehead square, broad, and *rather* overhanging. She has a very sweet voice, rather hesitates in choosing her expressions, but when chosen they seem without an effort, *admirable* and *just* befitting the occasion.' They talked a great deal together over their needlework and during the sight-seeing carriage drives which Sir James arranged; Mrs Gaskell was eager for the details of Charlotte's life. What she could not discover for herself she learned (not always accurately) from confidential gossip with Lady Kay-Shuttleworth, and in a mood of rare excitement wrote everything down. What struck her at almost every turn, in contrast to her own busy and happy life, was the evidence of loneliness in Charlotte's; her reactions were all those of a person wearily familiar with the extremes of solitude. 'I was struck by Miss Brontë's careful examination of the shape of the clouds and the signs of the heavens, in which she read, as from a book, what the coming weather would be. I told her that I saw she must have a view equal in extent at her own home. She said that I was right, but that the character of the prospect from Haworth was very different; that I had no idea what a companion the sky became to anyone living in solitude—more than any inanimate object on earth, more than the moors themselves.'

Each went home in the pleasant consciousness of having made a good impression, and they were soon exchanging letters. At this time Mrs Gaskell had one highly successful novel to her credit, and was contributing sketches to Dickens's *Household Words*: Charlotte felt that she could confide to her her own surprise that *Shirley* was everywhere rated inferior to *Jane Eyre*. 'Yet I took great pains with *Shirley*. I did not hurry; I tried to do my best, and my own impression was that it was not inferior to the former work; indeed, I had bestowed on it more time, thought, and anxiety; but a great part of it was written under the shadow of impending calamity; and the last volume, I cannot deny, was composed in the eager, restless endeavour to combat mental sufferings that were scarcely tolerable.'

These miseries were soon painfully revived, when Smith and Elder proposed to republish *Wuthering Heights* and *Agnes Grey*, which had been taken out of the hands of the dubious Newby: and Charlotte undertook the task of editing them and preparing a preface and biographical notice of her sisters. Since their deaths she had not dared to open her sisters' books, and she now found the task exquisitely painful. *Wuthering Heights* struck her afresh as a work of sombre genius. 'Its power fills me with renewed admiration; but yet I am oppressed: the reader is scarcely ever permitted a taste of unalloyed pleasure; every beam of sunshine is poured down through black bars of threatening cloud; every page is surcharged with a sort of moral electricity: and the writer was unconscious of all this—nothing could make her conscious of it.' The time was unpropitious for such a task: the return to Haworth alone, after the pleasant respite of the London visit, plunged her in depression; it was like returning to solitary confinement. 'There was a reaction that sunk me to the earth; the deadly silence, solitude, desolation, were awful; the craving for companionship, the hopelessness of relief, were what I should dread to feel again.' In this low ebb of the spirit, the dwelling on her sisters' work and thought revived the old horrors of neurasthenia. 'The reading over of papers, the renewal of remembrances brought back the pang of bereavement, and occasioned a depression of spirits well nigh intolerable. For one or two nights, I scarcely knew how to get on till morning; and when morning came, I was still haunted with a sense of sickening distress.' The preface and *Biographical Notice of Ellis and Acton Bell* which she wrote at this time contain some incomparable passages—the final and poetic expression of her love for Emily.

'If I say again what I have said already before, it is only to impress and re-impress upon my readers the dreary monotony of her life at this time. The dark, bleak season of the year brought back the long evenings, which tried her severely : all the more so, because her weak eyesight rendered her incapable of following any occupation but knitting by candle-light. For her father's sake, as well as for her own, she found it necessary to make some exertion to ward off settled depression of spirits. She accordingly accepted an invitation to spend a week or ten days with Miss Martineau at Ambleside.'

Harriet Martineau was a somewhat formidable character, the type of woman that has been lampooned for centuries as the strong-minded blue-stocking. Heroically hard-working, self-disciplined, indifferent to comfort, she would have been intimidating to Charlotte if it had not been for the warm-heartedness and striking intellectual honesty which made her attractive. As it was, though she found Miss Martineau overwhelmingly kind and was much stimulated by her company, Charlotte was a little appalled by the self-imposed rigours of her hostess's life.

'Her visitors enjoy the most perfect liberty; what she claims for herself she allows them. I rise at my own hour, breakfast alone (she is up at five, takes a cold bath, and a walk by starlight, and has finished breakfast and got to her work by seven o'clock). I pass the morning in the drawing-room

—she, in her study. At two o'clock we meet—work, talk, and walk together till five, her dinner-hour, spend the evening together, when she converses fluently and abundantly, and with the most complete frankness. I go to my own room soon after ten,—she sits up writing letters till twelve. She appears exhaustless in strength and spirits, and indefatigable in the faculty of labour. She is a great and a good woman; of course not without peculiarities, but I have seen none as yet that annoy me. She is both hard and warm-hearted, abrupt and affectionate, liberal and despotic. I believe she is not at all conscious of her own absolutism. When I tell her of it, she denies the charge warmly; then I laugh at her. I believe she almost rules Ambleside. Some of the gentry dislike her, but the lower orders have a great regard for her.'

Together they visited Fox How, celebrated as the home of the late Dr Arnold and made interesting by the presence of his wife and daughters, and by his eldest son, who had published a volume of verse. Charlotte was unfavourably impressed by Matthew Arnold, whom she thought conceited, affected, and a fop. She admitted, however, that in the course of conversation 'a real modesty appeared under his assumed conceit, and some genuine intellectual aspirations, as well as high educational acquirements, displaced superficial affectations. I was given to understand that his theological opinions were very vague and unsettled.' Matthew Arnold for his part found Miss Brontë 'past thirty and plain, with expressive grey eyes, though'. No spark of sympathy seems to have illuminated this visit.

Miss Martineau was a recent convert to mesmerism, having been cured by this means of a troublesome nervous ailment. She had learned as well to practise it herself, and Charlotte persuaded her to make a personal experiment, though Miss Martineau, shrewdly sensing the hysterical in Charlotte, was apprehensive. 'She was strangely pertinacious about that,' she told Mrs Gaskell, 'and I *most* reluctant to bring it before her at all, we being alone, and I having no confidence in her nerves. Day after day she urged me to mesmerise her. I always, and quite truly, pleaded that I was too tired for success, for we had no opportunity till the end of the day. At last, on Sunday evening, we returned from early tea somewhere; I could not say I was tired, and she insisted. I stopped the moment she called out that she was under the influence, and I would not resume it.' Charlotte was evidently disappointed, though pleased with Miss Martineau's cautious opinion that in time she would prove an excellent subject. Miss Martineau was evidently sensitive enough to perceive that Charlotte's temperament made her a ripe subject for hypnosis, though she knew nothing of the trance-like states which in the past had been self-induced by both Charlotte and Emily.

During the whole of this winter James Taylor, the partner in the firm of Smith and Elder who had carried Charlotte's manuscript to London, had been pressing her to marry him. It was a joyless proposal which brought her little pleasure; indeed, it was a somewhat saddening reflection that at this time of intolerable loneliness, when almost any escape from her present life might have tempted her, this sudden chance was one she could not take. Presentable and intelligent though he was, there was something about him from which her instincts shrank; he awoke in her some physical revulsion. Her first impression of him had not been auspicious, for after remarking to Ellen on his capacity and intelligence she had felt obliged to add, 'He has a determined, dreadful nose in the middle of his face which when poked into my countenance cuts into my soul like iron.' It was at this first meeting, however, that he himself had been strongly drawn to Charlotte, and his proposal of marriage (prompted, perhaps, by considerations of interest as well as liking) came soon after. It was not long before rumours of an engagement began to go about. 'Your poor mother,' Charlotte wrote to Ellen, 'is like Tabby, Martha and Papa; all these fancy I am somehow, by some mysterious process, to be married in London, or to engage myself to matrimony. . . . Papa seriously told me yesterday, that if I married and left him he should give up housekeeping and go into lodgings.' Mr Brontë did not take kindly to the idea; if she should ever wish to marry there would be, as Charlotte realised, many obstacles; 'the least allusion to such a thing is most offensive to Papa.'

James Taylor urged his suit with some persistence. It had been decided that he should go to India, to establish a branch publishing-house for the firm, and no doubt he would have liked to settle the matter before going. Charlotte's harsh impression was perceptibly softened by the frequency of his letters and kind attentions. 'The idea of the "little man" shocks me less,' she told Ellen early in 1851. '. . . . The fact is, there is a quiet constancy about this, my diminutive and red-haired friend, which adds a foot to his stature, turns his sandy locks dark, and altogether dignifies him a good deal in my estimation.' He was to go in April, and paid a final and determined visit to Haworth. Charlotte had thought long and earnestly on the matter, considering all the advantages of the marriage—security, escape from solitude, even the sur-prising fact that Mr Brontë liked him, and thought 'a pros-pective union, deferred for five years, with such a decorous reliable personage would be a very proper and advisable affair'—but when it came to the point and she 'saw him very near', the old obscure dislike hardened within her. 'As he stood near me, as he looked at me in his keen way, it was all I could do to stand my ground tranquilly and steadily, and not to recoil as before.' Taylor was refused once more and went away, and Charlotte began to wonder if she had been foolish. 'Now that he is away I feel far more gently towards him; it is only close by that I grow rigid, stiffening with a strange mixture of apprehension and anger, which nothing softens but his retreat and a perfect subduing of his manner.' She began almost to regret him, not from any real feeling of liking, but because it was a dreary thing to let go this last support, this half-serious possibility on which her mind had rested. She could not, she knew, ever have been happy with Mr Taylor. For all his good points, there was something essentially commonplace about him; and Charlotte, who had loved M Heger and was still on her guard about her feel-ings for George Smith, could not so grossly deceive herself. 'I could not find one gleam, I could not see one passing glimpse of true good breeding. . . . In mind too; though clever, he is second-rate, thoroughly second-rate. . . . Were I to marry him, my heart would bleed in pain and humiliation; I could not, *could* not look up to him. No,' she concluded, at the end of a long analysis of her feelings, '—if Mr Taylor be the only husband fate offers to me, single I must remain. But yet, at times, I grieve for him. . . .'

At the end of May Charlotte went once more to London at the invitation of the Smiths, to see the Great Exhibition and hear the lectures which Thackeray was giving at Willis's Rooms on *English Humorists of the Eighteenth Century*. She arrived in time for the second lecture, impressed afresh by Thackeray's great abilities, and alarmed at finding herself a centre of attraction. The lecture, she told Ellen, 'was a genuine treat to me, and I was glad not to miss it. It was given in Willis' Rooms, where the Almacks balls are held— a great painted and gilded saloon with long sofas for benches. The audience was said to be the cream of London society, and it looked so. I did not at all expect the great lecturer would know me or notice me under these circumstances, with admiring duchesses and countesses seated in rows before him; but he met me as I entered—shook hands—took me to his mother, whom I had not before seen, and introduced me. She is a fine, handsome, young-looking old lady; was very gracious, and called with one of her grand-daughters next day.

'Thackeray called too, separately. I had a long talk with him, and I think he knows me now a little better than he did: but of this I cannot yet be sure; he is a great and strange man.'

§ The lady, who accompanied Miss Brontë to the lecture at Thackeray's alluded to, says that, soon after they had taken their places, she was aware that he was pointing out her companion to several of his friends, but she hoped that Miss Brontë herself would not perceive it. After some time, however, during which many heads had been turned round, and many glasses put up, in order to look at the author of *Jane Eyre*, Miss Brontë said, 'I am afraid Mr Thackeray has been playing me a trick'; but she soon became too much absorbed in the lecture to notice the attention which was being paid to her.

As they were preparing to leave the room, her companion saw with dismay that many of the audience were forming themselves into two lines, on each side of the aisle down which they had to pass before reaching the door. Aware that any delay would only make the ordeal more trying, her friend took Miss Brontë's arm in hers, and they went along the avenue of eager and admiring faces. During this passage through the 'cream of society', Miss Brontë's hand trembled to such a degree, that her companion feared lest she should turn faint and be unable to proceed; and she dared not express her sympathy or try to give her strength by any touch or word, lest it might bring on the crisis she dreaded. §

The visit lasted a month, and was spoiled only by the frequent attacks of headache and sickness which poisoned her best enjoyments. 'I hoped to leave my headaches behind me at Haworth; but it seems I brought them carefully packed in my trunk, and very much have they been in my way since they came.' The Great Exhibition, housed in Paxton's palace of glass in Hyde Park, was visited five times, and proved rather more exhausting than enjoyable. On one occasion, however, the Smiths had arranged to go with Sir David Brewster, the Scottish natural philosopher, and she found to her surprise that in his kindly company the confusing array of exhibits became intelligible. 'I had rather dreaded this for Sir David is a man of profoundest science, and I feared it would be impossible to understand his explanations of the mechanism etc.; indeed, I hardly knew how to ask him questions. I was spared all trouble: without being questioned, he gave information in the kindest and simplest manner.' In spite of this, however, the Crystal Palace remained for Charlotte a place which she visited under coercion rather than for pleasure; a bustling, tiring, noisy, confusing experience for which she had little liking, but which provided excellent matter for her letters to Mr Brontë, to whom she described the railway engines and boilers.

More to her taste was a breakfast party with Samuel

Rogers, the poet, which 'proved a most calm, refined and intellectual treat'; and a visit to the theatre to see the acting of Rachel—'a wonderful sight—terrible as if the earth had cracked deep at your feet and revealed a glimpse of hell'. A confirmation by Cardinal Wiseman in the Spanish Ambassador's chapel she found 'impiously theatrical'; her protestantism was still easily affronted. A visit arranged by George Smith, however, by way of contrast, to a Quaker meeting, 'afforded her more amusement than edification'. Three eminent Church of England preachers struck her as decorously impressive, but 'Thackeray and Rachel have been the two points of attraction for me in town'.

A more frivolous expedition was made to a phrenologist, whom George Smith and Charlotte visited together, under assumed names. The practitioner, a Dr Browne, was much struck by the intellectual development of Charlotte's head, and wrote a long estimate of her talents and disposition which is curiously interesting. Her mental power and moral strength, her natural pessimism and self-distrust, combined with a great capacity for love, are all dwelt on. She was pronounced capable of great achievement, but Dr Browne did not discover that she was a writer.

On the way home Charlotte spent a couple of quiet days with Mrs Gaskell.

§ Miss Brontë returned from London by Manchester, and paid us a visit of a couple of days at the end of June. The weather was so intensely hot, and she herself so much fatigued with her London sight-seeing, that we did little but sit in-doors, with open windows, and talk. The only thing she made a point of exerting herself to procure was a present for Tabby. It was to be a shawl, or rather a large handkerchief, such as she could pin across her neck and shoulders, in the old-fashioned country manner. Miss Brontë took great pains in seeking out one which she thought would please the old woman. §

This interlude was a pleasant one, and strengthened the feeling of mutual respect and liking. 'The visit to Mrs Gaskell formed a cheering break in the journey. She is a woman of many fine qualities and deserves the epithet which I find is

277

generally applied to her—charming. Her family consists of four little girls—all more or less pretty and intelligent; these, scattered through the rooms of a somewhat spacious house, seem to fill it with liveliness and gaiety. Haworth Parsonage is rather a contrast. . . .' She had found the Gaskell children unexpectedly attractive, and had been surprised to find herself making friends with the youngest.

§ The child would steal her little hand into Miss Brontë's scarcely larger one, and each took pleasure in this apparently unobserved caress. Yet once when I told Julia to take and show her the way to some room in the house, Miss Brontë shrunk back : 'Do not *bid* her do anything for me,' she said; 'it has been so sweet hitherto to have her rendering her little kindnesses *spontaneously*.' §

'Could you manage,' she wrote at the end of a letter to Mrs Gaskell, to 'convey a small kiss to that dear, but dangerous little person, Julia? She surreptitiously possessed herself of a minute fraction of my heart, which has been missing ever since I saw her.' She was still ill at ease with children, however much she might occasionally be drawn to them. 'Whenever I see Florence and Julia again, I shall feel like a fond and bashful suitor, who views at a distance the fair personage to whom, in his clownish awe, he dare not risk a near approach. Such is the clearest idea I can give you of my feeling towards children I like, but to whom I am a stranger;—and to what children am I not a stranger?'

§ Before the autumn was far advanced, the usual effects of her solitary life, and of the unhealthy situation of Haworth Parsonage, began to appear in the form of sick headaches, and miserable, starting, wakeful nights. She does not dwell on this in her letters; but there is an absence of all cheerfulness of tone, and an occasional sentence forced out of her, which imply far more than many words could say. There was illness all through the Parsonage household—taking its accustomed forms of lingering influenza and low fever; she herself was outwardly the strongest of the family, and all domestic exertion fell for a time upon her shoulders. . . .

A visit from Miss Wooler at this period did Miss Brontë

much good for the time. She speaks of her guest's company as being 'very pleasant', 'like good wine', both to her father and to herself. But Miss Wooler could not remain with her long; and then again the monotony of her life returned upon her in all its force; the only events of her days and weeks consisting in the small changes which occasional letters brought. It must be remembered that her health was often such as to prevent her stirring out of the house in inclement or wintry weather. She was liable to sore throat, and depressing pain at the chest, and difficulty of breathing, on the least exposure to cold. §

Urged by her publisher, she had begun work, though with difficulty and heart-searching, on a third novel. She had vigorously resisted George Smith's suggestion that she should follow Dickens's and Thackeray's example and write one in serial form; she knew herself too well to suppose that she could stand the strain of seeing the early chapters in print before a book was finished. She had not, she insisted, 'the experience of a Thackeray or the animal spirit of a Dickens'; and even if she had, could never embark on their reckless hand-to-mouth methods.

What she had, at last, felt able to attempt was the creation of a second tale out of the undimmed memories of Brussels. Nearly eight years had gone by; she had forgotten nothing; but the passing of time, and the deep experiences she had been through since, had brought the old pain into a new perspective. There was no longer any compulsion to subdue it to the emotional *pianissimo* that had emasculated *The Professor*. She could bear, at last, to consider it with detachment, to break it up into fragments she could handle, to give it form as the most mature, and certainly the most autobiographical, of her novels. But the work went slowly. Depression and solitude lay on her spirits like a pall; the approach of winter brought back the anguish of that other winter when she had lost Emily and Anne. Stooping to write brought on a pain in the chest which was like an echo of their pain. Often, for weeks at a time and for sheer misery, the work had to be abandoned.

§ A little event which occurred about this time, did not

tend to cheer her. It was the death of poor old faithful Keeper, Emily's dog. He had come to the Parsonage in the fierce strength of his youth. Sullen and ferocious he had met with his master in the indomitable Emily. Like most dogs of his kind, he feared, respected, and deeply loved her who subdued him. He had mourned her with the pathetic fidelity of his nature, falling into old age after her death. And now, her surviving sister wrote: 'Poor old Keeper died last Monday morning, after being ill one night; he went gently to sleep; we laid his old faithful head in the garden.' §

At last it had to be admitted that she was ill. Sleeplessness, loss of appetite, headache and nausea had brought her to a pitch of dangerous weakness. A doctor was summoned, and the drastic medicines he prescribed reduced her further. Pain in the side, fever and sleeplessness continued; but in spite of these symptoms the physician pronounced her lungs to be sound, and diagnosed the condition as being due solely to derangement of the liver. Reassured, she very slowly began to mend, and was thankful for a few days of Ellen's company. 'Some long stormy days and nights there were, when I felt such a craving for support and companionship as I cannot express. Sleepless, I lay awake night after night, weak and unable to occupy myself. I sat in my chair day after day, the saddest memories my only company. It was a time I shall never forget.' It was now four months since she had made any progress with *Villette*, and she was determined not to leave home again, not to visit or be visited, until the book was finished. In June, nevertheless, she went alone to Scarborough, to revisit Anne's grave; she had long wished to correct some little inaccuracies in the lettering of the tombstone, and, this being done, went on to Filey, where she spent some weeks in the lodgings she and Ellen had occupied three years before. The lonely holiday seemed to do her good. She walked on the sands, bathed once (the water was bitterly cold) and became 'almost as sunburnt and weather-beaten as a fisherman' from the long unaccustomed days in the open air.

On her return home she was met by fresh anxiety. Mr

Brontë, who had got over his spring bronchitis, now suffered a slight stroke, which brought on an alarming return of his old blindness. Her work was once again laid aside while she nursed him back to health and sight, and she wrote anxiously to George Smith, begging him not to announce or even to discuss the new novel until the manuscript should be safely in his hands.

The summer dragged on, and autumn brought all its usual afflictions.

§ Haworth was in an unhealthy state, as usual; and both Miss Brontë and Tabby suffered severely from the prevailing epidemics. The former was long in shaking off the effects of this illness. In vain she resolved against allowing herself any society or change of scene until she had accomplished her labour. She was too ill to write; and with illness came on the old heaviness of heart, recollections of the past, and anticipations of the future. At last Mr Brontë expressed so strong a wish that her friend should be asked to visit her, and she felt some little refreshment so absolutely necessary, that on October the 9th she begged her to come to Haworth, just for a single week. §

Ellen's gentle company soothed and cheered her; with Ellen there she was able to sleep at night and, when she was gone, to work again with almost her old intensity. The first parcel of manuscript was at last posted to Cornhill. 'You must notify honestly what you think of *Villette*. . . . I can hardly tell you how I hunger to hear some opinion besides my own, and how I have sometimes desponded, and almost despaired, because there was no one to whom to read a line, or of whom to ask a counsel. *Jane Eyre* was not written under such circumstances, nor were two-thirds of *Shirley*. I got so miserable about it, I could bear no allusion to the book. It is not finished yet; but now I hope.' She was in a mood of doubt about the quality of the book, aware that she offered no social theme, as Harriet Martineau might have done, or Mrs Gaskell; yet sure of herself in this, that she had dealt with what she knew. 'You will see that *Villette* touches on no matter of public interest. I cannot write books handling the topics of the day; it is of no use trying. Nor can I write a book for its moral. Nor can I take up a philanthropic scheme, though I honour philanthropy.'

The first two volumes were now in George Smith's hands, and Charlotte had received with relief his letter of approval, and was discussing at length his various points of criticism. There was a piquancy in this situation of which she seems not to have been aware. John Graham Bretton, her ostensible hero, is a lively and admiring portrait of George Smith, and Mrs Bretton a shrewdly drawn impression of his mother; while Lucy Snowe (originally Lucy Frost) more than any other of her heroines embodies much of her own character and experience. She was now engaged in an intimate discussion of these characters with George Smith himself, secure, apparently, in the belief that he would never penetrate their disguises or speculate on their emotional relations. In this she was mistaken. 'Lucy must not marry Dr John,' she told him, preparing him in advance for the third volume; 'he is far too youthful, handsome, bright-spirited, and sweet-tempered; he is a "curled darling" of Nature and of Fortune, and must draw a prize in life's lottery. His wife must be young, rich, pretty; he must be made very happy indeed. If Lucy marries anybody, it must be the Professor—a man in whom there is much to forgive, much to "put up with". But I am not leniently disposed towards Miss Frost : from the beginning, I never meant to appoint her lines in pleasant places.' Mr Williams had offered some criticism on the development of Lucy's character, and to this she replied with the assurance of inner knowledge. 'You say that she may be thought morbid and weak, unless the history of her life may be more fully given. I consider that she *is* both morbid and weak at times; her character sets up no pretensions of unmixed strength, and anybody living her life would necessarily become morbid. It was no impetus of healthy feeling which urged her to the confessional, for instance; it was the semi-delirium of solitary grief and sickness.'

Mr Brontë was almost as eager as her publishers for the novel to be finished. He could not follow the work in progress or criticise it in detail, as Anne and Emily would have done;

but he had a general idea of the tale, enough to embarrass Charlotte at this point by urgent petitions for a happy ending.

§ Mr Brontë was anxious that her new tale should end well, as he disliked novels which left a melancholy impression upon the mind; and he requested her to make her hero and heroine (like the heroes and heroines in fairy-tales) 'marry, and live very happily ever after'. But the idea of M Paul Emanuel's death at sea was stamped on her imagination till it assumed the distinct force of reality; and she could no more alter her fictitious ending than if they had been facts which she was relating. All she could do in compliance with her father's wish was so to veil the fate in oracular words, as to leave it to the character and discernment of her readers to interpret her meaning. § The death of the heart which Charlotte had suffered after she had left Brussels could not be falsified; she could alter and disguise much, but not that. Her own love had had to burn itself out, without help or comfort, and Paul Emanuel could not be given to Lucy Snowe.

The third volume was finished at last, with a profound, an almost solemn, feeling of relief. 'I said my prayers when I had done it. Whether it is well or ill done, I don't know; D.V., I will now try and wait the issue quietly.' It was mid-November, 1852. The winter was already closing in on Haworth. The excitement and pressure of work was over, perhaps for many months to come. Nothing confronted her but months of noiseless solitude—a solitude scarcely broken by the presence of her father on the other side of the hall, where he still sat, read, dozed, smoked and ate alone. Charlotte was now thirty-six years old, fully aware that solitude, both before and after her father's inevitable death, was the future with which she must come to terms, or perish. She was schooling herself to put any lingering thoughts of marriage from her mind. Nothing had come of her friendship with George Smith. James Taylor, vaguely regretted now that he was gone, was half a world away and had ceased to write. To all this she was resigned; but resignation was singularly comfortless, for the enemy was not spinsterhood, but loneliness. She longed for Ellen, longed for the stimulus of London, yet forced herself to be still. She scarcely noticed the presence of Mr Nicholls, whom she encountered nearly every day and always on Sundays, and who occasionally invited himself to tea. His coming and going called for no remark; only his manner was changed of late; it was more subdued. He was now 'good, mild, uncontentious', she told Ellen.

XV: MR NICHOLLS

In writing of Mr Nicholls, of his long, painful, triumphant and tragic love story, Mrs Gaskell faced a difficulty seemingly insoluble. For there he sat, in his dark little stone-floored study which had once been the store-room, and which only a year ago had been papered and curtained by Charlotte in white and green, so that what little light came in was pale and greenish, as though filtering into a small and dark aquarium.

He had resisted the idea of the biography from the beginning, and had been sternly jealous of the privacy of his married life. What was Mrs Gaskell to say about that marriage—the slow and exquisitely painful story that preceded it, the doubts that surrounded it, the fears and misgivings with which, on Charlotte's part, it had been undertaken? Of all this, Mrs Gaskell knew too much. The only attitude open to her was a sort of reverent reticence, an attitude upon which her natural delicacy would in any case have insisted. He would never, she knew, have countenanced her at all if he had not believed her discreet, and discretion must be the mood of her final chapters. Yet it must often have galled her, as a novelist, to have to discard so much that was profoundly moving; so much that was relevant to Charlotte's character; so much that was true.

A few days before Christmas 1852, Mr Nicholls proposed. He had been curate at Haworth now for close on eight years, and though Charlotte had long been dimly aware of a certain intensity in his manner, he had given no hint of his real feelings. No hint, that is, beyond low spirits, and a tendency to talk despondently about his health, and to threaten to leave Haworth for good and become a missionary. He was making himself ill with emotional conflict, but was afraid to speak. This behaviour Charlotte observed with 'dim misgivings', and Mr Brontë, whom nothing escaped, 'with little sympathy and much indirect sarcasm'. The crisis came suddenly. 'On Monday evening Mr Nicholls was here to tea. I vaguely felt without clearly seeing, as without seeing I have felt for some time, the meaning of his constant looks, and strange, feverish restraint. After tea I withdrew to the dining-room as usual. As usual, Mr Nicholls sat with Papa till between eight and nine o'clock; I then heard him open the parlour door as if going. I expected the clash of the front door. He stopped in the passage: he tapped: like lightning it flashed on me what was coming. He entered—he stood before me. What his words were you can guess; his manner —you can hardly realise—never can I forget it. Shaking from head to foot, looking deadly pale, speaking low, vehemently yet with difficulty—he made me for the first time feel what it costs a man to declare affection where he doubts response. 'The spectacle of one ordinarily so statue-like, thus trembling, stirred and overcome, gave me a kind of strange shock. He spoke of sufferings he had borne for months, of sufferings he could endure no longer, and craved leave for some hope. I could only entreat him to leave me then and promise a reply on the morrow. I asked him if he had spoken to Papa. He said, he dared not. I think I half led, half put him out of the

286

room. When he was gone I immediately went to Papa, and told him what had taken place. Agitation and anger disproportionate to the occasion ensued; if I had *loved* Mr Nicholls and had heard such epithets applied to him as were used, it would have transported me past my patience; as it was, my blood boiled with a sense of injustice, but Papa worked himself into a state not to be trifled with, the veins on his temples started up like whipcord, and his eyes became suddenly bloodshot. I made haste to promise that Mr Nicholls should on the morrow have a distinct refusal.' Mr Brontë's violence, which was an explosion of outraged pride, exacerbated by his contempt for the obscure curate whose miserable wages he paid (Mr Nicholls had never had more than £100 a year) defeated its object. If Mr Brontë had been more moderate, Charlotte's own indifference would have been his ally. As it was, her pity and indignation were aroused, and she found herself looking with wonder at the despised curate who was as capable as herself of suffering and passion. 'Papa's vehement antipathy to the bare thought of anyone thinking of me as a wife,' she wrote to Ellen, 'and Mr Nicholls's distress, both give me pain. Attachment to Mr Nicholls you are well aware I never entertained, but the poignant pity inspired by his state on Monday evening, by the hurried revelation of his sufferings for many months, is something galling and irksome. That he cared something for me, and wanted me to care for him, I have long suspected, but I did not know the degree or strength of his feelings.'

The next few days were passed in acute discomfort. Mr Nicholls took sanctuary in his lodgings, alarming his landlady by 'entirely rejecting his meals', and replying by letter to the pitiless attacks of Mr Brontë, who pursued him with 'a hardness not to be bent and a contempt not to be propitiated'. 'I only wish,' Charlotte told Ellen, 'you were here to see Papa in his present mood: you would know something of him . . . he says that the match would be a degradation, that I should be throwing myself away; that he expects me, if I marry at all, to do very differently; in short, his manner of viewing the subject is, on the whole, far from being one with which I can sympathise.' Charlotte was so much shocked by her father's behaviour that she felt compelled to write to Mr Nicholls herself, since although he 'must never expect me to reciprocate the feeling he had expressed, yet at the same time I wished to disclaim participation in sentiments calculated to give him pain'. She could not share her father's wrath, but her own objections were almost as unanswerable—'a sense of incongruity and uncongeniality in feelings, tastes, principles. . . .' Even the sexton, with whom he lodged, even the parsonage servant took sides against him. He was, Charlotte observed, 'the one . . . person whom nobody pities but me. Martha is bitter against him. John Brown says *he should like to shoot him.* They don't understand the nature of his feelings—but I see now what they are. Mr N. is one of those who attach themselves to very few, whose sensations are close and deep—like an underground stream, running strong but in a narrow channel. He continues restless and ill. . . .'

Believing the situation to be hopeless, and knowing that he could no longer endure to stay in Haworth if it were, Mr Nicholls resigned his curacy, and his resignation was accepted with triumph by Mr Brontë. He then, in the spirit of one who can be relieved only by some desperate act, wrote to the Society for the Propagation of the Gospel and offered himself as a missionary. He was perfectly unencumbered, he told the secretary, having neither wife nor personal property. Haworth had been his only curacy; he was not in debt. His health he described as 'very good—except that I have been affected with rheumatism this winter'; and he expressed—perhaps because it lay at the greatest possible physical distance from Haworth—a preference for Australia. In making this application he was obliged to submit references, and now, at the very crisis of their mutual hostility, was compelled to ask for one from Mr Brontë. This he may well have done with some misgiving, but if he did, his apprehensions were unfounded. Mr Brontë was only too pleased to send him to Australia, and his written reference (still, by a happy chance, in the archives of the Society) strikes precisely that note of hollow enthusiasm to be found in the references of servants who are under notice. His other testimonials, all of them from fellow clergymen in the diocese, were excellent; but the Society took a long time to deliberate, and Mr Nicholls remained in Haworth in a state of gloom, uncertainty, and discomfort.

In the midst of this unpleasantness it was a relief to Charlotte to accept an invitation from the Smiths. The proofs of *Villette* were ready, and it was suggested that she should correct them in London, and stay with Mrs Smith until the book was published. She went thankfully. Mrs Gaskell had written, begging that *Villette* should be delayed for a week or two, so as not to clash with her own new novel, *Ruth* : and to this Charlotte and her publishers had agreed. There was thus nearly a month in which she would escape from the painful embarrassments of Haworth and enjoy a little congenial society.

This last visit to London, however, seems to have been quieter in tone than the preceding ones, and tinged with a faintly perceptible disappointment. George Smith had apparently little time to spend with her; he was working at great pressure in Cornhill, and she was now an established author rather than a sensational discovery. Besides, he was engaged to be married, and his manner, though charming and friendly as ever, was subtly changed. Left largely to her own devices, and allowed to choose her sight-seeing, Charlotte followed her own instinct for life and drama. 'Being allowed,' she told Ellen, 'to have my own choice of sights this time, I selected the *real* rather than the decorative side of life. I have been over two prisons ancient and modern—Newgate and Pentonville —also the Bank, the Exchange, the Foundling Hospital, and today if all be well I go with Dr Forbes to see Bethlehem Hospital. Mrs S. and her daughters are, I believe, a little amazed at my gloomy tastes, but I take no notice.'

Villette was published at the end of January 1853, and was received with almost universal praise. The only dissentient voice was, to Charlotte's chagrin and amazement, Harriet Martineau's : that uncompromising lady having taken offence— as many readers of *Jane Eyre* had done before—at the novel's unmistakable note of passion. Miss Martineau liked to think that sexual love was an emotion to which sensible women paid no great attention, and she was affronted by the depth of feeling, and the implicit erotic quality of that feeling, in *Villette*. 'I do not like the love,' she told Charlotte in a letter, 'either the degree or the kind of it'; and in her review of the book in the *Daily News* she elaborated this theme, complaining that all the female characters of *Villette* passionately felt the need of being loved; whereas, according to Miss Martineau, 'it is not thus in real life'. Charlotte was angered by both the letter and the review. 'I know,' she replied, 'what *love* is as I understand it; and if man or woman should be ashamed of feeling such love, then there is nothing right, noble, faithful, truthful, unselfish in this earth.' No criticism had such power to wound her as that which professed to find coarseness or indelicacy in her work; such fault-finding cast a slur on her own character, and puzzled as much as it offended her. It was particularly hurtful to have the old cry taken up by a friend she so much respected; one, moreover, whom she had recently refused to abandon when Miss Wooler had begged her to give up her friendship with one of known atheistical opinions. Now, she felt, the differences between them, both of opinion and of feeling, were too great to be bridged. 'In short, she has hurt me a good deal, and at present it appears very plain to me that she and I had better not try to be close friends.' On this conviction Charlotte declined a long-standing invitation to Ambleside, and did not write again. Miss Martineau was in consequence much offended—'and I know her bitterness will not be short-lived, but it cannot be helped'.

At Haworth again for the coldest weather of February, Charlotte found the atmosphere of the parsonage in no way ameliorated. At the beginning of March the Bishop of Ripon (that Dr Longley who was later to become Archbishop of Canterbury) was expected on a pastoral visit. He would stay the night and expect to be entertained and to meet the local clergy. It was a diversion, however troublesome, and Charlotte welcomed it. Extra help was enlisted in the kitchen, and the surrounding parsons were invited to supper and tea. The Bishop proved, when he came, to be delightful, 'a most charming little Bishop; the most benignant little gentleman that ever put on lawn sleeves'; and everything went off well, apart from the fact that Mr Nicholls, whose nerves were at breaking point, behaved 'not quite pleasantly'. 'I thought he made no effort to struggle with his dejection, but gave way to it in a manner to draw notice; the Bishop was obviously puzzled by it.' (She later learned that the Bishop had not been puzzled, but had divined the trouble; and being sorry for Mr Nicholls had singled him out for a kind word and a handshake at parting.) Charlotte, however, found her old antipathy revive under this sulking, which was the sheer folly of misery, but which the servant, who was against him, contrived to dramatise until it appeared quite sinister. He had even 'showed temper once or twice in speaking to Papa. Martha was beginning to tell me of certain "flaysome" looks also, but I desired not to hear of them. The fact is,' Charlotte confessed, 'I shall be thankful when he is well away; I pity him, but I don't like that dark gloom of his. He dogged me up the lane after the evening service in no pleasant manner; he stopped also in the passage after the Bishop and the other clergy were gone into the room, and it was because I drew away and went upstairs that he gave me that look that filled Martha's soul with horror. She, it seems, meantime, was making it her business to watch him from the kitchen door. . . .'

At this crucial moment a letter arrived from the missionary society, asking Mr Nicholls to go to London for an interview. He had been pressing the society for just this, but now he seems to have been thrown into something of a panic. He had not yet actually left Haworth; his boats were still unburned. If the interview were favourable, and he were recruited for Australia, could he ever, in any circumstances, honourably withdraw? He wrote hastily to the Society, playing for time. 'Some doubts have occurred to me as to the desirableness of leaving the country at present—when I have fully made up my mind upon the point I will again communicate with you.' He seems suddenly to have felt, perhaps owing to the Bishop's kindness or to some chance word of Charlotte's, that there was a glimmer of hope, and even asked Mr Brontë if he might withdraw his resignation. Finding his enemy thus delivered into his hands, Mr Brontë made an ultimatum: Mr Nicholls might remain at Haworth if he signed an undertaking never again to mention the subject of marriage. Mr Nicholls refused, so the resignation must stand. He retired to his own rooms in silence and misery. Charlotte observed him with sympathy whenever she dared, but could do nothing. 'He looks ill and miserable. . . . I pity him inexpressibly. We never meet nor speak, nor dare I look at him; silent pity is just all I can give him, and as he knows nothing about that, it does not comfort. He is now grown so gloomy and reserved, that nobody seems to like him; his fellow curates shun trouble in that shape, the lower orders dislike it. Papa has a perfect antipathy to him, and he, I fear, to Papa. Martha hates him. I think he might almost be *dying* and they would not speak a friendly word. . . . In this state of things I must be, and I am, *entirely passive*. I may be losing the purest gem, and to me far the most precious life can give—genuine attachment—or I may be escaping the yoke of a morose temper.' Once again she was glad to escape from the discomfort of Haworth, this time on a brief visit to Mrs Gaskell.

§ When Easter, with its duties arising out of sermons to be preached by strange clergymen who had afterwards to be entertained at the Parsonage,—with Mechanics' Institute Meetings, and school tea-drinkings, was over and gone, she came, at the close of April, to visit us in Manchester. We had a friend, a young lady, staying with us. Miss Brontë had expected to find us alone; and although our friend was gentle and sensible after Miss Brontë's own heart, yet her presence was enough to create a nervous tremor. I was aware that both our guests were unusually silent; and I saw a little shiver run from time to time over Miss Brontë's frame. I could account for the modest reserve of the young lady; and the next day Miss Brontë told me how the unexpected sight of a strange face had affected her.

It was now two or three years since I had witnessed a similar effect produced on her, in anticipation of a quiet evening at Fox How; and since then she had seen many and various people in London: but the physical sensations produced by shyness were still the same; and on the following day she laboured under severe headache. I had several opportunities of perceiving how this nervousness was ingrained in her constitution, and how acutely she suffered in striving to overcome it. One evening we had, among other guests, two sisters who sang Scottish ballads exquisitely. Miss Brontë had been sitting quiet and constrained till they began *The Bonnie House of Airlie*, but the effect of that and *Carlisle Yetts*, which followed, was as irresistible as the playing of the Piper of Hamelin. The beautiful clear light came into her eyes; her lips quivered with emotion; she forgot herself, rose, and crossed the room to the piano, where she asked eagerly for song after song. The sisters begged her to come and see them the next morning, when they would sing as long as ever she liked; and she promised gladly and thankfully. But on reaching the house her courage failed. We walked some time up and down the street; she upbraiding herself all the while for folly and trying to dwell on the sweet echoes in her memory rather than on the thought of a third sister who would have to be faced if we went in. But it was of no use; and dreading lest this struggle with herself might bring on one of her trying headaches, I entered at last and made the best apology I could for her non-appearance. Much of this nervous dread of encountering strangers I ascribed to the idea of her personal ugliness which had been strongly impressed upon her imagination early in life, and which she exaggerated to herself in a remarkable manner. 'I notice,' said she, 'that after a stranger has once looked at my face, he is careful not to let his eyes wander to that part of the room again!' A more untrue idea never entered into anyone's head. Two gentlemen who saw her during this visit, without knowing at the time who she was, were singularly attracted by her appearance; and this feeling of attraction towards a pleasant countenance, sweet voice, and gentle, timid manners, was so strong in one as to conquer a dislike he had previously entertained to her works. §

She returned to Haworth; the weeks went by; and soon it was Mr Nicholls's last Sunday. It was Whitsunday, in the middle of May, and Charlotte, who had looked forward to his departure as a relief, found herself shocked once more into emotional sympathy. Mr Nicholls was taking the Communion Service, and when he reached Charlotte with the wafer 'he struggled, faltered, then lost command over himself, stood before my eyes and in the sight of all the communicants, white, shaking, voiceless. Papa was not there, thank God! Joseph Redman spoke some words to him. He made a great effort, but could only with difficulty whisper and falter through the service.' Mr Brontë had not been there, but the sexton or some other well-wisher hastened to report. It 'excited only anger, and such expressions as "unmanly driveller" '. Compassion or relenting, Charlotte wrote bitterly, 'is no more to be looked for from Papa than sap from firewood'. As for herself, 'I never saw a battle more sternly fought with the feelings than Mr Nicholls fights with his, and when he yields momentarily, you are almost sickened by the sense of the strain upon him.'

Nor was this all, though the presentation, from which Mr Brontë absented himself, of a gold watch and a testimonial from the parishioners would seem to have brought the situation into some final decorum. There was still the last leave-taking, and this was exquisitely painful. After taking his formal farewell of Mr Brontë, 'he went out thinking he was not to see me, and indeed, till the very last moment, I thought it best not. But perceiving that he stayed long before going out at the gate, and remembering his long grief, I took courage and went out trembling and miserable. I found him leaning against the garden door in a paroxysm of anguish, sobbing as women never sob. Of course I went straight to him. Very few words were interchanged, those few barely articulate. Several things I should have liked to ask him were swept entirely from my memory. Poor fellow! But he wanted such hope and such encouragement as I *could* not give him.'

Mr Nicholls went to the south of England for a few weeks, then to the curacy of Kirk Smeaton, near Pontefract. Another of the troublesome race of curates, a Mr de Renzy, succeeded him at Haworth, and gradually an exhausted peace settled on the place.

The summer followed the pattern of most Haworth summers. Mr Brontë was not well; Charlotte caught cold, and then was ill with influenza; Mrs Gaskell's proposed visit was postponed. Charlotte made an attempt at gaiety by going to Scotland with the Joseph Taylors (Amelia Ringrose, a friend of Ellen's, had married Mary Taylor's brother, and had long been an object of impatient interest to Charlotte—the sort of friend with whom she had nothing in common, but whose virtues she strove to see for Ellen's sake) but the expedition ended ludicrously. On the first night away from home the Taylors' baby was unwell, and the parents in panic hurried back to Yorkshire. Charlotte accepted the disappointment in her own fashion, as a lesson against ever anticipating pleasure.

September came, and now Mrs Gaskell was to pay her visit. She found the parsonage less bleak within than she had imagined, for not long before, and rather against Mr Brontë's wishes, Charlotte had provided crimson curtains for the dining-room, and had had the walls papered; the rest of the parsonage was frugally furnished and unchanged. 'I don't know,' wrote Mrs Gaskell to a friend, in a letter which she was later to copy almost word for word into her biography, 'that I ever saw a spot more exquisitely clean; the most dainty place for that I ever saw. To be sure, the life is like clockwork. No one comes to the house; nothing disturbs the deep repose; hardly a voice is heard; you catch the ticking of the clock in the kitchen, or the buzzing of a fly in the parlour, all over the house. Miss Brontë sits alone in her parlour; breakfasting with her father in his study at nine o'clock. She helps in the housework; for one of their servants, Tabby, is nearly ninety, and the other only a girl. Then I accompanied her in her walks on the sweeping moors: the heather-bloom had been blighted by a thunder-storm a day or two before, and was all of a livid brown colour, instead of the blaze of purple glory it ought to have been. Oh! those high, wild, desolate moors, up above the whole world, and the very realms of silence! Home to dinner at two. Mr Brontë has his dinner sent in to him. All the small table arrangements had the same dainty simplicity about them. Then we rested, and talked over the clear, bright fire; it is a cold country, and the fires were a pretty warm dancing light all over the house. The parlour had been evidently refurnished within the last few years, since Miss Brontë's success has enabled her to have a little more money to spend. Everything fits into, and is in harmony with, the idea of a country parsonage, possessed by people of very moderate means. The prevailing colour of the room is crimson, to make a warm setting for the cold grey landscape without. There is her likeness by Richmond, and an engraving from Lawrence's picture of Thackeray; and two recesses, on each side of the high, narrow, old-fashioned mantel-piece, filled with books,—books given to her, books she has bought, and which tell of her individual pursuits and tastes; *not* standard books.

'She cannot see well, and does little beside knitting. . . . I soon observed that her habits of order were such that she could not go on with the conversation, if a chair was out of its place; everything was arranged with delicate regularity. . . .

'We have generally had another walk before tea, which is at six; at half-past eight, prayers; and by nine, all the household are in bed, except ourselves. We sit up together till ten, or past; and after I go, I hear Miss Brontë come down and walk up and down the room for an hour or so.'

§ Copying this letter has brought the days of that pleasant visit very clear before me,—very sad in their clearness. We were so happy together; we were so full of interest in each other's subjects. The day seemed only too short for what we had to say and to hear. I understand her life the better for seeing the place where it had been spent—where she had loved and suffered.

Mr Brontë was a most courteous host; and when he was with us,—at breakfast in his study, or at tea in Charlotte's parlour,—he had a sort of grand and stately way of describing past times, which tallied well with his striking appearance. He never seemed quite to have lost the feeling that Charlotte was a child to be guided and ruled, when she was present; and she herself submitted to this with a quiet docility that half amused, half astonished me. But when she had to leave the room, then all his pride in her genius and fame came out. He eagerly listened to everything I could tell him of the high admiration I had at any time heard expressed for her works. He would ask for certain speeches over and over again, as if he desired to impress them on his memory. §

In the course of several undisturbed evenings by the fire Mrs Gaskell learned the story of Mr Nicholls; Charlotte did not conceal the fact that she was worrying about him. Who was looking after him at Kirk Smeaton? Was his health suffering? 'I was aware,' Mrs Gaskell was later to write discreetly in her biography, 'that she had a great anxiety on her mind at this time; and being acquainted with its nature, I could not but deeply admire the patient docility which she displayed in her conduct towards her father.'

Part of Charlotte's anxiety was due to a deep feeling of guilt where her father was concerned. She was secretly in communication with Mr Nicholls, and knew that this, despite her apparent obedience, was complete treachery to his wishes. She had been drawn into correspondence against her will, and once she had answered Mr Nicholls's letters, and had even consented to a meeting, it was difficult to retreat. 'He wrote to her very miserably,' Mrs Gaskell discovered, 'wrote six times, and then she answered him—a letter exhorting him to heroic submission to his lot, etc. He sent word it had comforted him so much that he must have a little more, and so she came to write to him several times.' This concession encouraged Mr Nicholls to visit his friend Mr Grant, vicar of Oxenhope, the next village to Haworth—unknown, of course, to Mr Brontë; and several brief and secret meetings were arranged. Charlotte's sensitive conscience tormented her perpetually about this; but she was beginning to see a side of Mr Nicholls's character which had been hidden before, and she could not bring herself to throw away a devotion which might, after all, be worth saving.

After a short visit to Ellen and another to Miss Wooler, she spent a silent Christmas with her father. She worried continually about Mr Nicholls and about her own part in the affair, and her peace of mind was further troubled by a mysterious and unexplained estrangement from Ellen. It seems possible that Mr. Nicholls was the subject of this quarrel, for in February 1854 Mary Taylor was writing to Ellen with characteristic astringency. 'Does your strange morality mean that she should refuse to ameliorate her lot when it is in her power? How would she be inconsistent with herself in marrying? Because she considers her own pleasure? If this is so new for her to do, it is high time she began to make it more common. It is an outrageous exaction to expect her to give up her choice in a matter so important, and I think her to blame in having been hitherto so yielding that her friends can think of making such an impudent demand. . . .'

Charlotte's choice, then, was beginning to veer in Mr Nicholls's direction. Without love, without great liking, without any feeling, indeed, warmer than respect and pity, she had 'decided that she could make him happy, and that his love was too good to be thrown away by one so lonely as she is'. The quarrel with Ellen was made up in March, and Charlotte continued to send her news of the courtship. He had called at the parsonage, it seems, in January, and had been received 'not pleasantly'; now, he was expected at Oxenhope for Easter, and Charlotte had talked her father into some sort of grudging promise of better manners. He came at the beginning of April, after a difficult passage between Charlotte and her father, in which she had insisted that Mr Nicholls should be given his chance. The visit, though constrained, was momentous. Mr Brontë at last consented to an engagement. 'Matters have progressed thus since July,' Charlotte wrote to Ellen. 'He renewed his visit in September, but then matters so fell out that I saw little of him. He continued to write. The correspondence pressed on my mind. I grew very miserable in keeping it from Papa. At last sheer pain made me gather courage to break it—I told all. It was very hard and rough work at the time—but the issue after a few days was that I obtained leave to continue the communication. Mr Nicholls came in January; he was ten days in the neighbourhood. I saw much of him. I had stipulated with Papa for opportunity to become better acquainted—I had it, and all I learnt inclined me to esteem, and, if not love, at least affection. Still, Papa was very, very hostile—bitterly unjust. I told Mr Nicholls the great obstacles that lay in his way. He has persevered. The result of this, his last visit, is, that

Papa's consent is gained—that his respect, I believe, is won, for Mr Nicholls has in all things proved himself disinterested and forbearing. He has shown, too, that while his feelings are exquisitely keen, he can freely forgive. Certainly I must respect him, nor can I withhold from him more than mere cool respect. In fact, dear Ellen, I am engaged.'

Charlotte's pleading had not been the only thing to influence Mr Brontë. There was something else, and that something may, of the two, have been the more persuasive. The new curate, Mr de Renzy, was not giving satisfaction. Mr Brontë had grown accustomed to the method and thoroughness of Mr Nicholls's ministry, and everything seemed troublesome now that he was gone. If he married Charlotte, he could come back to Haworth. They were both solicitous in assuring Mr Brontë that his privacy should be respected; that they would not expect to share the parlour or to have meals with him; that none of the domestic arrangements need be disturbed. The store-room could be turned into a study, and out of his hundred a year Mr Nicholls would contribute to the household. Mr Brontë began to perceive that the marriage might even have its practical advantage.

In the light of this happy change, there is no mystery about the sudden collapse of Mr Nicholls's missionary ambitions. 'As, owing to the severity of the weather,' he wrote in his final letter to the missionary society, 'the rheumatic affection with which I have been troubled during the winter has not abated as rapidly as I expected, I have been induced by friends to relinquish for the present my intention of going abroad. . . .' He took no further interest in Australia.

Preparations for the wedding were quietly begun. 'I am still very calm, very inexpectant,' Charlotte confessed to Ellen. 'What I taste of happiness is of the soberest order. I trust to love my husband—I am grateful for his tender love to me. I believe him to be an affectionate, a conscientious, a high-principled man; and if, with all this, I should yield to regrets, that fine talents, congenial tastes and thoughts are not added, it seems to me I should be most presumptuous and thankless.' She was still haunted by a sense of treachery towards her father, and tried to soothe her sick conscience with the reflection that she had considered his comfort at least as much as her own. 'My hope is that in the end this arrangement will turn out more truly to Papa's advantage than any other it was in my power to achieve. Mr Nicholls only in his last letter refers touchingly to his earnest desire to prove his gratitude to Papa, by offering support and consolation to his declining age.' This anxious, self-justifying note is sounded again and again, as though in a long struggle with self-reproach. 'On one feature in the marriage I can dwell with unmingled satisfaction, with a *certainty* of being right. It takes nothing from the attention I owe to my father. I am not to leave him— my future husband consents to come here—thus Papa secures by the step a devoted and reliable assistant in his old age.' But from Mrs Gaskell she did not conceal that her father, indeed everyone, regarded the match as the shabbiest of disappointments. 'I could almost cry sometimes that in this important action in my life I cannot better satisfy Papa's perhaps natural pride.'

Mrs Gaskell herself was in two minds about the matter. She wished for the marriage for Charlotte's sake, but did not care for what she had heard of Mr Nicholls. 'I am terribly afraid he won't let her go on being intimate with us heretics. . . . I fancy him very good, but *very* stern and bigoted. . . . However, with all his bigotry and sternness it must be charming to be loved with all the strength of his heart, as she sounds to be.' With her usual perception she had sensed something in Charlotte which might even respond to this aspect of Mr Nicholls. 'I am sure that Miss Brontë could never have borne not to be well ruled and ordered. . . . I mean that she would never have been happy but with an exacting, rigid, law-giving, passionate man.'

§ At the beginning of May, Miss Brontë left home to pay three visits before her marriage. The first was to us. She only remained three days, as she had to go to the neighbourhood of Leeds, there to make such purchases as were required for her marriage. Her preparations, as she said, could neither be expensive nor extensive; consisting chiefly in a modest replenishing of her wardrobe, some re-papering

300

and repainting in the Parsonage; and, above all, converting the small flagged passage-room, hitherto used only for stores (which was behind her sitting room), into a study for her husband. On this idea, and plans for his comfort, as well as her father's, her mind dwelt a good deal.

. . .

It was fixed that the marriage was to take place on the 29th of June. Her two friends arrived at Haworth Parsonage the day before; and the long summer afternoon and evening were spent by Charlotte in thoughtful arrangements for the morrow, and for her father's comfort during her absence from home. When all was finished—the trunk packed, the morning's breakfast arranged, the wedding-dress laid out,—just at bedtime, Mr Brontë announced his intention of stopping at home while the others went to church. What was to be done? Who was to give the bride away? There were only to be the officiating clergyman, the bride and bridegroom, the bridesmaid, and Miss Wooler present. The Prayer-book was referred to; and there it was seen that the Rubric enjoins that the Minister shall receive 'the woman from her father's or *friend's* hands', and that nothing is specified as to the sex of the 'friend'. So Miss Wooler, ever kind in emergency, volunteered to give her old pupil away.

. The news of the wedding had slipt abroad before the little party came out of church, and many old and humble friends were there, seeing her look 'like a snow-drop', as they say. Her dress was white embroidered muslin, with a lace mantle, and white bonnet trimmed with green leaves, which perhaps might suggest the resemblance to the pale wintry flower. §

Mrs Gaskell's delicacy forbade her to do more than hint at the sudden and surprising happiness which Charlotte found in marriage. It was a change that depended wholly on her discovery of Mr Nicholls's character. Indeed, in the letters of the next few months it is wonderful to see how, in the sudden climate of happiness, he blossoms and improves. There were no great disclosures; only the gentle unfolding of his tenderness; and the revelation, for Charlotte, of the contentment, even the rare emotional experience, which outwardly unpromising people can bestow.

After the wedding they left by train for North Wales, and after a tolerable railway journey and a romantic drive through the mountains from Llanberis to Beddgelert, reached Conway and spent the night at a comfortable inn. Thence, by way of Bangor, where they also spent a night, they crossed from Holyhead to Dublin, and after an interlude of sightseeing went on to Banagher. Here Charlotte was agreeably surprised by everything she saw. Dr Bell's house, where Mr Nicholls had been brought up, was 'very large and looks externally like a gentleman's country seat; within, most of the rooms are lofty and spacious and some—the drawing-room, dining-room, etc.,—handsomely and commodiously furnished'. The note of surprise, though decorous, is unmistakable. Remembering her father's peasant origins, perhaps, she had clearly prepared herself for something humble; but the house was quite imposing and the other male members of the family seemed 'thoroughly educated gentlemen'. 'I must say,' she told Miss Wooler, 'I like my new relations. My dear husband too appears in a new light here in his own country.' And to Miss Wooler's sister, 'I was very much pleased with all I saw—but I was also greatly surprised to find so much of English order and repose in the family habits and arrangements. I had heard a great deal about Irish negligence. . . .'

They travelled on to Killarney and the south-west coast, Charlotte all the way deriving an exquisite and specially feminine pleasure from 'the kind and ceaseless protection which has ever surrounded me, and made travelling a different matter to me from what it has heretofore been'; and finding to her delight, when at last they confronted the wild and grand Atlantic, that Mr Nicholls was by no means an insensitive companion. 'My husband is not a poet or a poetical man,' she wrote, '—and one of my grand doubts before marriage was about "congenial tastes" and so on. The first morning we went out on the cliffs and saw the Atlantic coming in all white foam. I did not know whether I should get leave or time to take the matter in my own way. I did not want to talk—but I *did* want to look and be silent. Having hinted a petition, licence was not refused; covered with a rug to keep off the spray I was allowed to sit where I chose; and he only interrupted me when he thought I crept too near the edge of the cliff. So far he is always good in this way—and this protection which does not interfere or pretend is I believe a thousand times better than any half sort of pseudo sympathy. I will try with God's help to be as indulgent to him whenever indulgence is needed.'

He was changing, under Charlotte's very eyes, into something she had hardly believed possible. The toad was becoming, if not a prince, at least something very interesting and likeable. He now looked 'quite strong and hale', and had gained twelve pounds during the four weeks in Ireland. Now, in letters to Ellen, he is no longer Mr Nicholls, but 'Arthur—excuse the name, it has grown natural to use it now'; and soon he is 'my dear Arthur', 'my dear boy', and the letters are full of him. The only flaws in these singularly happy weeks were the cold which Charlotte had caught at her wedding, and could not shake off, and her obsession of anxiety about her father. They had been away too long . . . he must be unwell . . . she had done wrong to leave him. At length she could bear her self-reproaches no longer, and they returned to Haworth. 'May God preserve him to us yet for some years! The wish for his continued life, together with a certain solicitude for his happiness and health seems—I scarcely know why—stronger in me now than before I was married.' She marvelled at the equanimity with which Mr Brontë now accepted his son-in-law. 'So far the understanding between Papa and Mr Nicholls seems excellent; if only it continues thus I shall be truly grateful. Papa has taken no duty since we returned, and each time I see Mr Nicholls put on gown or surplice, I feel comforted to think that this marriage has secured Papa good aid in his old age.'

Mr Nicholls had, indeed, quietly shouldered the whole work of the parish, and was insistent that Charlotte should share in everything he did. 'My life,' she told Ellen, 'is changed indeed—to be wanted continually—to be constantly called for and occupied seems so strange.' He was proving, in short, fond, authoritative, possessive. Even when, with clerical gravity, he took it upon himself to censor her letters to Ellen, she was too much amused by his strictures to resent them.

In spite of the many and various demands on her time, which made it difficult for her even to write a letter without Mr Nicholls standing impatiently at her elbow, waiting to take her for a walk, Charlotte had begun work on a new novel, and was looking forward to a productive winter. Her scanty leisure, she knew, was all that she could now devote to writing. Her husband was not hostile to her fame, but he was a little jealous of it, he saw it, rightly, as a threat to his possessiveness, and as far from being the most important attribute of the woman he had married. But he had not discouraged her; he had even listened attentively to the early chapters of the new novel, *Emma*, and had warned her that the public might find the theme repetitive. She had made several beginnings, and though none of them entirely pleased her, she was encouraged by the presence of a critic who, while he could never take the place of her dead sisters, was at least a listener.

Her health, at the beginning of this winter, was wonderfully improved. 'It is long,' she told Miss Wooler, 'since I have known such comparative immunity from headache, sickness, and indigestion, as during the last three months. My life is different to what it used to be. May God make me thankful for it! I have a good, kind, attached husband, and every day makes my own attachment to him stronger.' Sir James Kay-Shuttleworth had recently paid them a visit, and had offered Mr Nicholls the living of Padiham in Lancashire, which was in his gift, and where the climate was said to be kinder than at Haworth. It was not, of course, possible to accept while Mr Brontë lived, though the stipend of £200 a year was very tempting. Still, the offer gave Charlotte pleasure—a 'gratifying proof', as she innocently observed, 'of respect for my dear Arthur'.

The first hint of anything amiss came in December. Mr Nicholls, who was a great walker and lover of fresh air, had called Charlotte away one morning from her letter-writing, and had taken her for a walk on the edge of the moor. 'We set off not intending to go far, but . . . when we had got about half a mile on the moors, Arthur suggested the idea of the waterfall—after the melted snow he said it would be fine. I had often wanted to see it in its winter power, so we walked on. It was fine indeed—a perfect torrent raving over the rocks, white and beautiful. It began to rain while we were watching it, and we returned home under a stormy sky.' That same night Charlotte was shivering with chill, and had a sore throat and a cold; but as this was a commonplace she was not unduly alarmed. Christmas passed and she seemed somewhat better, though the cold remained.

§ Early in the new year (1855), Mr and Mrs Nicholls went to visit Sir James Kay-Shuttleworth at Gawthorpe. They only remained two or three days, but it so fell out that she increased her lingering cold, by a long walk over damp ground in thin shoes.

Soon after her return, she was attacked by new sensations of perpetual nausea, and ever-recurring faintness. After this state of things had lasted for some time, she yielded to Mr Nicholls' wish that a doctor should be sent for. He came, and assigned a natural cause for her miserable indisposition; a little patience, and all would go right. She, who was ever patient in illness, tried hard to bear up and bear on. But the dreadful sickness increased and increased, till the very sight of food occasioned nausea. 'A wren would have starved on what she ate during those last six weeks,' says one. Tabby's health had suddenly and utterly given way, and she died in this time of distress and anxiety respecting the last daughter of the house she had served so long. Martha tenderly waited on her mistress, and from time to time tried to cheer her with the thought of the baby that was coming. 'I dare say I shall be glad some time,' she would say; 'but I am so ill—so weary——' §

It was not realised at first that, weakened by her long cold and by the sickness of early pregnancy, she had given way to the disease that had lain in wait for her from the beginning—the consumption which had killed Maria, Elizabeth, Branwell, Emily and Anne.

No great novelist has ever devised a more tragically fitting, or more poignant, ending than the famous, the almost unbearable last passages of Mrs Gaskell's biography. Slowly dying, Charlotte had written a last pencilled note to Ellen, crowning with one unforgettable chord the long sustained crescendo of Mr Nicholls's love. 'I must write one line out of my dreary bed. . . . I am not going to talk of my sufferings—it would be useless and painful. I want to give you an assurance, which I know will comfort you—and that is, that I find in my husband the tenderest nurse, the kindest support, the best earthly comfort that ever woman had. His patience never fails, and it is tried by sad days and broken nights. . . .'

§ I do not think she ever wrote a line again. Long days and longer nights went by; still the same relentless nausea and faintness, and still borne on in patient trust. About the third week in March there was a change; a low wandering delirium came on; and in it she begged constantly for food and even for stimulants. She swallowed eagerly now; but it was too late. Wakening for an instant from this stupor of intelligence, she saw her husband's woe-worn face, and caught the sound of some murmured words of prayer that God would spare her. 'Oh!' she whispered forth, 'I am not going to die, am I? He will not separate us, we have been so happy.'

Early on Saturday morning, March 31st, the solemn tolling of Haworth church-bell spoke forth the fact of her death to the villagers who had known her from a child, and whose hearts shivered within them as they thought of the two sitting desolate and alone in the old grey house. §

AUTHOR'S NOTE

It is perhaps superfluous to provide a complete Brontë bibliography, since an excellent and up to date one is to be found in *The Four Brontës* by Lawrence and E. M. Hanson (Oxford University Press, 1949). I should, however, like to offer the reader a short list of books and papers which I have found particularly rewarding, and to which I gratefully acknowledge my debt:

The Brontës: Their Lives, Friendships and Correspondence. The Shakespeare Head Brontë, edited by T. J. Wise and J. A. Symington. Blackwell, 1932.

Transactions of the Brontë Society. Published annually from 1895 to the present day.

Cowan Bridge: New Light from Old Documents. Edith M. Weir. Brontë Society Publications, 1946.

The Brontës' Web of Childhood. F. A. Ratchford. Columbia University Press, 1941.

The Brontës: Charlotte and Emily. Laura L. Hinkley. Hammond, 1947.

The Brontës. Irene Cooper-Willis. Duckworth, 1933.

The Authorship of 'Wuthering Heights'. Irene Cooper-Willis. 'The Trollopian', 1947.

The Brontës. Phyllis E. Bentley. Home and Van Thal, 1947.

The Complete Poems of Emily Jane Brontë. Edited by C. W. Hatfield. Columbia University Press, 1941.

The Psychology of Religious Mysticism. J. H. Leuba. Kegan Paul, 1929.

The Inner History of the Brontë-Heger Letters. Marion H. Spielmann. Reprinted from 'The Fortnightly Review', 1919.

Charlotte Brontë. George M. Smith. 'The Cornhill Magazine,' December 1900.

The Brontës: Their Lives Recorded by Their Contemporaries.
Compiled with an Introduction by E. M. Delafield. Hogarth
Press, 1935.
In the Steps of the Brontës. Ernest Raymond. Rich and
Cowan, 1948.
Elizabeth Gaskell: Her Life and Work. A. B. Hopkins. John
Lehmann, 1952.

I should also like to record my gratitude to the Brontë
Society for much generous help, and to Sir John Murray for
allowing me to see the unpublished letters of Mrs Gaskell and
Mr Nicholls in the archives at 50 Albemarle Street.

M.L.

INDEX

Fontana Literature

Simone de Beauvoir

The Woman Destroyed *35p*
'Immensely intelligent, basically passionless stories about the decay of passion. Simone de Beauvoir shares, with other women novelists, the ability to write about emotion in terms of direct experience ... The middle-aged women at the centre of the three stories in *The Woman Destroyed* all suffer agonisingly the pains of growing older and of being betrayed by husbands and children.'   *Sunday Times*

The Mandarins *60p*
'A magnificent satire by the author of *The Second Sex*. *The Mandarins* gives us a brilliant survey of the post-war French intellectual . . . a dazzling panorama.' *New Statesman.* 'A superb document . . . a remarkable novel.'   *Sunday Times*

Les Belles Images *35p*
Her totally absorbing story of upper-class Parisian life. 'A brilliant sortie into Jet Set France.' *Daily Mirror.* 'As compulsively readable as it is profound, serious and disturbing.'
Queen

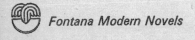

Fontana Modern Novels

Fontana Modern Novels

The First Circle   Alexander Solzhenitsyn   *60p*
The unforgettable novel of Stalin's post-war Terror. 'The
greatest novel of the 20th Century.' *Spectator*. 'An unqualified
masterpiece—this immense epic of the dark side of Soviet
life.' *Observer*. 'At once classic and contemporary . . . future
generations will read it with wonder and awe.' *New York
Times*

Doctor Zhivago   Boris Pasternak   *50p*
The world-famous novel of life in Russia during and after
the Revolution. '*Dr. Zhivago* will, I believe, come to stand
as one of the great events in man's literary and moral history.'
New Yorker. 'One of the most profound descriptions of love
in the whole range of modern literature.' *Encounter*

The Master and Margarita   Mikhail Bulgakov   *50p*
'The fantastic scenes are done with terrific verve and the
nonsense is sometimes reminiscent of Lewis Carroll . . . on
another level, Bulgakov's intentions are mystically serious.
You need not catch them all to appreciate his great imaginative power and ingenuity.' *Sunday Times*. 'A grim and
beautiful tale . . . just as you think the whole thing is a very
funny satire, a chilling wind out of the Ingmar Bergman
country blows, and, yet again, as you search for some moral
significance, there are pages of sheer and beautiful fantasy.'
Times Educational Supplement

The White Guard   Mikhail Bulgakov   *40p*
'A powerful reverie . . . the city is so vivid to the eye that it is
the real hero of the book.' *V. S. Pritchett, New Statesman*.
'Set in Kiev in 1918 . . . the tumultuous atmosphere of the
Ukrainian capital in revolution and civil war is brilliantly
evoked.' *Daily Telegraph*. 'A beautiful novel.' *The Listener*

Fontana Modern Novels

Fontana Modern Novels

The Tin Men Michael Frayn *30p*
'One knew, sourly, that this book was going to be funny; one
did not see how it could be so continuously funny . . . The
fun of *The Tin Men* is outrageous because it is so serious.'
Guardian

Ordinary Families E. Arnot Robertson *35p*
'The loves and jealousies, miseries and raptures of adolescence, woven with a very dexterous hand.' *Observer*. 'A
splendid book . . . It is one of the few books to yield treasures
on a second reading.' *Evening Standard*. 'A wise, witty and
brilliant book.' *Sunday Times*

The Once and Future King T. H. White *60p*
'T. H. White is much more than a spinner of good plots; his
prose gives as much pleasure as his matter. There are witty
and learned asides on every subject under the sun. He can
draw living people; he can describe a landscape; and he can
enter into the inmost minds of birds and beasts. This
ambitious work will long remain a memorial to an author
who is at once civilised, learned, witty and humane.'
Times Literary Supplement

The Towers of Trebizond Rose Macaulay *30p*
'Never was triumph better deserved. Beauty, wisdom, humour
. . . lunacy and love are blended to produce a kind of *Alice
Through the Looking Glass* of modern life. I never had more
pleasure in praising a book.' *Sir Compton Mackenzie*

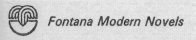 *Fontana Modern Novels*

Fontana Books

All Fontana books are available at your bookshop or news-agent; or can be ordered direct. Just fill in the form below and list the titles you want.

....

FONTANA BOOKS, Cash Sales Department, P.O. Box 4, Godalming, Surrey GU7 1JY. Please send purchase price plus 5p postage per book by cheque, postal or money order. No currency.

NAME (Block Letters) _____

ADDRESS _____

_____

_____